BY ROBERT SERVICE

VERSE

The Spell of the Yukon
Ballads of a Cheechako
Rhymes of a Rolling Stone
Rhymes of a Red Cross Man
Ballads of a Bohemian
Bar-Room Ballads
Songs of a Sun-Lover
Rhymes of a Roughneck
Lyrics of a Low Brow
Rhymes of a Rebel
Songs for My Supper
The Collected Poems
Carols of an Old Codger
More Collected Verse

NOVELS

The Trail of '98
The Pretender
The Poisoned Paradise
The Roughneck
The Master of the Microbe
The House of Fear

MISCELLANEOUS

Why Not Grow Young?

AUTOBIOGRAPHY

Ploughman of the Moon
Harper of Heaven

MORE COLLECTED VERSE

MORE
COLLECTED
VERSE

BY ROBERT SERVICE

1971

DODD, MEAD & COMPANY · NEW YORK

CONTENTS

CONTENTS

SONGS OF A SUN-LOVER

CONTENTS

DEDICATION TO PROVENCE

I loved to toy with tuneful rhyme,
My fancies into verse to weave;
For as I walked my words would chime
So bell-like I could scarce believe;
My rhythms rippled like a brook,
My stanzas bloomed like blossoms gay:
And that is why I deem this book
 A verseman's holiday.

The palm-blades brindle in the blaze
Of sunsets splendouring the sea;
The gloaming is a lilac haze
That impish stars stab eagerly. . . .
O Land of Song! O golden clime!
O happy me, whose work is play!
Please take this tribute of my rhyme:
 A verseman's holiday.

LOWLY LAUREATE

O Sacred Muse, my lyre excuse!—
My verse is vagrant singing;
Rhyme I invoke for simple folk
Of penny-wise upbringing:
For Grannies grey to paste away
Within an album cover;
For maids in class to primly pass,
And lads to linger over.

I take the clay of every day
And mould it in my fashion;
I seek to trace the commonplace
With humour and compassion.
Of earth am I, and meekly try
To be supremely human:
To please, I plan, the little man,
And win the little woman.

No evil theme shall daunt my dream
Of fellow-love and pity;
I tune my lute to prostitute,
To priest I pipe my ditty.
Though gutter-grime be in my rhyme,
I bow to altars holy. . . .
*Lord, humble me, so I may be
A Laureate of the Lowly.*

MACTAVISH

I do not write for love of pelf,
Nor lust for phantom fame;
I do not rhyme to please myself,
Nor yet to win acclaim:
No, strange to say it is my plan,
What gifts I have, to lavish
Upon a simple working man,
    MACTAVISH.

For that's the rather smeary name,
Of dreary toil a hinter,
That heads the galley proofs that came
This morning from my printer;
My patient pencil much they need,
Yet how my eyes they ravish,
As at the top of each I read:
    MACTAVISH.

Who is this meek and modest man,
Who puffs no doubt a pipe,
And has my manuscript to scan,
And put in magic type?
Somehow I'm glad that he is not
Iberian or Slavish—
I hail him as a brother Scot,
    MACTAVISH.

I do not want to bore him with
My work, I make it snappy;
For even though his name were Smith,
I'd like him to be happy.
I hope, because I'm stumped for rhyme,
He will not think me knavish,
If I should call him just this time:
MACTAYVISH.

Forgive me, Friend Mactavish, I
No doubt have cost you curses;
I'm sorry for you as you try
To put my type in verses;
And though new names I know you by,
When of new books creator,
I'll always look on you as my
COLLABORATOR.

INSPIRATION

How often have I started out
With no thought in my noddle,
And wandered here and there about,
Where fancy bade me toddle;
Till feeling faunlike in my glee
I've voiced some gay distiches,
Returning joyfully to tea,
A poem in my britches.

A-squatting on a thymy slope
With vast of sky about me,
I've scribbled on an envelope
The rhymes the hills would shout me;
The couplets that the trees would call,
The lays the breezes proffered . . .
Oh no, I didn't *think* at all—
I took what Nature offered.

For that's the way you ought to write—
Without a trace of trouble;
Be super-charged with high delight
And let the words out-bubble;
Be voice of vale and wood and stream
Without design or proem:
Then rouse from out a golden dream
To find you've made a poem.

So I'll go forth with mind a blank,
And sea and sky will spell me;
And lolling on a thymy bank
I'll take down what they tell me;
As Mother Nature speaks to me
Her words I'll gaily docket,
So I'll come singing home to tea
A poem in my pocket.

BIRTHDAY
(16th January 1949)

I thank whatever gods may be
For all the happiness that's mine;
That I am festive, fit and free
To savour women, wit and wine;
That I my game of golf enjoy,
And have a formidable drive:
In short, that I'm a gay old boy
Though I be
           Seventy-and-five.

My daughter thinks, because I'm old
(I'm not a crock, when all is said),
I mustn't let my feet get cold,
And should wear woollen socks in bed;
A worsted night-cap too, forsooth!
To humour her I won't contrive:
A man is in his second youth
When he is
           Seventy-and-five.

At four-score years old age begins,
And not till then, I warn my wife;
At eighty I'll recant my sins,
And live a staid and sober life.
But meantime let me whoop it up,
And tell the world that I'm alive:
Fill to the brim the bubbly cup—
Here's health to
           Seventy-and-five!

THE BATTLE OF THE BULGE

This year an ocean trip I took, and as I am a Scot
And like to get my money's worth I never missed a
    meal.
In spite of Neptune's nastiness I ate an awful lot,
Yet felt as fit as if we sailed upon an even keel.
But now that I am home again I'm stricken with dis-
    gust;
How many pounds of fat I've gained I'd rather not
    divulge:
Well, anyway I mean to take this tummy down or bust,
So here I'm suet-strafing in the
                                    Battle of the Bulge.

No more will sausage, bacon, eggs provide my breakfast
    fare;
On lobster I will never lunch, with mounds of *mayon-
    naise.*
At tea I'll Spartanly eschew the chocolate *éclair;*
Roast duckling and *pêche melba* shall not consummate
    my days.
No more nocturnal ice-box raids, midnight spaghetti
    feeds;
On slabs of *pâté de foie gras* I vow I won't indulge:
Let bran and cottage cheese suffice my gastronomic
    needs,
And lettuce be my ally in the
                                    Battle of the Bulge.

To hell with you, ignoble paunch, abhorrent in my
     sight!
I gaze at your rotundity, and savage is my frown.
I'll rub you and I'll scrub you and I'll drub you day and
     night,
But by the gods of symmetry I swear I'll get you down.
Your smooth and smug convexity, by heck! I will
     subdue,
And when you tucker in again with joy will I refulge;
No longer of my toes will you obstruct my downward
     view . . .
With might and main I'll fight to gain the
                              Battle of the Bulge.

VANITY

My tangoing seemed to delight her;
With me it was love at first sight.
I mentioned that I was a writer;
She asked me: "What is it you write?"
"Oh, only best-sellers," I told her.
Their titles? . . . She shook her blonde head;
The atmosphere seemed to grow colder:
Not *one* of my books had she read.

Oh, she was a beauty ensnaring,
And I was an author of note;
But little I saw she'd be caring
If never a novel I wrote.
Alas for the caprice of Cupid!
Alack for the phantom of Fame!
I thought her just homely and stupid:
She didn't know even my *name*.

I saw her a score of years after;
She gushed as I took off my hat;
But inwardly loud was my laughter,
For she was enormously fat.
Thank heaven I'd not made *that* error;
I saw Love drive off in a hearse;
But I too retreated in terror . . .
She started to quote me my verse.

MY DENTIST

Sitting in the dentist's chair,
Wishing that I wasn't there,
To forget and pass the time
I have made this bit of rhyme.

I had a *rendez-vous* at ten;
I rushed to get in line,
But found a lot of dames and men
Had waited there since nine;
I stared at them, then in an hour
Was blandly ushered in;
But though my face was grim and sour
He met me with a grin.

He told me of his horse of blood,
And how it "also ran";
He plans to own a racing stud—
(He seems a wealthy man.)
And then he left me there until
I growled: "At any rate,
I hope he'll not charge in his bill
For all the time I wait."

His wife has sables on her back,
With jewels she's ablaze;
She drives a stately Cadillac,
And I'm the mug who pays:
At least I'm one of those who peer
With pessimistic gloom
At magazines of yester-year
In his damn waiting room.

I am a Christian Scientist;
I don't believe in pain;
My dentist has a powerful wrist,
He tries and tries in vain
To make me grunt or groan or squeal
With probe or rasp or drill. . . .
But oh, what agony I feel
When HE PRESENTS HIS BILL !

Sitting in the dental chair,
Don't you wish you weren't there:
Well, your cup of woe to fill,
Just think of his infernal bill.

CANINE CONVERSATION

If dogs could speak, O Mademoiselle,
What funny stories they could tell!
For instance, take your little "peke,"
How awkward if the dear could speak!
How sad for you and all of us,
Who round you flutter, flirt and fuss:
Folks think you modest, mild and meek . . .
But would they—if Fi-fi could speak?

If dogs could tell, Ah Madame Rose,
What secrets could they not disclose!
If your pet poodle Angeline
Could hint one half of what she's seen,
Your reputation would, I fear,
As absolutely disappear
As would a snowball dropped in hell . . .
If Angeline could only tell.

If dogs could speak, how dangerous
It would be for a lot of us!
At what they see and what they hear
They wink an eye and wag an ear.
How fortunate for old and young
The darlings have a silent tongue!
We love them, but it's just as well
For all of us that—dogs can't tell.

POOCH

Nurse, won't you let him in?
He's barkin' an' scratchin' the door,
Makin' so dreffel a din
I jest can't sleep any more;
Out there in the dark an' the cold,
Hark to him scrape an' whine,
Breakin' his heart o' gold,
Poor little pooch o' mine.

Nurse, I was sat in ma seat
In front o' the barber shop,
When there he was lickin' ma feet
As if he would never stop;
Then all on a sudden I see
That dog-catcher moseyin' by:
"Whose mongrel is that?" says he;
"It's ma pedigree pup," says I.

Nurse, he was starved an' a-stray,
But his eyes was plumbful o' trust.
How could I turn him away?
I throwed him a bit o' a crust,
An' he choked as he gulped it up,
Then down at ma feet he curled:
Poor little pitiful pup!
Hadn't a friend in the world.

14

Nurse, I was friendless too,
So we was makin' a pair.
I'm black as a cast-off shoe,
But that li'le dog didn't care.
He loved me as much as though
Ma skin was pearly an' white:
Somehow dogs seem to know
When a man's heart's all right.

Nurse, we was thick as thieves;
Nothin' could pry us apart,
An' now to hear how he grieves
Is twistin' a knife in ma heart.
As I worked at ma shoe-shine stand
He'd watch me wi' eyes o' love,
A-wigglin' an' lickin' ma hand
Like I was a god above.

Nurse, I sure had no luck
That night o' the rain an' the fog;
There was that thunderin' truck,
And right in the way—ma dog.
Oh, I was a fool, I fear;
It's harder to think than to feel . . .
I dashed in, flung the pup clear,
But—I went under the wheel. . . .

Nurse, it's a-gittin' dark;
Guess ma time's about up:
Don't seem to hear him bark,
Poor, broken-hearted pup! . . .
Why, here he is, darn his skin!
Lickin' ma face once more:
How did the cuss git in?
Musta' busted the door.

God, I'm an ol' black coon,
But You ain't conscious o' race.
I gotta be goin' soon,
I'll be meetin' You face to face.
I'se been sinful, dice an' hooch,
But Lordy, before I die
I'se a-prayin': "Be good to ma pooch" . . .
That's all—little mut, good-bye.

16

BINGO

The daughter of the village Maire
Is very fresh and very fair,
    A dazzling eyeful;
She throws upon me such a spell
That though my love I dare not tell,
    My heart is sighful.
She has the cutest brown *caniche,*
The French for "poodle" on a leash,
    While I have Bingo;
A dog of doubtful pedigree,
Part pug or pom or chow maybe,
    But full of stingo.

The daughter of the village Maire
Would like to speak with me, I'll swear,
    In her sweet lingo;
But *parlez-vous* I find a bore,
For I am British to the core,
    And so is Bingo.
Yet just to-day as we passed by,
Our two dogs halted eye to eye,
    In friendly poses;
Oh, how I hope to-morrow they
Will wag their tails in merry play,
    And rub their noses.

    .   .   .   .   .

The daughter of the village Maire
To-day gave me a frigid stare,
　　My hopes are blighted.
I'll tell you how it came to pass . . .
Last evening in the Square, alas!
　　My sweet I sighted;
And as she sauntered with her pet,
Her dainty, her adored Frolette,
　　I cried: "By Jingo!"
Well, call it chance or call it fate,
I made a dash . . . Too late, too late!
　　Oh, naughty Bingo!

Dear daughter of the village Maire,
That you'll forgive me, is my prayer
　　And also Bingo.
You should have shielded your *caniche;*
You saw my dog strain on his leash
　　And like a spring go.
They say that Love will find a way—
It definitely did, that day . . .
　　Oh, canine noodles!
Now it is only left to me
To wonder—will your offspring be
　　Poms, pugs or poodles?

TRIXIE

Dogs have a sense beyond our ken—
At least my little Trixie had:
Tail-wagging when I laughed, and when
I sighed, eyes luminously sad.
And if I planned to go away,
She'd know, oh, days and days before:
Aye, dogs I think are sometimes *fey*,
They seem to sense our fate in store.

Now take the case of old Tom Low;
With flowers each week he'd call on me.
Dear Trixie used to love him so,
With joyous jump upon his knee.
Yet when he wandered in one day,
Her hair grew sudden stark with dread;
She growled, she howled, she ran away . . .
Well, ten hours later Tom was dead.

Aye, dogs hear sounds we cannot hear,
And dogs see sights we cannot see;
And that is why I took the fear
That one day she would glare at me
As if a Shape cowered on my bed,
And with each hair on end she'd creep
Beneath the couch and whine with dread . . .
And so I've had her *put to sleep*.

Now Trixie's gone, the only one
Who loved me in my lonely life,
And here I wait, my race nigh run,
My ill too grievous for the knife.
My hand of ice she'll never lick,
My heedless mask she'll never see:
No heartbreak—just a needle prick. . . .
Oh, Doctor, do the same for me!

YELLOW

One pearly day of early May
I strolled upon the sand,
And saw, say half-a-mile away
A man with gun in hand;
A dog was cowering to his will,
As slow he sought to creep
Upon a dozen ducks so still
They seemed to be asleep.

When like a streak the dog dashed out,
The ducks flashed up in flight;
The fellow gave a savage shout
And cursed with all his might.
Then as I stood somewhat amazed
And gazed with eyes agog,
With bitter rage his gun he raised
And blazed and shot the dog.

You know how dogs can yelp with pain;
Its blood soaked in the sand,
And yet it crawled to him again
And tried to lick his hand.
"Forgive me, Lord, for what I've done,"
It seemed as if it said,
But once again he raised his gun:
This time he shot it—dead.

What could I do? What could I say?
'Twas such a lonely place.
Tongue-tied I saw him stride away,
I never saw his face.
I should have bawled the bastard out:
A yellow dog he slew;
But worse, he proved beyond a doubt
That—I was yellow too.

BOOK BORROWER

I am a mild man, you'll agree,
    But red my rage is,
When folks who borrow books from me
    Turn down their pages.

Or when a chap a book I lend,
    And find he's loaned it
Without permission to a friend—
    As if *he* owned it.

But worst of all I hate those crooks
    (May hell-fires burn them!)
Who beg the loan of cherished books
    And don't return them.

My books are tendrils of myself
    No shears can sever . . .
May he who rapes one from its shelf
    Be damned forever.

BOOK LOVER

I keep collecting books I know
I'll never, never read;
My wife and daughter tell me so,
And yet I never heed.
"Please make me," says some wistful tome,
"A wee bit of yourself."
And so I take my treasure home,
And tuck it in a shelf.

And now my very shelves complain;
They jam and over-spill.
They say: "Why don't you ease our strain?"
"Some day," I say, "I will."
So book by book they plead and sigh;
I pick and dip and scan;
Then put them back, distrest that I
Am such a busy man.

Now, there's my Boswell and my Sterne,
My Gibbon and Defoe;
To savour Swift I'll never learn,
Montaigne I may not know.
On Bacon I will never sup,
For Shakespeare I've no time;
Because I'm busy making up
These jingly bits of rhyme.

Chekov is caviare to me,
While Stendhal makes me snore;
Poor Proust is not my cup of tea,
And Balzac is a bore.
I have their books, I love their names,
And yet alas! they head,
With Lawrence, Joyce and Henry James,
My Roster of Unread.

I think it would be very well
If I commit a crime,
And get put in a prison cell
And not allowed to rhyme;
Yet given all these worthy books
According to my need,
I now caress with loving looks,
But never, never read.

MY LIBRARY

Like prim Professor of a College
I primed my shelves with books of knowledge;
And now I stand before them dumb,
Just like a child that sucks its thumb,
And stares forlorn and turns away,
With dolls or painted bricks to play.

They glour at me, my tomes of learning.
"You dolt!" they jibe; "you undiscerning
Moronic oaf, you made a fuss,
With highbrow swank selecting us;
Saying: 'I'll read you *all* some day'—
And now you yawn and turn away.

"Unwanted wait we with our store
Of facts and philosophic lore;
The scholarship of all the ages
Snug packed within our uncut pages;
The mystery of all mankind
In part revealed—but you are blind.

"You have no time to read, you tell us;
Oh, do not think that we are jealous
Of all the trash that wins your favour,
The flimsy fiction that you savour:
We only beg that sometimes you
Will spare us just an hour or two.

"For all the minds that went to make us
Are dust if folk like you forsake us,
And they can only live again
By virtue of your kindling brain;
In magic print they packed their best:
Come—try their wisdom to digest. . . ."

Said I: "Alas! I am not able;
I lay my cards upon the table,
And with deep shame and blame avow
I am too old to read you now;
So I will lock you in glass cases
And shun your sad, reproachful faces."

.   .   .   .

My library is noble planned,
Yet in it desolate I stand;
And though my thousand books I prize,
Feeling a witling in their eyes,
I turn from them in weariness
To wallow in the Daily Press.

For, oh, I never, never will
The noble field of knowledge till:
I pattern words with artful tricks,
As children play with painted bricks,
And realize with futile woe,
Nothing I know—*nor want to know.*

My library has windowed nooks;
And so I turn from arid books
To vastitude of sea and sky,
And like a child content am I
With peak and plain and brook and tree,
Crying: "Behold! the books for me:
Nature, be thou my Library!"

DUNCE

At school I never gained a prize,
Proving myself the model ass;
Yet how I watched with wistful eyes,
And cheered my mates who topped the class.
No envy in my heart I found,
Yet none was worthier to own
Those precious books in vellum bound,
Than I, a dreamer and a drone.

No prize at school I ever gained
(Shirking my studies, I suppose):
Yes, I remember being caned
For lack of love of Latin prose.
For algebra I won no praise,
In grammar I was far from bright:
Yet, oh, how Poetry would raise
In me a rapture of delight!

I never gained a prize at school;
The dullard's cap adorned my head;
My masters wrote me down a fool,
And yet—I'm sorry they are dead.
I'd like to go to them and say:
"Yours is indeed a tricky trade.
My honoured classmates, where are they?
Yet I, the dunce, brave books have made."

Oh, I am old and worn and grey,
And maybe have not long to live;
Yet 'tis my hope at some Prize Day
At my old school the Head will give
A tome or two of mine to crown
Some pupil's well-deserved success—
Proving a scapegrace and a clown
May win at last to worthiness.

STOWAWAY

We'd left the sea-gulls long behind,
And we were almost in mid-ocean;
The sky was soft and blue and kind,
The boat had scarcely any motion;
Except that songfully it sped,
And sheared the foam swift as an arrow . . .
When on my deck chair as I read
There fluttered down a city sparrow.

I stared with something of surprise;
The apparition mocked my seeming;
In fact I gently rubbed my eyes
And wondered if I were not dreaming.
It must, I mused, at Montreal
Have hopped abroad, somewhere to nestle,
And failed to hear the warning call
For visitors to leave the vessel.

Well, anyway a bird it was,
With winky eyes and wings a-twitter,
Unwise to Emigration Laws,
From Canada a hardy flitter;
And as it hopped about the deck
So happily I wondered whether
It wasn't scramming from Quebec
For London's mild and moister weather.

My rover's heart went out to it,
That vain, vivacious little devil;
And as I watched it hop and flit
I hoped it would not come to evil;
It planed above the plangent sea
(A foolish flight, I'd never risk it),
And then it circled back to me
And from my palm picked crumbs of biscuit.

Well, voyages come to an end
(We make them with that understanding);
One morn I missed my feathered friend,
And hope it made a happy landing.
Oh may she ever happy be
(If 'twas a "she"), with eggs to sit on,
And rest on our side of the sea,
A brave, brown, cheery, chirping Briton.

EUTHANASIA

A sea-gull with a broken wing
I found upon the kelp-strewn shore.
It sprawled and gasped; I sighed: "Poor thing!
I fear your flying days are o'er;
Sad victim of a savage gun,
So ends your soaring in the sun."

I only wanted to be kind;
Its icy legs I gently caught,
Thinking its fracture I might bind,
But fiercely in its fear it fought;
Till guessing that I meant no ill,
It glared and gaped, but lay quite still.

I took it home and gave it food,
And nursed its wing day after day.
Alas for my solicitude,
It would not eat, but pined away.
And so at last with tender hands
I took it to its native sands.

"I'll leave it where its kindred are,"
I thought, "And maybe they will cheer
And comfort it": I watched afar,
I saw them wheeling swiftly near. . . .
Awhile they hovered overhead,
Then darted down and—stabbed it dead.

When agonized is human breath,
And there's of living not a chance,
Could it not be that gentle death
Might mean divine deliverance?
Might it not seep into our skulls
To be as merciful as gulls?

FLIGHT

On silver sand where ripples curled
I counted sea-gulls seven;
Shy, secret, screened from all the world,
And innocent as heaven.
They did not of my nearness know,
For dawn was barely bright,
And they were still, like spots of snow
In that pale, pearly light.

Then one went forth unto the sea
That rippled up in gold,
And there were rubies flashing free
From out its wing-unfold;
It ducked and dived in pretty play,
The while the other six
So gravely sat it seemed that they
Were marvelled by its tricks.

Then with a sudden flurry each
Down-rushed to join its mate,
And in a flash that sickle beach
With rapture was elate.
With joy they pranked till everyone
Was diamonded with spray,
Then flicked with flame to greet the sun
They rose and winged away.

But with their going, oh, the surge
Of loss they left in me!
For in my heart was born the urge,
The passion to be free.
And where each dawn with terror brings
Some tale of bale and blight,
Who would not envy silver wings,
The sea-gull in its flight!

Let me not know the coils of woe
That chain this stricken earth;
Let me forget the fear and fret
That bind men from their birth;
Let me be one with wind and sun,
With earth and sky and sea. . . .
Oh, let me teach in living speech
God's glory—Liberty.

COURAGE

Ten little brown chicks scattered and scuffled,
Under the blue-berries hiding in fear;
Mother-grouse cackling, feathers all ruffled,
Dashed to defend them as we drew near.
Heart of a heroine, how I admired her!
Of such devotion great poets have sung;
Homes have been blest by the love that inspired her,
Risking her life for the sake of her young.

Ten little chicks on her valour reliant,
Peered with bright eyes from the bilberry spray;
Fiercely she faced us, dismayed but defiant,
Rushed at us bravely to scare us away.
Then my companion, a crazy young devil
(After, he told me he'd done it for fun)
Pretended to tremble, and raised his arm level,
And ere I could check him he blazed with his gun.

Headless she lay, from her neck the blood spouted,
And dappled her plumage, the poor, pretty thing!
Ten little chicks—oh, I know for I counted,
Came out and they tried to creep under her wing.
Sickened I said: "Here's an end to *my* killing;
I swear, nevermore bird or beast will I slay;
Starving I may be, but no more blood-spilling . . ."
That oath I have kept, and I keep it to-day.

WORMS

Worms finer for fishing you couldn't be wishing;
I delved them dismayed from the velvety sod;
The rich loam upturning I gathered them squirming,
Big, fat, gleamy earthworms, all ripe for my rod.
Thinks I, without waiting, my hook I'll be baiting,
And flip me a fish from the foam of the pool;
Then Mother beholding, came crying and scolding:
"You're late, ye young divil! Be off to the school."
So grabbing me bait-tin I dropped them fat worms in,
With gobs of green turf for their comfort and cheer;
And there, clean forgotten, no doubt dead and rotten,
I left them to languish for nigh on a year.

One day to be cleaning the byre I was meaning,
When seeing that old rusty can on a shelf,
Says I: "To my thinking, them worms must be stink-
     ing:
Begorrah! I'd better find out for myself."
So I opened the tin, held my nose and looked in;
And what did I see? Why, most nothing at all.
Just darkness and dank, and . . . a something that stank,
Tucked down in a corner, a greasy grey ball.
My worms—no, not dead, but thin as a thread,
Each seemed to reproach me, protesting its worth:
So softly I took them and tenderly shook them
Back into the bosom of mothering earth.

I'm now in the City; 'tis grand, but I pity
The weariful wretches that crawl in its grime;
The dregs and the scum and the spawn of the slum,
And the poor little childer that's cradled in crime.
Sure I see them in terms of my pitiful worms,
Surviving despite desperation and doom,
And I wish I was God, with a smile and a nod
To set them all down in a valley of bloom,
Saying: "Let these rejoice with a wonderful voice
For mothering earth and for fathering sea,
And healing of sun, for each weariful one
Of these poor human worms is a wee bit of me. . . .
Let yours be the blame and yours be the shame:
What ye do unto them ye do also to ME."

WINDOW SHOPPER

I stood before a candy shop
Which with a Christmas radiance shone;
I saw my parents pass and stop
To grin at me and then go on.
The sweets were heaped in gleamy rows;
On each I feasted—what a game!
Against the glass with flatted nose,
Gulping my spittle as it came;
So still I stood, and stared and dreamed,
Savouring sweetness with my eyes,
Devouring dainties till it seemed
My candy shop was Paradise.

I had, I think, but five years old,
And though three-score and ten have passed,
I still recall the craintive cold,
The grimy street, the gritty blast;
And how I stared into that shop,
Its gifts so near and yet so far,
Of marzipan and toffee drop,
Of chocolate and walnut bar;
Imagining what I would buy
Amid delights so rich and rare . . .
The glass was misted with my sigh:
"If just one penny Pop could spare!"

And then when I went home to tea
Of bread with butter sparsely spread,
Oh, how my parents twitted me:
"You stood for full an hour," they said.
"We saw you as we passed again;
Your eyes upon the sweets were glued;
Your nose was flattened to the pane,
Like someone hypnotized you stood."
But when they laughed as at a joke,
A bitterness I could not stem
Within my little heart awoke. . . .
Oh, I have long forgiven them;
For though I know they did not own
Pennies to spare, they might, it seems
More understanding love have shown
More sympathy for those vain dreams,
Which make of me with wistful gaze
God's Window Shopper all my days.

MY HOLIDAY

I love the cheery bustle
Of children round the house,
The tidy maids a-hustle,
The chatter of my spouse;
The laughter and the singing,
The joy on every face:
With frequent laughter ringing,
Oh, Home's a happy place!

Aye, Home's a bit of heaven;
I love it every day;
My line-up of eleven
Combine to make it gay;
Yet when in June they're leaving
For Sandport by the sea,
By rights I should be grieving,
But gosh! I just feel *free*.

I'm left with parting kisses,
The guardian of the house;
The romp, it's true, one misses,
I'm quiet as a mouse.
In carpet slippers stealing
From room to room alone
I get the strangest feeling
The place is all my own.

It seems to nestle near me,
It whispers in my ear;
My books and pictures cheer me,
Hearth never was so dear.
In peace profound I lap me,
I take no stock of time,
And from the dreams that hap me,
I make (like this) a rhyme.

Oh, I'm ashamed of saying
(And think it's mean of me),
That when the kids are staying
At Sandport on the sea,
And I evoke them clearly
Disporting in the spray,
I love them still more dearly
Because . . . they're far away.

EYRIE

The little pink house is high on the hill
And my heart is not what it used to be;
It will kick up a fuss I know, but still
I must toil up that twisty trail to see
What that empty old house can mean to me.

For a Poet lived there for donkey's years,
A Poet of parts and founded fame.
He took to the bottle, it appears,
And hid up there to enjoy his shame . . .
Oh, no, I'll never betray his name.

Then gaily he drank himself to death,
But, oh, on the rarest of mellow wine;
An exquisite way to end one's breath—
Lachrimae Christi, I'd choose for mine,
To sip and souse in the sweet sunshine.

They say that poets are half divine;
I question if that is always true;
At least, our Poet was partly swine,
Drunk each day, with a drab or two,
Till Presto! he vanished from our view.

Maybe he was weary of woe and sin,
Or sick, and crawled like a dog to die;
Where the olives end and the pines begin,
He sought the peace of the sun and sky . . .
He would see no one, and I wonder why?

44

And so I must climb up, up some day
And try to picture my Poet there;
He sprawled on his rose-bowered porch, they say,
To smoke and fuddle and dream and stare
At the sapphire sea through the amber air.

He gave up the ghost with none to see;
In his bed, no doubt, though I'd fain surmise
It was yonder under the ilex tree,
Watching the sun in splendour rise,
With the glory of God-light in his eyes.

Well, he was a Lord of Radiant Rhyme;
His gift was godlike, one can't deny,
But he quit in the glory of his prime
As if he despised us—I wonder why?
As if he found, where yon mountains soar,
Far from men-folk and heaven-high,
Peace and Beauty forever more . . .
Peace and Beauty—Ah! so would I.

ESCAPE

Tell me, Tramp, where I may go
To be free from human woe;
Say where I may hope to find
Ease of heart and peace of mind;
Is there not some isle you know
Where I may leave Care behind?

So spoke one in sore distress,
And I answered softly: "Yes,
There's an isle so sweet and kind
So to clemency inclined,
So serene in loveliness
That the blind may lead the blind.

"Where there is no shade of fear,
For the sun shines all the year,
And there hangs on every tree
Fruit and food for you and me:
With each dawn so crystal clear
How like heaven earth can be!

"Where in mild and friendly clime
You will lose all count of time,
See the seasons blend in one,
Under sovereignty of sun;
Day with day resolve in rhyme,
Reveries and nothings done.

"You will mock the ocean roar,
Knowing you will evermore
Bide beside a lorn lagoon,
Listen to the ripples croon
On the muteness of the shore,
Silver-shattered in the moon.

"Come, let's quit this sorry strife,
Seek a sweeter, saner life,
Go so far, so very far
It just seems another star.
Go where joy and love are rife,
Go where peace and plenty are."

But he answered: "Brother, no,
To your isle I'll never go,
For the pity in my heart
Will not let me live apart
From God's world of want and woe:
I will stay and play my part,
Strive and suffer . . . Be it so."

PORTENT

Courage mes gars:
La guerre est proche.

I plant my little plot of beans,
I sit beneath my cyprus tree;
I do not know what trouble means,
I cultivate tranquillity . . .
But as to-day my walk I made
In all serenity and cheer,
I saw cut in an *agave* blade:
"Courage, my comrades, war is near!"

Seaward I went, my feet were slow,
Awhile I drowsed upon the shore;
And then I roused with fear for lo!
I saw six grisly ships of war.
A grim, grey line of might and dread
Against the skyline looming sheer:
With horror to myself I said:
"Courage, my comrades, war is near."

I saw my cottage on the hill
With rambling roses round the door;
It was so peaceful and so still
I sighed . . . and then it was no more.
A flash of flame, a rubble heap;
I cried aloud with woe and fear . . .
And woke myself from troubled sleep—
My home was safe, war was not near.

48

Oh, I am old, my step is frail,
My carcase bears a score of scars,
And as I climbed my homeward trail
Sadly I thought of other wars.
And when that *agave* leaf I saw
With vicious knife I made a blear
Of words clean-cut into the raw:
"Courage, my comrades, war is near."

Who put them there I do not know—
One of these rabid reds, no doubt;
But I for freedom struck my blow,
With bitter blade I scraped them out.
There now, said I, I will forget,
And smoke my pipe and drink my beer—
Yet in my mind these words were set:
"Courage, my comrades, war is near."

"Courage, my comrades, war is near."
I hear afar its hateful drums;
Its horrid din assails my ear:
I hope I die before it comes. . . .
Yet as into the town I go,
And listen to the rabble cheer,
I think with heart of weary woe:
War is not coming—WAR IS HERE.

NO MORE MUSIC

The porch was blazoned with geranium bloom;
Myrtle and jasmine meadows lit the lea;
With rose and violet the vale's perfume
Languished to where the hyacinthine sea
Dreamed tenderly . . . "And I must go," said he.

He spoke in that dim, ghostly voice of his:
"I was a singer; then the War . . . and GAS."
(I had to lean to him, no word to miss.)
"We bought this little *café* nigh to Grasse;
With sun and flowers my last few days will pass.

"And music too. I have my mandolin:
Say! Maybe you can strum on yon guitar . . .
Come on—we two will make melodious din,
While Madame sings to us behind the bar:
You'll see how sweet Italian folk-songs are."

So he would play and I would thrum the while;
I used to go there every lovely day;
His wife would listen with a sunny smile,
And when I left: "Please come again," she'd say.
"He seems quite sad when you have gone away."

Alas! I had to leave without good-bye,
And lived in sooty cities for a year.
Oh, how my heart ached for that happy sky!
Then, then one day my *café* I drew near—
God! it was strange how I was gripped with fear.

So still it was; I saw no mandolin,
No gay guitar with ribbons blue and red;
Then all in black, stone-faced the wife came in . . .
I did not ask; I looked, she shook her head:
"La musique est fini," was all she said.

TRANQUILLITY

This morning on my pensive walk
I saw a fisher on a rock,
Who watched his ruby float careen
In waters bluely crystalline,
While silver fishes nosed his bait,
Yet hesitated ere they ate.

Nearby I saw a mother mild
Who knitted by her naked child,
And watched him as he romped with glee,
In golden sand, in singing sea,
Her eyes so blissfully love-lit
She gazed and gazed and ceased to knit.

And then I watched a painter chap,
Grey-haired, a grandfather, mayhap,
Who daubed with delicate caress
As if in love with loveliness,
And looked at me with vague surmise,
The joy of beauty in his eyes.

Yet in my Morning Rag I read
Of paniked peoples, dark with dread,
Of flame and famine near and far,
Of revolution, pest and war;
The fall of this, the rise of that,
The writhing proletariat. . . .

I saw the fisher from his hook
Take off a shiny perch to cook;
The mother garbed her laughing boy,
And sang a silver lilt of joy;
The artist, packing up his paint,
Went home serenely as a saint.

The sky was gentleness and love,
The sea soft-crooning as a dove;
Peace reigned so brilliantly profound
In every sight, in every sound. . . .
Alas, what mockery for me!
Can peace be mine till Man be free?

PANTHEIST

Lolling on a bank of thyme
Drunk with Spring I made this rhyme. . . .

Though peoples perish in defeat,
And races suffer to survive,
The sunshine never was so sweet,
So vast the joy to be alive;
The laughing leaves, the glowing grass
Proclaim how good it is to be;
The pines are lyric as I pass,
The hills hosannas sing to me.

Pink roses ring yon placid palm,
Soft shines the blossom of the peach;
The sapphire sea is satin calm,
With bell-like tinkle on the beach;
A lizard lazes in the sun,
A bee is bumbling to my hand;
Shy breezes whisper: "You are one
With us because you understand."

Yea, I am one with all I see,
With wind and wave, with pine and palm;
Their very elements in me
Are fused to make me what I am.
Through me their common life-stream flows,
And when I yield this human breath,
In leaf and blossom, bud and rose,
Live on I will . . . There is no Death.

Oh, let me flee from woeful things,
And listen to the linnet's song;
To solitude my spirit clings,
To sunny woodlands I belong.
O foolish men! Yourselves destroy.
But I from pain would win surcease. . . ,
O Earth, grant me eternal joy!
O Nature—everlasting peace!

                    Amen.

A VERSEMAN'S APOLOGY

Alas! I am only a rhymer,
I don't know the meaning of Art;
But I learned in my little school primer
To love Eugene Field and Bret Harte.
I hailed Hoosier Ryley with pleasure,
To John Hay I took off my hat;
These fellows were right to my measure,
And I've never gone higher than that.

The Classics! Well, most of them bore me,
The Moderns I don't understand;
But I keep Burns, my kinsman, before me,
And Kipling, my friend, is at hand.
They taught me my trade as I know it,
Yet though at their feet I have sat,
For God-sake don't call me a poet,
For I've never been guilty of that.

A rhyme-rustler, rugged and shameless,
A Bab Balladeer on the loose;
Of saccarine sonnets I'm blameless,
My model has been—Mother Goose.
And I fancy my grave-digger griping
As he gives my last lodging a pat:
"That guy wrote McGrew;
'Twas the best he could do" . . .
So I'll go to my Maker with that.

NO SOURDOUGH

To be a *bony feed* Sourdough
You must, by Yukon Law,
Have killed a moose,
And robbed a sluice,
AND BUNKED UP WITH A SQUAW. . . .

Alas! Sourdough I'll never be.
Oh, sad is my excuse:
My shooting's so damn bad, you see . . .
I've never killed a moose.

KATHLEEN

It was the steamer *Alice May* that sailed the Yukon
 foam,
And touched at every river camp from Dawson down
 to Nome.
It was her builder, owner, pilot, Captain Silas Geer,
Who took her through the angry ice, the last boat of
 the year;
Who patched her cracks with gunny sacks and wound
 her pipes with wire,
And cut the spruce upon the banks to feed her boiler
 fire;
Who headed her into the stream and bucked its mighty
 flow,
And nosed her up the little creeks where no one else
 would go;
Who bragged she had so small a draft, if dew was on
 the grass,
With gallant heart and half a start his little boat would
 pass.
Aye, ships might come and ships might go, but steady
 every year
The *Alice May* would chug away with Skipper Silas
 Geer.

Now though Cap Geer had ne'er a fear the devil he
 could bilk,
He owned a gastric ulcer and his grub was mostly milk.
He also owned a Jersey cow to furnish him the same,
So soft and sleek and mild and meek, and Kathleen was
 her name.

And as his source of nourishment he got to love
    her so
That everywhere the Captain went the cow would also
    go;
And though his sleeping quarters were ridiculously
    small,
He roped a section of them off to make Kathleen a stall.
So every morn she'd wake him up with mellifluous
    moo,
And he would pat her on the nose and go to wake the
    crew.
Then when he'd done his daily run and hitched on to
    the bank,
She'd breathe above his pillow till to soothing sleep he
    sank.
So up and down the river seeded sourdoughs would
    allow,
They made a touching tableau, Captain Silas and his
    cow.

Now as the Captain puffed his pipe and Kathleen
    chewed her cud,
There came to him a poetess, a Miss Belinda Budd.
"An epic I would write," said she, "about this mighty
    stream,
And from your gallant bark 'twould be romantic as a
    dream."
Somewhat amazed the Captain gazed at her and shook
    his head:
"I'm sorry, Miss, but we don't take *she* passengers," he
    said.

"My boat's a freighter, we have no accommodation space
For women-folk—my cabin is the only private place.
It's eight foot small from wall to wall, and I have, any-
    how,
No room to spare, for half I share with Kathleen, that's
    my cow."
The lady sighed, then soft replied: "I love your Yukon
    scene,
And for its sake your room I'll take, and put up with
    Kathleen."

Well, she was so dead set to go the Captain said: "By
    heck!
I like your spunk; you take my bunk and I'll camp on
    the deck."
So days went by then with a sigh she sought him out
    anew:
"Oh, Captain Geer, Kathleen's a dear, but does she
    have to moo?
In early morn like motor horn she bellows overhead,
While all the night without respite she snorts above my
    bed.
I know it's true she dotes on you, your smile she seems
    to miss;
She leans so near I live in fear my brow she'll try to
    kiss.
Her fond regard makes it *so* hard my Pegasus to
    spur. . . .
Oh, please be kind and try to find another place for
    her."

60

Bereft of cheer was Captain Geer; his face was glazed
   with gloom:
He scratched his head: "There ain't," he said, "another
   inch of room.
With freight we're packed; it's stowed and stacked—
   why even on the deck.
There's seven salted sourdoughs and they're sleeping
   neck and neck.
I'm sorry, Miss, that Kathleen's kiss has put your muse
   to flight;
I realize her amber eyes abstract you when you write.
I used to love them orbs above a-shining down on me,
And when she'd chew my whiskers you can't calculate
   my glee.
I ain't at all poetical, but gosh! I guess your plight,
So I will try to plan what I can fix up for to-night."

Thus while upon her berth the wan and weary Author
   Budd
Bewailed her fate, Kathleen sedate above her chewed
   her cud;
And as he sought with brain distraught a steady course
   to steer,
Yet find a plan, a worried man was Captain Silas Geer.
Then suddenly alert was he, he hollered to his mate:
"Hi, Patsy, press our poetess to climb on deck and
   wait.
Hip-hip-hooray! Bid her be gay and never more de-
   spair:
My search is crowned—by heck! I've found an answer
   to her prayer."

To Patsy's yell like glad gazelle came bounding Bardess
 Budd;
No more forlorn, with hope new-born she faced the
 foaming flood;
While down the stair with eager air was seen to dis-
 appear,
Like one inspired (by genius fired) exultant Captain
 Geer.
Then up he came with eye aflame and honest face
 aglow,
And oh, how loud he laughed, as proud he led her
 down below.
"Now you may write by day or night upon our Yukon
 scene,
For I," he cried, "have clarified the problem of Kath-
 leen.
I thought a lot, then like a shot the remedy I found:
I jest unhitched her rope and switched the loving crea-
 ture round.
No more her moo will trouble you, you'll sleep right
 restful now.
Look, Lady, look!—I'm giving you . . . *the tail end of*
 the cow."

MONTREAL MAREE

You've heard of Belching Billy, likewise known as
    Windy Bill,
As punk a chunk of Yukon scum as ever robbed a
    sluice;
A satellite of Soapy Smith, a capper and a shill,
A slimy tribute-taker from the Ladies on the Loose.
But say, you never heard of how he aimed my gore to spill
(That big gorilla gunnin' for a little guy like me,)
A-howlin' like a malamute an' ravin' he would drill
Me full of holes and all because of Montreal Maree.

Now Spike Mahoney's Nugget Bar was stiff with
    roarin' drunks,
And I was driftin' lonesome-like, scarce knowin' what
    to do,
So come I joined a poker game and dropped a hundred
    plunks,
And bein' broke I begged of Spike to take my I.O.U.
Says he: "Me lad, I'll help ye out, but let me make
    this clear:
If you don't pay by New Year's day your wage I'll
    garnishee."
So I was broodin' when I heard a whisper in my ear:
"What ees zee trouble, leetle boy?" said Montreal
    Maree.

Now dance-hall gels is good and bad, but most is in
    between;
Yeh, some is scum and some is dumb, and some is jest
    plumb cold;

But of straight-shootin' Dawson dames Maree was
   rated queen,
As pretty as a pansy, wi' a heart o' Hunker gold.
And so although I didn't know her more than passin'
   by,
I told how Spike would seek my Boss, and jobless I
   would be;
She listened sympathetic like: "Zut! Baby, don't you
   cry:
I lend to you zee hundred bucks," said Montreal Maree.

Now though I zippered up my mug somehow the story
   spread
That I was playin' poker and my banker was Maree;
And when it got to Windy Bill, by Golly, he saw red,
And reachin' for his shootin' iron he started after me.
For he was batty for that babe and tried to fence her in.
And if a guy got in his way, say, he was set to kill;
So fortified with barbwire hooch and wickeder than sin:
"I'll plug that piker full of lead," exploded Windy Bill.

That night, a hundred smackers saved, with joy I
   started out
To seek my scented saviour in her cabin on the hill;
But barely had I paid my debt, when suddenly a
   shout . . .
I peered from out the window, and behold! 'twas
   Windy Bill.
He whooped and swooped and raved and waved his
   gun as he drew near.
Now he was kickin' in the door, no time was there to
   flee;

No place to hide: my doom was sealed . . . then softly
in my ear:
"Quick! creep beneez my petticoat," said Montreal
Maree.

So pale as death I held my breath below that billowed
skirt,
And as she sat I wondered at her voice so calm and clear;
Serene and still she spoke to Bill like he was so much dirt:
"*Espèce de skunk!* You jus' beeg drunk. You see no
man is here."
Then Bill began to cuss and ran wild shootin' down the
hill,
And all was hushed, and how I wished that bliss could
ever be,
When up she rose in dainty pose beside the window sill:
"He spill hees gun, run Baby, run," cried Montreal
Maree.

I've heard it said that she got wed and made a wonder
wife.
I guess she did; that careless kid had mother in her
heart.
But anyway I'll always say she saved my blasted life,
For other girls may come and go, and each may play
their part:
But if I live a hundred years I'll not forget the thrill,
The rapture of that moment when I kissed a dimpled
knee,
And safely mocked the murderous menace of Windy
Bill,
Snug hid beneath the petticoat of Montreal Maree.

THE THREE BARES

Ma tried to wash her garden slacks but couldn't get 'em
    clean
And so she thought she'd soak 'em in a bucket o' ben-
    zine.
It worked all right. She wrung 'em out then wondered
    what she'd do
With all that bucket load of high explosive residue.
She knew that it was dangerous to scatter it around,
For Grandpa liked to throw his lighted matches on the
    ground.
Somehow she didn't dare to pour it down the kitchen
    sink,
And what the heck to do with it, poor Ma jest couldn't
    think.

Then Nature seemed to give the clue, as down the
    garden lot
She spied the edifice that graced a solitary spot,
Their Palace of Necessity, the family joy and pride,
Enshrined in morning-glory vine, with graded seats in-
    side;
Jest like that cabin Goldylocks found occupied by three,
But in this case B-E-A-R was spelt B-A-R-E—
A tiny seat for Baby Bare, a medium for Ma,
A full-sized section sacred to the Bare of Grandpapa.

Well, Ma was mighty glad to get that worry off her
    mind,
And hefting up the bucket so combustibly inclined,
She hurried down the garden to that refuge so discreet,

And dumped the liquid menace safely through the
   centre seat.

Next morning old Grandpa arose; he made a hearty
   meal,
And sniffed the air and said: "By Gosh! how full of
   beans I feel.
Darned if I ain't as fresh as paint; my joy will be
   complete
With jest a quiet session on the usual morning seat;
To smoke me pipe an' meditate, an' maybe write a
   pome,
For that's the time when bits o' rhyme gits jiggin' in
   me dome."

He sat down on that special seat slicked shiny by his
   age,
And looking like Walt Whitman, jest a silver-whiskered
   sage,
He filled his corn-cob to the brim and tapped it snugly
   down,
And chuckled: "Of a perfect day I reckon this the
   crown."
He lit the weed, it soothed his need, it was so soft and
   sweet:
And then he dropped the lighted match *clean through
   the middle seat.*

His little grand-child Rosyleen cried from the kitchen
   door:
"Oh, Ma, come quick; there's sompin wrong; I heared
   a dreffel roar;

Oh, Ma, I see a sheet of flame; it's rising high and
higher . . .
Oh, Mummy dear, I sadly fear our comfort-cot's
caught fire."

Poor Ma was thrilled with horror at them words o'
Rosyleen.
She thought of Grandpa's matches and that bucket of
benzine;
So down the garden geared on high, she ran with all her
power,
For regular was Grandpa, and she knew it was his hour.
Then graspin' gaspin' Rosyleen she peered into the fire,
A roarin' soarin' furnace now, perchance old Grandpa's
pyre. . . .

But as them twain expressed their pain they heard a
hearty cheer—
Behold the old rapscallion squattin' in the duck-pond
near,
His silver whiskers singed away, a gosh-almighty wreck,
Wi' half a yard o' toilet seat entwined about his
neck. . . .

He cried: "Say, folks, oh, did ye hear the big blow-out
I made?
It scared me stiff—I hope you-uns was not too much
afraid?
But now I best be crawlin' out o' this dog-gasted
wet. . . .
For what I aim to figger out is—WHAT THE HECK
I ET?

MY MASTERS

Of Poetry I've been accused,
But much more often I have not;
Oh, I have been so much amused
By those who've put me on the spot,
And measured me by rules above
Those I observe with equal love.

An artisan of verse am I,
Of simple sense and humble tone;
My Thesaurus is handy by,
A rhyming lexicon I own;
Without them I am ill at ease—
What bards would use such aids as these?

Bad poets make good verse, they say;
The Great have not disdained to woo
The modest muse of every day;
Read Longfellow and Byron through,
The fabric test—much verse you'll see
Compared with what is poetry.

Small blame; one cannot always soar
To heights of hyaline sublime;
Melodious prose one must deplore,
And fetters of rebellious rhyme:
Keats, Browning—that's another tale,
But even Giants fall and fail.

I've worshipped Ryley, Harte and Field,
And though their minstrelsy I lack,
To them heart-homage here I yield,
And follow with my verseman's pack:
To them with gratitude I look,
For briefing me to make this book.

THE YUKONER

He burned a hole in frozen muck,
He pierced the icy mould,
And there in six-foot dirt he struck
A sack or so of gold.

He burned holes in the Decalogue,
And then it came about,
For Fortune's just a lousy rogue,
His "pocket" petered out.

And lo! 'twas but a year all told,
When there in shadow grim,
In six feet deep of icy mould
They burned a hole for him.

MY TYPEWRITER

I used to think a pot of ink
Held magic in its fluid,
And I would ply a *pen* when I
Was hoary as a Druid;
But as I scratch my silver thatch
My battered old Corona
Calls out to me as plaintively
As dying Desdemona.

"For old time's sake give me a break:
To you I've been as loyal
As ever could an Underwood,
Or Remington or Royal.
The globe we've spanned together and
Two million words, maybe,
For you I've tapped—it's time you rapped
A rhyme or two for me.

"I've seen you sit and smoke and spit
With expletives profane,
Then tear with rage the virgin page
I tendered you in vain.
I've watched you glare in dull despair
Through hours of brooding thought,
Then with a shout bang gaily out
The 'word unique' you sought.

"I've heard you groan and grunt and moan
That rhyme's a wretched fetter;
That after all you're just a small
Fat-headed verse-begetter;
You'd balance me upon your knee
Like any lady friend,
Then with a sigh you'd lay me by
For weeks and weeks on end.

"I've known when you were mighty blue
And hammered me till dawn,
Dire poverty! But I would be
The last thing you would pawn.
Days debt-accurst! Then at its worst
The sky, behold, would clear;
A poem sold, the garret cold
Would leap to light and cheer.

"You've toted me by shore and sea
From Mexico to Maine;
From Old Cathay to Mandalay,
From Samarkand to Spain.
You've thumped me in the battle's din
And pounded me in peace;
By air and land you've lugged me and
Your shabby old valise.

"But now my keys no more with ease
To your *two* fingers yield;
With years of use my joints are loose,
With wear of flood and field.
And even you are slipping too:
You're puffy, stiff and grey:
Old Sport, we're done, our race is run—
Why not call it a day?"

. . . . .

Why not? You've been, poor old machine!
My tried and faithful friend.
With fingertip your keys I'll flip
Serenely to the end.
For even though you're stiff and slow,
No other will I buy,
And though each word be wan and blurred
I'll tap you till I die.

THE LIVING DEAD

Since I have come to years sedate
I see with more and more acumen
The bitter irony of Fate,
The vanity of all things human.
Why, just to-day some fellow said,
As I surveyed Fame's outer portal:
"By gad! I thought that you were dead."
Poor me, who dreamed to be immortal!

But that's the way with many men
Whose name one fancied time-defying;
We thought that they were dust, and then
We found them living by their dying.
Like dogs we penmen have our day,
To brief best-sellerdom elected;
And then, "thumbs down," we slink away
And die forgotten and neglected.

Ah well, my lyric fling I've had;
A thousand bits of verse I've minted;
And some, alas! were very bad,
And some, alack! were best unprinted.
But if I've made my muse a bawd
(Since I am earthy as a ditch is),
I'll answer humbly to my God:
Most men at times have toyed with bitches.

Yes, I have played with Lady Rhyme,
And had a long and lovely innings;
And when the Umpire calls my time
I'll blandly quit and take my winnings.
I'll hie me to some Sleepydale,
And feed the ducks and pat the poodles,
And prime my paunch with cakes and ale,
And blether with the village noodles.

And then some day you'll idly scan
The Times obituary column,
And say: "Dear me, the poor old man!"
And for a moment you'll look solemn.
"So all this time he's been alive—
In realms of rhyme a second-rater . . .
But gad! to live to ninety-five:
Let's toast his ghost—a sherry, waiter!"

HOBO

A father's pride I used to know,
A mother's love was mine;
For swinish husks I let them go,
And bedded with the swine.
Since then I've come on evil days
And most of life is hell;
But even swine have winsome ways
When once you know them well.

One time I guessed I'd cease to roam,
And greet the folks again;
And so I rode the rods to home
And through the window pane
I saw them weary, worn and grey . . .
I gazed from garden gloom,
And like sweet, shiny saints were they
In that sweet, shiny room.

D'ye think I hollered out: "Hullo!"
The prodigal to play,
And eat the fatted calf? Ah no,
I cursed and ran away.
My eyes were blears of whisky tears
As to a pub I ran:
But once at least I beat the beast
And proved myself a man.

Oh, some day I am going back,
But I'll have gold galore;
I'll wear a suit of sober black
And knock upon the door.
I'll tell them how I've made a stake,
We'll have the grandest time. . . .
*"Say, Mister, give a guy a break:
For Crissake, spare a dime."*

DRIFTER

God gave you guts: don't let Him down;
Brace up, be worthy of His giving.
The road's a rut, the sky's a frown;
I know you're plumb fed up with living.
Fate birches you, and wry the rod . . .
Snap out, you fool! Don't let down God.

Oh, yes, you're on misfortune's shift,
And weary is the row you're hoeing;
You have no home, you drift and drift,
Seems folks don't care the way you're going . . .
Well, make them care—you're not afraid:
Step on the gas—you'll make the grade.

Believe that God has faith in you,
In you His loving light is shining;
All of you that is fine and true
Is part of Him, so quit your whining . . .
Buck up, son, for your Maker's sake:
Don't let Him down—give God a break.

HOT DIGITTY DOG

Hot digitty dog! Now, ain't it queer,
I've been abroad for over a year;
Seen a helluva lot since then,
Killed, I reckon, a dozen men;
Six was doubtful, but six was sure,
Three in Normandy, three in the Ruhr.
Four I got with a hand grenade,
Two I shot in a midnight raid:
Oh, I ain't sorry, except perhaps
To think that my jerries wasn't japs.

Hot digitty dog! Now ain't it tough;
I oughta be handed hero stuff—
Bands and banquets, and flags and flowers,
Speeches, peaches, confetti showers;
"Welcome back to the old home town,
Colour Sergeant Josephus Brown.
Fought like a tiger, one of our best,
Medals and ribands on his chest.
Cheers for a warrior, fresh from the fight . . ."
Sure I'd 'a got 'em--had I been *white*.

Hot digitty dog! It's jist too bad,
Gittin' home an' nobody glad;
Sneakin' into the Owl Drug Store
Nobody knowin' me any more;
Admirin' my uniform fine and fit—
Say, I've certainly changed a bit
From the lanky lad who used to croon
To a battered banjo in Shay's Saloon;
From the no-good nigger who runned away
After stickin' his knife into ol' man Shay.

They'd a lynched me, for he was white,
But he raped my sister one Sunday night;
So I did what a proper man should do,
And I sunk his body deep in the slough.
Oh, he taunted me to my dark disgrace,
Called me nigger, spat in my face;
So I buried my jack-knife in his heart,
Laughin' to see the hot blood start;
Laughin' still, though it's long ago,
And nobody's ever a-gonna know.

Nobody's ever a-gonna tell
How Ol' Man Shay went straight to hell;
Nobody's gonna make me confess—
And what is a killin' more or less.
My skin may be black, but by Christ! I fight;
I've slain a dozen, and each was white,
And none of 'em ever did me no harm,
And my conscience is clear—I've no alarm:
So I'll go where I sank Ol' Man Shay in the bog,
And spit in the water . . . *Hot digitty dog!*

OLD ED

Our cowman, old Ed, hadn't much in his head,
And lots of folks thought him a witling;
But he wasn't a fool, for he always kept cool,
And his sole recreation was whittling.
When I'd spill him my woes (infantile, I suppose),
He'd harken and whittle and whittle;
Then when I had done, turn his quid and say: "Son,
Ye're a-drownin' yerself in yer spittle."

He's gone to his grave, but the counsel he gave
I've proved in predicaments trying;
When I got in a stew, feeling ever so blue,
My failures and faults magnifying,
I'd think of old Ed as he sniffed and he said:
"Shaw! *them* things don't matter a tittle.
Ye darned little cuss, why make such a fuss?
Ye're a-drownin' yerself in yer spittle."

When you're tangled with care till you're up in the air,
And worry and fear have you quaking,
When each tiny trouble seems bigger than double,
Till mountains of mole-hills you're making:
Go easy, my friend, things click in the end,
But maybe 'twill help you a little,
If you take Ed's advice (though it may not *sound* nice):
"Don't be drownin' yerself in yer spittle."

SCHIZOPHRENIC

Each morning as I catch my bus,
A-fearing I'll be late,
I think: there are in all of us
Two folks quite separate;
As one I greet the office staff
With grim, official mien;
The other's when I belly-laugh,
And Home Sweet Home's the scene.

I've half a hundred men to boss,
And take my job to heart;
You'll never find me at a loss,
So well I play my part.
My voice is hard, my eye is cold,
My mouth is grimly set;
They all consider me, I'm told,
A "bloody martinet."

But when I reach my home at night
I'm happy as a boy;
My kiddies kiss me with delight,
And dance a jig of joy.
I slip into my oldest clothes,
My lines of care uncrease;
I mow the lawn, unhook the hose,
And glow with garden peace.

It's then I wonder which I am,
The boss with hard-boiled eye,
Or just the gay don't-care-a-damn
Go-lucky garden guy?
Am I the starchy front who rants
As round his weight he throws,
Or just old Pop with patchy pants,
Who sings and sniffs a rose?

BABETTE

My Lady is dancing so lightly,
The belle of the Embassy Ball;
I lied as I kissed her politely,
And hurried away from it all.
I'm taxiing up to Montmartre,
With never a pang of regret,
To toy for awhile with the garter
Of her whom I know as Babette.

My Lady's an exquisite creature,
As rare as a queen on a throne;
She's faultless in form and in feature,
But oh, she is cold as a stone.
And so from her presence I hurry,
Her iciness quick to forget
In sensuous joy as I bury
My face in the breast of Babette.

She's only a flower of the pavement;
With Paris and Spring in her eyes;
Yet I who foresaw what the grave meant
Of passion behold with surprise,
When she greets me as gay as a linnet,
Afar from life's fever and fret,
I'm twenty years younger the minute
I enter the room of Babette.

The poor little supper she offers
Is more than a banquet to me;
A diffident *bif-tik* she proffers,
Pommes frit and a morsel of *Brie;*
We finish with coffee and kisses,
Then sit on the sofa and pet . . .
At the Embassy *Mumm* never misses,
But *pinard's* my drink with Babette.

Somehow and somewhere to my thinking,
There's a bit of *apache* in us all;
In *bistros* I'd rather be drinking,
Than dance at the Embassy Ball.
How often I feel I would barter
My place in the social set,
To roam in a moonlit Montmartre,
Alone with my little Babette.

I'm no longer young and I'm greying;
I'm tailored, top-hatted, kid-gloved,
And though in dark ways I be straying,
It's heaven to love and be loved;
The passion of youth to re-capture. . . .
My Lady's perfection and yet
When I kiss her I think of the rapture
I find in the charms of Babette—
Entwined in the arms of Babette.

NO LILIES FOR LISETTE

Said the Door: "She came in
With no shadow of sin;
Turned the key in the lock,
Slipped out of her frock,
The robe she liked best
When for supper she dressed.
Then a letter she tore . . .
What a wan look she wore!"
      Said the Door.

Said the Chair: "She sat down
With a pitiful frown,
And then (oh, it's queer)
Just one lonely tear
Rolled down her pale cheek.
How I hoped she would speak
As she let down her hair,"
      Said the Chair.

Said the Glass: "Then she gazed
Into me like one dazed;
As with delicate grace
She made up her face,
Her cheeks and her lips
With rose finger-tips,
So lovely—alas!
Then she *turned on the gas*,"
      Said the Glass.

Said the Bed: "Down she lay
In a weariful way,
Like an innocent child,
To her fate reconciled;
Hands clasped to her breast,
In prayer or in rest:
'Dear Mother,' she said,
Then pillowed her head,"
      Said the Bed.

Said the Room: "Then the gleam
Of the moon like a dream,
Soft silvered my space,
And it fell on her face
That was never so sweet
As her heart ceased to beat . . .
Then the moon fled and gloom
Fell like funeral plume,"
      Said the Room.

"Just a whore,"
Said the Door;
"Yet so fair,"
Said the Chair;
"Frail, alas!"
Said the Glass;
"Now she's dead,"
Said the Bed;
"Sorry doom,"
Said the Room. . . .

Then they all,
Floor and wall,
Quiet grew,
Ceiling too;
Like a tomb
Was the room;
With hushed breath
Hailing Death:
Soul's release,
Silence, Peace.

THE CHRISTMAS TREE

In the dank and damp of an alley cold,
Lay the Christmas tree that hadn't been sold;
By a shopman dourly thrown outside,
With the ruck and rubble of Christmas-tide;
Trodden deep in the muck and mire,
Unworthy even to feed a fire. . . .
So I stooped and salvaged that tarnished tree,
And this is the story it told to me:

"My Mother was Queen of the forest glade,
And proudly I prospered in her shade;
For she said to me: 'When I am dead,
You will be monarch in my stead,
And reign, as I, for a hundred years,
A tower of triumph amid your peers.
When I crash in storm I will yield you space;
Son, you will worthily take my place.'

"So I grew in grace like a happy child,
In the heart of the forest free and wild;
And the moss and the ferns were all about,
And the craintive mice crept in and out;
And a wood-dove swung on my highest twig,
And a chipmunk chattered: 'So big! So big!'
And a shy fawn nibbled a tender shoot,
And a rabbit nestled under my root. . . .
Oh, I was happy in rain and shine
As I thought of the destiny that was mine!
Then a man with an axe came cruising by
And I knew that my fate was to fall and die.

"With a hundred others he packed me tight,
And we drove to a magic city of light,
To an avenue lined with Christmas trees,
And I thought: may be I'll be one of these,
Tinselled with silver and tricked with gold,
A lovely sight for a child to behold;
A-glitter with lights of every hue,
Ruby and emerald, orange and blue,
And kiddies dancing, with shrieks of glee—
One might fare worse than a Christmas tree.

"So they stood me up with a hundred more
In the blaze of a big department store;
But I thought of the forest dark and still,
And the dew and the snow and the heat and the chill;
And the soft chinook and the summer breeze,
And the dappled deer and the birds and the bees. . . .
I was so homesick I wanted to cry,
But patient I waited for someone to buy.
And some said 'Too big,' and some 'Too small,'
While some passed on saying nothing at all.
Then a little boy cried: 'Ma, buy that one,'
But she shook her head: 'Too dear, my son.'
So the evening came, when they closed the store,
And I was left on the littered floor,
A tree unwanted, despised, unsold,
Thrown out at last in the alley, cold."

Then I said: "Don't sorrow; at least you'll be
A bright and beautiful New Year's tree,
All shimmer and glimmer and glow and gleam,
A radiant sight like a fairy dream.
For there is a little child I know,
Who lives in poverty, want and woe;
Who lies abed from morn to night,
And never has known an hour's delight. . . ."

So I stood the tree at the foot of her bed:
"Santa's a little late," I said.
"Poor old chap! Snowbound on the way,
But he's here at last, so let's be gay."
Then she woke from sleep and she saw you there,
And her eyes were love and her lips were prayer.
And her thin little arms were stretched to you
With a yearning joy that they never knew.
She woke from the darkest dark to see
Like a heavenly vision, that Christmas Tree.

Her mother despaired and feared the end,
But from that day she began to mend,
To play, to sing, to laugh with glee. . . .
Bless you, O little Christmas Tree!
You died, but your life was not in vain:
You helped a child to forget her pain,
And let hope live in our hearts again.

WHITE CHRISTMAS

My folks think I'm a serving maid
Each time I visit home;
They do not dream I ply a trade
As old as Greece or Rome;
For if they found I'd fouled their name
And was not white as snow,
I'm sure that they would die of shame . . .
Please God, they'll never know.

I clean the paint from off my face,
In sober black I dress;
Of coquetry I leave no trace
To give them vague distress;
And though it causes me a pang
To play such sorry tricks,
About my neck I meekly hang
A silver crucifix.

And so with humble step I go
Just like a child again,
To greet their Christmas candle-glow,
A soul without a stain;
So well I play my contrite part
I make myself believe
There's not a stain within my heart
On Holy Christmas Eve.

With double natures we are vext,
And what we feel, we are;
A saint one day, a sinner next,
A red light or a star;
A prostitute or proselyte,
And in each part sincere:
So I become a vestal white
One week in every year.

For this I say without demur
From out life's lurid lore,
Each righteous woman has in her
A tincture of the whore;
While every harpy of the night,
As I have learned too well;
Holds in her heart a heaven-light
To ransom her from hell.

So I'll go home and sweep and dust;
I'll make the kitchen fire,
And be of model daughters just
The best they could desire;
I'll fondle them and cook their food,
And Mother dear will say:
"Thank God! my darling is as good
As when she went away."

But after New Year's Day I'll fill
My bag and though they grieve,
I'll bid them both good-bye until
Another Christmas Eve;
And then . . . a knock upon the door:
I'll find them waiting there,
And angel-like I'll come once more
In answer to their prayer.

Then Lo! one night when candle-light
Gleams mystic on the snow,
And music swells of Christmas bells,
I'll come, no more to go:
The old folks need my love and care,
Their gold shall gild my dross,
And evermore my breast shall bear
My little silver cross.

REVERENCE

I saw the Greatest Man on Earth,
Aye, saw him with my proper eyes.
A loin-cloth spanned his proper girth,
But he was naked otherwise,
Excepting for a grey sombrero;
And when his domelike head he bared,
With reverence I stared and stared,
As mummified as any Pharaoh.

He leaned upon a little cane,
A big cigar was in his mouth;
Through spectacles of yellow stain
He gazed and gazed towards the South;
And then he dived into the sea,
As if to Corsica to swim;
His side stroke was so strong and free
I could not help but envy him.

A fitter man than I, I said,
Although his age is more than mine;
And I was strangely comforted
To see him battle in the brine.
Thought I: We have no cause for sorrow;
For one so dynamic to-day
Will gird him for the future fray
And lead us lion-like to-morrow.

The Greatest Man in all the world
Lay lazying like you or me,
Within a flimsy bathrobe curled
Upon a mattress by the sea:
He reached to pat a *tou-tou's* nose,
And scratched his torso now and then,
And scribbled with a fountain pen
What I assumed was jewelled prose.

And then methought he looked at me,
And hailed me with a gesture grand;
His fingers made the letter "V,"
So I, too, went to raise my hand;—
When nigh to me the barman glided
With liquid gold, and then I knew
He merely called for cock-tails two,
And so abjectly I subsided.

Yet I have had my moment's glory,
A-squatting nigh that Mighty Tory,
Proud Hero of our Island Story.

EXTERNALISM

The Greatest Writer of to-day
(With Maupassant I almost set him)
Said to me in a weary way,
The last occasion that I met him:
"Old chap, this world is more and more
Becoming bourgeois, *blasé,* blousy:
Thank God I've lived so long before
It got so definitely lousy."

Said I: "Old Chap, I don't agree.
Why should one so dispraise the present?
For gainful guys like you and me,
It still can be extremely pleasant.
Have we not Woman, Wine and Song—
A gleeful trio to my thinking;
So blithely we can get along
With laughing, loving, eating, drinking."

Said he: "Dear Boy, it may be so,
But I'm fed up with war and worry;
I would escape this world of woe,
Of wrath and wrong, of hate and hurry.
I fain would gain the peace of mind
Of Lamas on Thibetan highlands,
Or maybe sanctuary find
With beach-combers on coral islands."

Said I: "Dear Boy, don't go so far:
Just live a life of simple being;
Forgetting all the ills that are,
Be satisfied with hearing, seeing.
The sense of smell and taste and touch
Can bring you bliss in ample measure:
If only you don't *think* too much,
Your programme can be packed with pleasure.

"But do not try to probe below
This fairy film of Nature's screening;
Look on it as a surface show,
Without a purpose or a meaning.
Take no account of social strife,
And dread no coming cataclysm:
Let your philosophy of life
Be what I call: EXTERNALISM.

"The moon shines down with borrowed light,
So savants say—I do not doubt it.
Suffice its silver trance my sight,
That's all I want to know about it.
A fig for science—'how' and 'why'
Distract me in my happy dreaming:
Through line and form and colour I
Am all content with outward seeming. . . ."

The Greatest Writer of to-day
(I would have loved to call him Willie),
Looked wry at me and went his way—
I think he thought me rather silly.
Maybe I am, but I insist
My point of view will take some beating:
Don't mock this old Externalist—
The pudding's proof is in the eating.

PEDLAR

Pedlar's coming down the street,
Housewives beat a swift retreat.
Don't you answer to the bell;
Heedless what she has to sell.
Latch the door—Oh, do not hide:
Just discreetly go inside.
We must hang a board, I fear:
PEDLARS NOT PERMITTED HERE.

I'm trying to sell what nobody wants to buy;
They turn me away, but still I try and try.
My arms are aching and my feet are sore;
Heartsick and worn I drag from door to door.
I ring bells, meekly knock, hold out my tray,
But no one answers, so I go away.
I am so weary; oh, I want to cry,
Trying to sell what no one wants to buy.

I do not blame them. Maybe in their place
I'd slam the door shut in a pedlar's face.
I do not know; perhaps I'd raise their hopes
By looking at their pens and envelopes,
Their pins and needles, pencils, spools of thread,
Cheap tawdry stuff, before I shake my head
And go back to my cosy kitchen nook
Without another thought or backward look.
I would not see their pain nor hear their sigh,
Trying to sell what no one wants to buy.

I know I am a nuisance. I can see
They only buy because they pity me.
They may . . . I've had a cottage of my own,
A husband, children—now I am alone,
Friendless in all the world. The bitter years
Have crushed me, robbed me of my dears.
All, all I've lost, my only wish to die,
Selling my trash that no one wants to buy.

Pedlar's beating a retreat—
Poor old thing, her face is sweet,
Her figure frail, her hair snow-white;
Dogone it! Every door's shut tight. . . .
"Say, Ma, how much for all you've got?
Hell, here's ten bucks . . . I'll take the lot.
Go, get yourself a proper feed,
A little of the rest you need.
I've got a mother looks like you—
I'd hate her doing what you do. . . .
No, don't get sloppy, can the mush,
Praying for me—all that slush;
But please don't come again this way,
Ten bucks is all I draw a day."

WALLFLOWER

Till midnight her needle she plied
To finish her pretty pink dress;
"Oh, bless you, my darling," she sighed;
"I hope you will be a success."
As she entered the Oddfellows' Hall
With the shy thrill of maiden romance
She felt like the belle of the Ball,
But . . . nobody asked her to dance.

Her programme was clutched in her hand;
Her smile was a tiny bit wan;
She listened, applauding the band,
Pretending she *liked* to look on.
Each girl had her favourite swain,
She watched them retreat and advance;
She waited and waited in vain,
But nobody asked her to dance.

Said Mother to me: "You'll agree
That any young girl who wears specs,
However so clever she be,
Is lacking in glamour of sex."
Said I: "There is one by the wall
Who doesn't seem having a chance.
She's ready to weep—Dash it all,
I'm going to ask her to dance."

I caught her just slipping away
So quietly no one would know;
But bravely she tried to seem gay,
Though her heart might be aching with woe.
Poor kid! She looked only sixteen,
And she gave me a half frightened glance
When I bowed as if she were a Queen,
And I begged: "May I please have this dance?"

She gave me her card; what a bluff!
She'd written "Sir G." and "Sir G."
So I cut out that Galahad stuff,
And I scribbled "M.E." and "M.E.";
She looked so forlorn and so frail,
Submitting like one in a trance,
So I acted the conquering male,
And guided her into the dance.

Then lo! to my joy and surprise
Her waltzing I found was divine;
And she took those damn specs from her eyes,
And behold, they were jewels a-shine;
No lipstick nor rouge she had on,
But no powder and paint could enhance
On her cheeks the twin roses that shone
As I had with her dance after dance.

Then all of a sudden I knew
As we waltzed and reversed round the hall
That all eyes were watching us two,
And that she was the Belle of the Ball.
The fellows came buzzing like bees,
With swagger and posture and prance,
But her programme was full of "M.E.",s,
So she couldn't afford them a dance.

Said Mother: "You've been a nice boy,
But had a good time, I suppose.
You've filled that poor kid's heart with joy,
From now she'll have plenty of beaus." . . .
So fellows, please listen to me:
Don't look at a wallflower askance;
If a girl sitting lonely you see,
Just bow, smile and *beg* for a dance.

STAMP COLLECTOR

My worldly wealth I hoard in albums three,
My life collection of rare postage stamps;
My room is cold and bare as you can see,
My coat is old and shabby as a tramp's;
Yet more to me than balances in banks,
My albums three are worth a million francs.

I keep them in that box beside my bed,
For who would dream such treasures it could hold;
But every day I take them out and spread
Each page, to gloat like miser o'er his gold:
Dearer to me than could be child or wife,
I would defend them with my very life.

They *are* my very life, for every night
Over my catalogues I pore and pore;
I recognize rare items with delight,
Nothing I read but philatelic lore;
And when some specimen of choice I buy,
In all the world there's none more glad than I.

Behold my gem, my British penny black;
To pay its price I starved myself a year;
And many a night my dinner I would lack,
But when I bought it, oh, what radiant cheer!
Hitler made war that day—I did not care,
So long as my collection he would spare.

Look——my triangular Cape of Good Hope.
To purchase it I had to sell my car.
Now in my pocket for some *sous* I grope
To pay my omnibus when home is far,
And I am cold and hungry and footsore,
In haste to add some beauty to my store.

This very day, ah, what a joy was mine,
When in a dingy dealer's shop I found
This *franc* vermillion, eighteen forty-nine . . .
How painfully my heart began to pound!
(It's weak, they say), I paid the modest price
And tremblingly I vanished in a trice.

But oh, my dream is that some day of days,
I might discover a Mauritius blue,
Poking among the stamp-bins of the *quais;*
Who knows! They say there are but two;
Yet if a third one I should ever spy,
I think——God help me! I should faint and die. . . .

Poor Monsieur Pons, he's cold and dead,
One of those stamp-collecting cranks.
His garret held no crust of bread,
But albums worth a million francs.
On them his income he would spend,
By philatelic frenzy driven:
What did it profit in the end. . . .
You can't take stamps to Heaven.

OLD TROUPER

I was Mojeska's leading man
And famous parts I used to play,
But now I do the best I can
To earn my bread from day to day;
Here in this Burg of Breaking Hearts,
Where one wins as a thousand fail,
I play a score of scurvy parts
Till Time writes Finis to my tale.

My wife is dead, my daughters wed,
With heaps of trouble of their own;
And though I hold aloft my head
I'm humble, scared and all alone . . .
To-night I burn each photograph,
Each record of my former fame,
And oh, how bitterly I laugh
And feed them to the hungry flame!

Behold how handsome I was then—
What glowing eye, what noble mien;
I towered above my fellow men,
And proudly strode the painted scene.
Ah, Vanity! What fools are we,
With empty ends and foolish aims . . .
There now, I fling with savage glee
My *David Garrick* to the flames.

"Is this a dagger that I see":
Oh, how I used to love that speech;
We were old-fashioned—"hams" maybe,
Yet we Young Arrogance could teach.
"Out, out brief candle!" There are gone
My *Lear*, my *Hamlet* and *Macbeth;*
And now by ashes cold and wan
I wait my cue, my prompter Death.

This life of ours is just a play;
Its end is fashioned from the start;
Fate writes each word we have to say,
And puppet-like we strut our part.
Once I wore laurels on my brow,
But now I wait, a sorry clown,
To make my furtive, farewell bow . . .
Haste Time! Oh, ring the Curtain down.

SENTIMENTAL SHARK

Give me a cabin in the woods
Where not a human soul intrudes;
Where I can sit beside a stream
Beneath a balsam bough and dream,
And every morning see arise
The sun like bird of paradise;
Then go down to the creek and fish
A speckled trout for breakfast dish,
And fry it at an ember fire—
Ah! there's the life of my desire.

Alas! I'm tied to Wall Street where
They reckon me a millionaire,
And sometimes in a day alone
I gain a fortune o'er the 'phone.
Yet I to be a man was made,
And here I ply this sorry trade
Of Company manipulation,
Of selling short and stock inflation:
I whom God meant to rope a steer,
Fate made a Wall Street buccaneer.

Old Timer, how I envy you
Who do the things I long to do.
Oh, I would swap you all my riches
To step into your buckskin britches.
Your ragged shirt and rugged health
I'd take in trade for all my wealth.
Then shorn of fortune you would see
How drunk with freedom I would be;
I'd kick so hard, I'd kick so high,
I'd kick the moon clean from the sky.

Aye, gold to me is less than brass,
And jewels mean no more than glass.
My gold is sunshine and my gems
The glint of dew on grassy stems . . .
Yet though I hate my guts it's true
Time sorta makes you used to you;
And so I will not gripe too much
Because I have the Midas touch,
But doodle on my swivel chair,
Resigned to be a millionaire.

PULLMAN PORTER

The porter in the Pullman car
Was charming, as they sometimes are.
He scanned my baggage tags: "Are you
The man who wrote of Lady Lou?"
When I said "yes" he made a fuss—
Oh, he was most assiduous;
And I was pleased to think that he
Enjoyed my brand of poetry.

He was forever at my call,
So when we got to Montreal
And he had brushed me off, I said:
"I'm glad my poems you have read.
I feel quite flattered, I confess,
And if you give me your address
I'll send you (autographed, of course)
One of my little books of verse."

He smiled—his teeth were white as milk;
He spoke—his voice was soft as silk.
I recognized, despite his skin,
The perfect gentleman within.
Then courteously he made reply:
"I thank you kindly, Sir, but I
With many other cherished tome
Have all your books of verse at home.

"When I was quite a little boy
I used to savour them with joy;
And now my daughter, aged three,
Can tell the tale of Sam McGee;
While Tom, my son, that's only two
Has heard the yarn of Dan McGrew. . . .
Don't think your stuff I'm not applaudin'—
My taste is Eliot and Auden."

So as we gravely bade adieu
I felt quite snubbed—and so would you.
And yet I shook him by the hand,
Impressed that he could understand
The works of those two tops I mention,
So far beyond *my* comprehension—
A humble bard of boys and barmen,
Disdained, alas! by Pullman carmen.

THE LOCKET

From out her shabby rain-coat pocket
The little Jew girl in the train
Produced a dinted silver locket
With pasted in it portraits twain.
"These are my parents, sir," she said;
"Or were, for now I fear they're dead.

"I know to Belsen they were sent;
I never heard of them again.
So many were like that—they went,
Our woeful quest was all in vain.
I was in London with a friend,
Or I, too, would have shared their end.

"They could have got away, I'm told,
And joined me here in Marylebone,
But Grannie was so sick and old,
They could not leave her there alone.
When they were seized she cried and cried:
Thank God! 'Twas in her *bed* she died.

"How did *they* die? I cannot bear
To think of that—it crazes me.
My mother was so sweet, so fair;
My father handsome as you see . . .
I'm sure no daughter ever had
More lovely parents . . . Yes, it's sad.

"But for their loss I shall not grieve;
I'll hug the hope they still survive;
Oh, I must make myself believe
Somehow, somewhere they're still alive. . . .

"Well, that's my only souvenir,
A locket stained with many a tear."

THE MYSTERY OF MISTER SMITH

For supper we had curried tripe.
I washed the dishes, wound the clock;
Then for awhile I smoked my pipe—
Puff! Puff! We had no word of talk.
The Misses sewed—a sober pair;
Says I at last: "I need some air."

I don't know why I acted so;
I had no thought, no plot, no plan.
I did not really mean to go—
I'm such a docile little man;
But suddenly I felt that I
Must change my life or I would die.

A sign I saw: A ROOM TO LET.
It had a musty, dusty smell;
It gloated gloom, it growled and yet
Somehow I felt I liked it well.
I paid the rent a month ahead:
That night I *smoked my pipe in bed.*

From out my world I disappeared;
My walk and talk changed over-night.
I bought black glasses, grew a beard—
Abysmally I dropped from sight;
Old Tax Collector, Mister Smith
Became a memory, a myth.

I see my wife in widow's weeds;
She's gained in weight since I have gone.
My pension serves her modest needs,
She keeps the old apartment on;
And living just a block away
I meet her nearly every day.

I hope she doesn't mourn too much;
She has a sad and worried look.
One day we passed and chanced to touch,
But as with sudden fear I shook,
So blankly in my face she peered,
I had to chuckle in my beard.

Oh, comfort is a blessed thing,
But forty years of it I had.
I never drank the wine of Spring,
No moon has ever made me mad.
I never clutched the skirts of Chance
Nor daftly dallied with Romance.

And that is why I seek to save
My soul before it is too late,
To put between me and the grave
A few years of fantastic fate:
I've won to happiness because
I've killed the man that once I was.

I've murdered Income Taxer Smith,
And now I'm Johnny Jones to you.
I have no home, no kin, no kith,
I do the things I want to do.
No matter though I've not a friend,
I've won to freedom in the end.

Bohemian born, I guess, was I;
And should my wife her widowhood
By wedlock end I will not sigh,
But pack my grip and go for good,
To live in lands where laws are lax,
And innocent of Income Tax.

EQUALITY

The Elders of the Tribe were grouped
And squatted in the Council Cave;
They seemed to be extremely pooped,
And some were grim, but all were grave:
The subject of their big To-do
Was axe-man Chow, the son of Choo.

Then up spoke Tribal Wiseman Waw:
"Brothers, to-day I talk to grieve:
As an upholder of the Law
You know how deeply we believe
In Liberty, Fraternity,
And likewise in Equality.

"A chipper of the flint am I;
I make the weapons that you use,
And though to hunt I never try,
To bow to hunters I refuse:
But stalwart Chow, the son of Choo
Is equal to us any two.

"He is the warrior supreme,
The Super-caveman, one might say;
The pride of youth, the maiden's dream,
And in the chase the first to slay.
Where we are stunted he is tall:
In short, a menace to us all.

"He struts with throwing stone and spear;
And is he not the first to wear
Around his waist with bully leer
The pelt of wolf and baby bear!
Admitting that he made the kill,
Why should he so *exploit* his skill?

"Comrades, grave counsel we must take,
And as he struts with jest and jibe,
Let us act swiftly lest he make
Himself Dictator of our Tribe:
The Gods have built him on *their* plan:
Let us reduce him to a man."

And so they seized him in the night,
And on the sacrificial stone
The axe-men of the Tribe did smite,
Until one limb he ceased to own.
There! They had equalized the odds,
Foiling unfairness of the Gods.

So Chow has lost his throwing arm,
And goes around like every one;
No longer does he threaten harm,
And tribal justice has been done.
For men are equal, let us seek
To grade the Strong down to the weak.

FLIES

I never kill a fly because
I think that what we have of laws
To regulate and civilize
Our daily life—we owe to flies.

Apropos, I'll tell you of Choo, the spouse
Of the head of the hunters, Wung;
Such a beautiful cave they had for a house,
And a brood of a dozen young.
And Wung would start by the dawn's red light
On the trailing of bird or beast,
And crawl back tired on the brink of night
With food for another feast.

Then the young would dance in their naked glee,
And Choo would fuel the fire;
Fur and feather, how good to see,
And to gorge to heart's desire!
Flesh of rabbit and goose and deer,
With fang-like teeth they tore,
And laughed with faces a bloody smear,
And *flung their bones on the floor.*

But with morning bright the flies would come,
Clouding into the cave;
You could hardly hear for their noisy hum,
They were big and black and brave.
Darkling the day with gust of greed
They'd swarm in the warm sunrise
On the litter of offal and bones to feed—
A million or so of flies.

Now flies were the wife of Wung's despair;
They would sting and buzz and bite,
And as her only attire was hair
She would itch from morn to night:
But as one day she scratched her hide,
A thought there came to Choo:
"If I were to throw the bones outside,
The flies would go there too."

That spark in a well-nigh monkey mind,
Nay, do not laugh to scorn;
For there in the thought of Choo you'll find
Was the sense of Order born;
As she flung the offal far and wide,
And the fly-cloud followed fast,
Battening on the bones outside
The cave was clear at last.

And Wung was pleased when he came at night,
For the air was clean and sweet,
And the cave-kids danced in the gay firelight,
And fed on the new-killed meat;
But the children Choo would chide and boss,
For her cleanly floor was her pride,
And even the baby was taught to toss
His bit of a bone outside.

Then the cave crones came and some admired,
But others were envious;
And they said: "She swanks, she makes us tired
With her complex modern fuss."
However, most of the tribe complied,
Though tradition dourly dies,
And a few Conservatives crossly cried:
"We'll keep our bones and our flies."

So Reformer Choo was much revered
And to all she said: "You see
How my hearth is clean and my floor is cleared,
And there ain't no flies on me" . . .
And that was how it all began,
Through horror of muck and mess,
Even in prehistoric Man,
LAW, ORDER and CLEANLINESS.

And that is why I never kill
A fly, no matter how obscene;
For I believe in God's good will:
He gave us vermin to make us clean.

RHYME-SMITH

Oh, I was born a lyric babe
(That last word is a bore—
It's only rhyme is "astrolabe,"
Whose meaning I ignore.)
From cradlehood I lisped in numbers,
Made jingles even in my slumbers.
Said Ma: "He'll be a bard, I know it."
Said Pa: "Let's hope he will outgrow it."

Alas! I never did, and so
A dreamer and a drone was I,
Who persevered in want and woe
His misery to versify.
Yea, I was doomed to be a failure
(Old Browning rhymes that last with "pale lure"):
And even starving in the gutter,
My macaronics I would utter.

Then in a poor, cheap book I crammed,
And to the public maw I tossed
My bitter Dirges of the Damned,
My biting Lyrics of the Lost.
"Let carping critic flay and flout
My Ditties of the Down and Out—
"There now," said I, "I've done with verse,
My love, my weakness and my curse."

Then lo! (As I would fain believe,
Before they crown, the Fates would shame us)
I went to sleep one bitter eve,
And woke to find that I was famous. . . .
And so the sunny sequels were a
Gay villa on the Riviera,
A bank account, a limousine, a
Life patterned *dolce e divina.*

Oh, yes, my lyric flight is flighty;
My muse is much more mite than mighty:
But poetry has been my friend,
And rhyming's saved me in the end.

THE ORDINARY MAN

If you and I should chance to meet,
I guess you wouldn't care;
I'm sure you'd pass me in the street
As if I wasn't there;
You'd never look me in the face,
My modest mug to scan,
Because I'm just a commonplace
    And Ordinary Man.

But then, it may be, you are too
A guy of every day,
Who does the job he's told to do
And takes the wife his pay;
Who makes a home and kids his care,
And works with pick or pen. . . .
Why, Pal, I guess we're just a pair
    Of Ordinary Men.

We plug away and make no fuss,
Our feats are never crowned;
And yet it's common coves like us
Who make the world go round.
And as we steer a steady course
By God's predestined plan,
Hats off to that almighty Force:
    THE ORDINARY MAN.

MY BOSS

My Boss keeps sporty girls, they say;
His belly's big with cheer.
He squanders in a single day
What I make in a year.
For I must toil with bloody sweat,
And body bent and scarred,
While my whole life-gain he could bet
Upon a single card.

My Boss is big and I am small;
I slave to keep him rich.
He'd look at me like scum and call
Me something of a bitch . . .
Ah no! he wouldn't use that phrase
To designate my mother:
Despite his high and mighty ways,
My Boss is *my twin-brother*.

Conceived were we in common joy
And born in common pain;
But while I was a brawny boy
My brother stole my brain.
As dumb was I as he was smart,
As blind as he could see;
And so it was, bang from the start
He got the best of me.

I'm one of many in his pay;
From him I draw my dough;
But he would fire me right away
If he should hap to know
A week ago he passed me by;
I heard his wheezing breath,
And in his pouched and blood-shot eye
I saw, stark-staring—Death.

He has his women, cards and wine;
I have my beans and bread.
But oh, the last laugh will be mine
The day I hear he's dead.
Aye, though we shared a common womb
(I gloat to think of it)
Some day I'll stand beside his tomb
And loose my gob and . . . *spit*.

THE TUNNEL

Toil's a tunnel, there's no way out
For fellows the likes o' me;
A beggar wi' only a crust an' a clout
At the worst o' the worst is free;
But I work to eat, an' I eat to work;
It's always the same old round,
And I dassent fail for the day I shirk
They'll shovel me underground.

I guess God meant it to be that way,
For a man must make his bread;
I was born to bondage, to earn my pay,
To slave to the day I'm dead;
To live in a tunnel, to die in a ditch—
That's just what us fellows do;
For the poor must be makin' the rich more rich,
An' the many must serve the few.

Aye, we live in a tunnel, most o' us,
A-fearin' to lose our job;
But who has the right to gripe an' cuss
So the goblet's hot on the hob.
An' I mustn't be havin' the wife complain,
An' I can't let the childer fast:
So I'll toil in my tunnel an' drag my chain,
Clank! Clank! Clank! to the last.

RIPE FRUIT

Through eyelet holes I watch the crowd
Rain of confetti fling;
Their joy is lush, their laughter loud,
For Carnival is King.
Behind his chariot I pace
To earn my petty pay;
They laugh to see my monster face:
"Ripe Fruit," I hear them say.

I do not laugh: my shoulders sag;
No heart have I for glee,
Because I hold aloft a hag
Who grins enough for me;
A hideous harridan who bears
In crapulous display,
Like two grub-eaten mouldy pears
Her bubbies on a tray.

Ripe Fruit! Oh, God! It's hell to think
How I have drifted down
Through vice and dice and dope and drink
To play the sordid clown;
That I who held the golden key
To operatic fame,
Should gnaw the crust of misery
And drain the dregs of shame.

What matter! I'll get soused to-night,
And happy I will be,
To sit within a tavern bright,
A trollop on my knee. . . .
So let the crazy pipers pipe,
And let the rapture ring:
Ripe fruit am I—yea, rotten ripe,
And Carnival is King.

DRAM-SHOP DITTY

I drink my fill of foamy ale
I sing a song, I tell a tale,
I play the fiddle;
My throat is chronically dry,
Yet *savant* of a sort am I,
And Life's my riddle.

For look! I raise my arm to drink—
A voluntary act, you think
(Nay, Sir, you're grinning).
You're wrong: this stein of beer I've drained
To emptiness was pre-ordained
Since Time's beginning.

But stay! 'Tis I who err, because
Time has no birth; it always was,
It will be ever;
And trivial though my act appears,
Its repercussion down the years
Will perish never.

It will condition ages hence,
But its most urgent consequence,
You'll not deny, Sir,
Is that it should be filled again
To goad my philosophic brain,
If you will buy, Sir.

There is no great, there is no small;
Fate makes a tapestry of all,
Each stitch is needed . . .
The gods be praised! that barman chap
Manipulates his frothing tap—
My plea is heeded.

Two foaming tankards over-spill,
And soon, ah! not too soon, they will
Our thirst be slaking.
Stout lad! he does not dream that he
A page of history maybe
Is blandly making.

For Sir, it was ordained that you
Buy me a drink (or maybe two)
Since ages hoary;
And doubtless it is predestined
Our meeting shall affect in kind
Earth's Cosmic Story.

The fathomless, eternal Past,
The Future infinitely vast,
We two are linking;
So let us fitly celebrate
This moment of immortal Fate
In drinking, drinking.

But though I toss a hearty pot,
Kind stranger, do not think I'm not
For Truth a groper . . .
Another? Thanks, I won't refuse,
I am a tippler, if you choose,
But not a toper.

A nice distinction! . . . Well, life's good;
Just give me beer, rich greasy food,
And let me fiddle;
Enough of dull philosophy;
To-night we'll merry, merry be . . .
Hi-diddle-diddle.

REPTILES AND ROSES

So crystal clear it is to me
That when I die I cease to be,
All else seems sheer stupidity.

All promises of Paradise
Are wishful thinking, preacher's lies,
Dogmatic dust flung in our eyes.

Yea, *life's* immortal, swift it flows
Alike in reptile and in rose,
But as it comes, so too it goes.

Dead roses will not bloom again;
The lifeless lizard writhes in vain;
Cups shattered will not hold champagne.

Our breath is brief, and being so
Let's make our heaven here below,
And lavish kindness as we go.

For when dour Death shall close the door
There will be darkness evermore;
So let us kneel in prayer before

Each day and let our duty be
To fight that Mankind may be free . . .
There is our Immortality.

FRUSTRATION

Gazing to gold of seraph wing,
With wistful wonder in my eyes,
A blue-behinded ape, I swing
Upon the palms of Paradise.

A parakeet of gaudy hue
Upon a flame tree smugly rocks;
Oh, we're a precious pair, we two,
I gibber while the parrot squawks.

"If I had but your wings," I sigh,
How ardently would I aspire
To soar celestially high
And mingle with yon angel choir."

His beady eye is bitter hard;
Right mockingly he squints at me;
As critic might review a bard
His scorn is withering to see.

And as I beat my breast and howl,
"Poor fool," he shrills, my bliss to wreck.
So . . . so I steal behind that fowl
And grab his claw and screw his neck.

And swift his scarlet wings I tear;
Seeking to soar, with hope divine,
I frantically beat the air,
And crash to earth and—snap my spine.

Yet as I lie with shaken breaths
Of pain I watch my seraph throng. . . .
Oh, I would die a dozen deaths
Could I but sing one deathless song!

FINALITY

When I am dead I will not care
How future generations fare,
For I will be so unaware.

Though fields their slain has carpeted,
And seas be salt with tears they shed,
Not one I'll waste, for I'll be dead.

Though atom bombs in ashes lay
Their skyey cities of to-day,
With carrion lips I cannot pray.

Though ruin reigns and madness raves,
And cowering men creep back to caves,
I cannot help to dig their graves.

Though fools for knowledge delve too deep,
And wake dark demons from their sleep,
I will not have the eyes to weep.

I will not care, I cannot care,
For I will be no longer there
To share their sorrow and despair.

And nevermore my heart will bleed
When on my brain the blind-worms feed,
For I'll be dead, *dead*, DEAD indeed.

And when I rot and cease to be,
It matters not a jot to me
What may be man's dark destiny.

Ah! there you have the hell of it,
As in the face of Fate I spit
I know she doesn't mind a bit.

A thousand millions clot this earth,
And billions more await their birth—
For what? . . . *Ye gods, enjoy your mirth!*

FORTITUDE

Time, the Jester, jeers at you;
Your life's a fleeting breath;
Your birth's a flimsy I.O.U.
To that old devil, Death.
And though to glory you attain,
Or be to beauty born,
Your pomp and vanity are vain:
Time ticks you off with scorn.

Time, the Cynic, sneers at you,
And stays you in your stride;
He flouts the daring deeds you do,
And pillories your pride.
The triumph of your yesterday
He pages with the Past;
He taunts you with the grave's decay
And calls the score at last.

All this I know, yet what care I!
Despite his dusty word,
I hold my tattered banner high,
And swing my broken sword.
In blackest night I glimpse a gleam,
And nurse a faith sublime,
To do, to dare, to hope, to dream,
To fight you, Foeman Time;
Yea, in the dark a deathless beam
To smite you, Tyrant Time.

GOD'S BATTLE-GROUND

God dwells in you; in pride and shame,
In all you do to blight or bless;
In all you are of praise or blame,
In beauty or in ugliness.
"Divine Creation"—What a fraud!
God did not make you . . . *You make God.*

God lives in me, in all I feel
Of love and hate, of joy and pain,
Of grace and greed, of woe and weal,
Of fear and cheer, of loss and gain:
For good or evil I am He,
Yea, saint or devil, One are we.

God fends and fights in each of us;
His altars we, or bright or dim;
So with no sacerdotal fuss
But worthy act let's worship Him:
Goodness is Godness—let us be
Deserving of Divinity.

And of His presence be aware,
And by our best His love express;
A gentle word is like a prayer,
A kindly act is holiness:
Don't let God down; let Him prevail
And write his AMEN to our tale.

SUCCESS

You ask me what I call Success—
Is it, I wonder, Happiness?

It is not wealth, it is not fame,
Nor rank nor power nor honoured name.
It is not triumph in the Arts—
Best-selling books or leading parts.
It is not plaudits of the crowd,
The flame of flags, processions proud.
The panegyrics of the Press
Are but the mirage of Success.
You may have all of them, my friend,
Yet be a failure in the end.

I've known proud Presidents of banks
Who've fought their way up from the ranks,
And party leaders of renown
Who played as boys in Shantytown.
Strong, self-made men, yet seek to trace
Benignity in any face;
Grim purpose, mastery maybe,
Yet never sweet serenity;
Never contentment, thoughts that bless—
That mellow joy *I* deem Success.

Then haply seek some humble hearth,
Quite poor in goods yet rich in mirth,
And see a man of common clay
Watching his little ones at play;
A laughing fellow full of cheer,
Health, strength and faith that mocks at fear;
Who for his happiness relies
On joys he lights in other eyes;
He loves his home and envies none. . . .
Who happier beneath the sun?

Aye, though he walk in lowly ways,
Shining Success has crowned his days.

AGNOSTIC APOLOGY

I am a stout materialist;
With abstract terms I can't agree,
And so I've made a little list
Of words that don't make sense to me.
To fool my reason I refuse,
For honest thinking is my goal;
And that is why I rarely use
      Vague words like *Soul*.

In terms of matter I am sure
This world of ours can be defined;
And so with theories obscure
I will not mystify my mind;
And though I use it more or less,
Describing alcoholic scenes,
I do not know, I must confess,
      What *Spirit* means.

When I survey this cosmic scene,
The term "Creator" seems absurd;
The Universe has always been,
Creation *never* has occurred.
But in my Lexicon of Doubt
It strikes me definitely odd,
One word I never dare to flout,
One syllable the mountains shout,
Three letters that the stars spell out:
      GOD.

REGRET

It's not for laws I've broken
That bitter tears I've wept,
But solemn vows I've spoken
And promises unkept;
It's not for sins committed
My heart is full of rue,
But gentle acts omitted,
Kind deeds I did not do.

I have outlived the blindness,
The selfishness of youth;
The canker of unkindness,
The cruelty of truth;
The searing hurt of rudeness . . .
By mercies great and small,
I've come to reckon goodness
The greatest gift of all.

Let us be helpful ever
To those who are in need,
And each new day endeavour
To do some gentle deed;
For faults beyond our grieving,
What kindliness atone;
On earth by love achieving
A Heaven of our own.

ROSY-KINS

As home from church we two did plod,
"Grandpa," said Rosy, "What is God?"
Seeking an answer to her mind,
This is the best that I could find. . . .

God is the Iz-ness of the Is,
The One-ness of our Cosmic Biz;
The high, the low, the near, the far,
The atom and the evening star;
The lark, the shark, the cloud, the clod,
The whole darned Universe—that's **God.**

Some deem that other gods there be,
And to them humbly bend the knee;
To Mumbo Jumbo and to Joss,
To Bud and Allah—but the Boss
Is mine . . . While there are suns and seas
My timeless God shall dwell in these.

In every glowing leaf He lives;
When roses die His life he gives;
God is not outside and apart
From Nature, but her very heart;
No Architect (as I of verse)
He is Himself the Universe.

Said Rosy-kins: "Grandpa, how odd
Is your imagining of God.
To me he's always just appeared
A huge Grandfather with a beard.

145

PRAYER

You talk o' prayer an' such—
Well, I jest don't know how;
I guess I got as much
Religion as a cow.
I fight an' drink an' swear;
Red hell I often raise,
But never said a prayer
    In all my days.

I'm honest, right enough;
Don't take no stock in crimes;
I'm jest a dockside tough,
An' yet . . . an' yet sometimes,
If I should happen by
A church-door open wide
The chances are that I
    Will sneak inside.

It's kind o' peaceful there,
Jest sittin' in a pew;
There's sompin' in the air
That rests me through an' through;
It does me heaps o' good
To see them candles glow,
So soothin' to the mood . . .
    Why?—I don't know.

Unless that sittin' still
Can be a kind o' prayer;
My heart jest seems to fill
Wi' peace . . . Oh, God don't care
For guys the likes o' me;
I just ain't in His line:
But when the CROSS I see,
    I make the sign.

SILENCE

When I was cub reporter I
Would interview the Great,
And sometimes they would make reply,
And sometimes hesitate;
But often they would sharply say,
With bushy eyebrows bent:
"Young man, your answer for to-day
    Is—No Comment."

Nigh sixty years have called the tune,
And silver is my pate;
No longer do I importune
Important men of state;
But time has made me wise, and so
When button-holed I shake
My head and say: "To-day I've no
    Comment to make."

Oh, Silence is a mighty shield,
Verbosity is vain;
Let others wordy warfare wield,
From argument abstain;
When faced with dialectic foes
Just shrug and turn away:
Be sure your wisest words are those
    You do not say.

148

Yea, Silence is a gleaming sword
Whose wounds are hard to heal;
Its quiet stuns the spoken word
More than a thunder peal;
Against it there is no defence,
For like the grave-yard sod
Its hush is Heaven's eloquence,
    The VOICE OF GOD.

REMORSE

That scathing word I used in scorn
(Though half a century ago)
Comes back to me this April morn,
Like boomerang to work me woe;
Comes back to me with bitter blame
(Though apple boughs are blossoming),
And oh! the anguish of my shame
Is sharper than a serpent's sting!

Age sensitizes us to pain,
And when remembrance of some word
We spoke in wrath returns again,
Its stab is like a driven sword. . . .
And if in some celestial span
Our hearts in penitence may bleed
For all the hurt we've done to man—
Ah, that would be a hell indeed!

So friends, be careful of your words,
Though other breasts may meet their steel,
Lest they return like vengeful swords,
Till *yours* the wounds that never heal.
For Age the heart to mercy mellows;
Foul memories haunt like evil elves:
Let us be gentle to our fellows,
And win God's mercy for ourselves.

THE UNDYING

She was so wonderful I wondered
If wedding me she had not blundered;
She was so pure, so high above me,
I marvelled how she came to love me:
Or did she? Well, in her own fashion—
Affection, pity, never passion.

I knew I was not worth her love;
Yet oh, how wistfully I strove
To be her equal in some way;
She knew I tried, and I would pray
Some day she'd hold her head in pride,
And stand with praising by my side.

A weakling, I—she made me strong;
My finest thoughts to her belong;
Through twenty years she mothered me,
And then one day she smothered me
With kisses, saying wild with joy:
"Soon we'll be three—let's hope, a boy."

"Too old to bear a child," they said;
Well, they were right, for both are dead. . . .
Ah no, not *dead*—she is with me,
And by my side she'll ever be;
Her spirit lingers, half divine:
All good I do is hers, not mine.

God, by my works O let me strive
To keep her gentleness alive!
Let in my heart her spirit glow,
And by my thought for others show
She is not dead: she'll never die
While love for humankind have I.

YOUR POEM

My poem may be yours indeed
In melody and tone,
If in its rhythm you can read
A music of your own;
If in its pale woof you can weave
Your lovelier design,
'Twill make my lyric, I believe,
     More yours than mine.

I'm but a prompter at the best;
Crude cues are all I give.
In simple stanzas I suggest—
'Tis you who make them live.
My bit of rhyme is but a frame,
And if my lines you quote,
I think, although they bear my name,
     'Tis you who wrote.

Yours is the beauty that you see
In any words I sing;
The magic and the melody
'Tis you, dear friend, who bring.
Yea, by the glory and the gleam,
The loveliness that lures
Your thought to starry heights of dream,
     The poem's yours.

AN OLD STORY
(Retold in Rhyme)

They threw him in a prison cell;
He moaned upon his bed,
And when he crept from coils of hell:
"Last night you killed," they said.

"Last night in drunken rage you slew
A being brave with breath;
A radiant soul, because of you,
Lies dark in death."

"Last night I killed," he moaned distraught,
"When I was wild with wine;
I slew, and I remember naught . . .
O Mother, Mother mine!

"To what unbridled rage may lead
You taught me at your knee.
Why did I not your warning heed . . .
And now—the gallows tree.

"O Mother, Mother, come to me,
For I am sore distrest,
And I would kneel beside your knee
And weep upon your breast. . . ."

They stared at him; their lips were dumb,
Their eyes tear-filled;
Then spoke the Priest: "She cannot come . . .
'Twas she you killed."

WHY?

He was our leader and our guide;
He was our saviour and our star.
We walked in friendship by his side,
Yet set him where our heroes are.

He taught disdain of fame and wealth;
With courage he inspired our youth;
He preached the purity of health,
And held aloft the torch of truth.

He bade us battle for the Right,
And led us in the carnage grim;
He was to us a living light,
And like a God we worshipped him.

He raised us from the grievous gloom,
And brimmed our hearts with radiant cheer;
And then he climbed up to his room,
And . . . cut his throat from ear to ear.

Let us not judge his seeming lapse;
His secret soul we could not see;
He smiled and left us, and perhaps
Death was his crowning victory.

THE LAST SUPPER

Marie Vaux of the Painted Lips,
And the mouth so mocking gay,
A wanton you to the finger-tips,
Who break men's hearts in play;
A thing of dust I have striven for,
Honour and manhood given for,
Headlong to ruin driven for,
And this is the last, you say. . . .

Drinking your wine with dainty sips,
Marie Vaux of the Painted Lips.

Marie Vaux of the Painted Lips,
Long have you held your sway;
I have laughed at your merry quips—
Now is my time to pay.
What we sow we must reap again;
When we laugh we must weep again;
So to-night we will sleep again,
Nor wake until Judgement Day. . . .

'Tis a poisoned wine that your palate sips,
Marie Vaux of the Painted Lips.

Marie Vaux of the Painted Lips,
Down on your knees and pray;
Pray your last ere the moment slips,
Pray ere the dark and the terror grips,
And the bright world fades away.
Pray for the good unguessed of us,
Pray for the peace and rest of us:
Here comes the Shape in quest of us,
Now we must go away. . . .

You and I in the grave's eclipse,
Marie Vaux of the Painted Lips.

NO NECK-TIE PARTY *

A prisoner speaks:

Majority of twenty-three,
I face the Judge with joy and glee;
For am I not a lucky chap—
No more hanging, no black cap;
A "lifer," yes, but well I know
In fifteen years they'll let me go;
For I'll be pious in my prison,
Sing with gusto: Christ Is Risen;
Serve the hymn-books out on Sunday,
Sweep the chapel clean on Monday:
Such a model lag I'll be
In fifteen years they'll set me free.

Majority of twenty-three,
You've helped me cheat the gallows tree.
I'm twenty now, at thirty-five
How I will laugh to be alive!
To leap into the world again
And bless the fools miscalled "humane,"
Who say the gibbet's wrong and so
At thirty-five they let me go,
That I may sail across the sea,
A killer unsuspect and free,
To change my name, to darkly thrive
By hook or crook at thirty-five.

* By a majority of twenty-three the House of Commons voted the abolition of the death penalty.

O silent dark and beastly wood
Where with my bloodied hands I stood!
O piteous child I raped and slew!
Had she been *yours*, would you and you
Have pardoned me and set me free,
Majority of twenty-three?
Yet by your solemn vote you willed
I shall not die though I have killed;
Although I did no mercy show,
In mercy you will let me go. . . .
That he who kills and does not pay
May live to kill another day.

CASINO CALYPSO

Although of gold I am not rich in,
And have of jewels none at all,
I'm dreaming in what's called the Kitchen
Of earth's most famous gambling hall.
I linger in a lonely corner,
And though the croupier entreats,
Of Lady Luck I am a scorner:
  I'm reading Keats.

The plunging players pack the tables,
Beneath the bunched electric's glare;
The tumult is the Tower of Babel's,
As strong as Camembert the air.
The counters click, the balls are spinning,
The number eight three times repeats—
There was a fortune for my winning:
  What price John Keats?

Yet (in parenthesis) it's funny
That I, of this gain-goaded throng,
Alone should mock the might of money,
And lose myself in golden song.
I wonder which of us is crazy,
I, toying with my rhymed conceits,
Or they, the mob with eyes greed-glazy—
  Enlight me, Keats.

Your little book of limp green leather
I sadly fear that I profane,
Because we two are linked together
In this rococo hall of gain;
That I a piddling poetaster,
A nuzzler of the muse's teats,
Should in this *milieu* con the Master—
    Forgive me, Keats.

Well, supper calls, I must be going
To whirl spaghetti from a plate;
But on my way behold I'm throwing
A louis on my number, *eight*. . . .
By gad! I've won, I've made a killing;
I'll dine on pheasant, fruit and sweets,
And golden Asti I'll be spilling
To your sweet memory, God willing,
    Divine John Keats:
Aye, fluted glasses I'll be filling
    To toast you, Keats.

RIVIERA HONEYMOON

Beneath the trees I lounged at ease
And watched them speed the pace;
They swerved and swung, they clutched and clung,
They leapt in roaring chase;
The crowd was thrilled, a chap was killed:
It was a splendid race.

Two men, they say, went West that day,
But I knew only one;
Geranium-red his blood was spread
And blazoned in the sun;
A lightning crash . . . Lo! in a flash
His racing days were done.

I did not see—such sights to me
Appallingly are grim;
But for a girl of sunny curl
I would not mention him,
That English lad with grin so glad,
And racing togs so trim.

His motor bike was painted like
A postal box of red.
'Twas gay to view . . . "We bought it new,"
A voice beside me said.
"Our little bit we blew on it
The day that we were wed.

"We took a chance: through sunny France
We flashed with flaunting power.
With happy smiles a hundred miles
Or more we made an hour.
Like flame we hurled into a world
A-foam with fruit and flower.

"Our means were small; we risked them all
This famous race to win,
So we can take a shop and make
Our bread—one must begin.
We're not afraid; Jack has his trade:
He's bright as brassy pin.

"Hark! Here they come; uphill they hum;
My lad has second place;
They swing, they roar, they pass once more,
Now Jack sprints up the pace.
They're whizzing past . . . At last, at last
He leads—he'll *win* the race.

Another round . . . They leap, they bound,
But—where O where is he?"
And then the girl with sunny curl
Turned chalk-faced unto me,
Within her eyes a wild surmise
It was not good to see.

They say like thunder-bolt he crashed
Into a wall of stone;
To bloody muck his face was mashed,
He died without a moan;
In borrowed black the girl went back
To London Town alone.

Beneath the trees I lounged at ease
And saw them pep the pace;
They swerved and swung, they clutched and clung
And roaring was the chase:
Two men, they say, were croaked that day--—
It was a glorious race.

WRESTLING MATCH

What guts he had, the Dago lad
Who fought that Frenchman grim with guile;
For nigh an hour they milled like mad,
And mauled the mat in rare old style.
Then up and launched like catapults,
And tangled, twisted, clinched and clung,
Then tossed in savage somersaults,
And hacked and hammered, ducked and swung;
And groaned and grunted, sighed and cried,
Now knotted tight, now springing free;
To bend each other's bones they tried,
Their faces crisped in agony. . . .

Then as rage rose, with tiger-bound,
They clashed and smashed, and flailed and flung,
And tripped and slipped, with hammer-pound,
And streaming sweat and straining lung.
The mighty mob roared out their joy,
And wild I heard a wench near-by
Shriek to the Frenchman: "Atta Boy!
Go to it, Jo-jo—kill the guy."

The boy from Rome was straight and slim,
And swift and springy as a bow;
The man from Metz was gaunt and grim,
But all the tricks he seemed to know.
'Twixt knee and calf with scissors-lock,
He gripped the lad's arm like a vice;
The prisoned hand went white as chalk,
And limp as death and cold as ice.

And then he tried to break the wrist,
And kidney-pounded with his knee,
But with a cry and lightning twist
The Roman youth had wrested free. . . .

Then like mad bulls they hooked and mauled,
And blindly butted, bone on bone;
Spread-eagled on the mat they sprawled,
And writhed and rocked with bitter moan.
Then faltered to their feet and hung
Upon the ropes with eyes of woe;
And then the Frenchman stooped and flung
The wop among the mob below,
Who helped to hoist him back again,
With cheers and jeers and coarse cat-calls,
To where the Gaul with might and main
Hung poised to kick his genitals
And drop him senseless in the ring. . . .
And then an old man cried: "My son!"
The maddened mob began to fling
Their chairs about—the fight was done.

Soft silver sandals tapped the sea;
Palms listened to the lack of sound;
The lucioles were lilting free,
The peace was precious and profound.
Oh had it been an evil dream? . . .
A chapel of the Saints I sought,
And there before the altar gleam
I clasped my hands and thought and thought. . . .

SOLDIER BOY

My soldier boy has crossed the sea
    To fight the foeman;
But he'll come back to make of me
    An honest woman.
So I am singing all day long,
    Despite blood-shedding;
For though I know he's done me wrong,
    We'll end by wedding.

My soldier boy is home again,
    So bold and scathless;
But oh, my heart is numb with pain
    Because he's faithless.
He's brought with him a French Mam'selle;
    They plan a marriage;
Maybe I'll go—no one will know
    Of my miscarriage.

My soldier boy has made his choice,
    She'll hold him to it;
I tell myself that I rejoice,
    May he not rue it.
But oh, that starry month of May,
    Love-words wild spoken!
I stand alone and make no moan . . .
    My heart is broken.

VILLAGE VIRTUE

Jenny was my first sweetheart;
Poor lass! she was none too smart.
Though I swore she'd never rue it,
She would never let me do it.
When I tried she made a fuss,
So damn pure and virtuous.
Girls should cozen all they can,
Use their wiles to get their man.

June, my second, was no prude;
Too good-looking to be good;
Wanton and a giddy-gadder,
Never knew who might have had her;
Kept me mad and jumping jealous,
Tempting all the other fellows
Like a wayside flower to pluck her:
So at last I had to chuck her.

Now I'm settled down with Jill,
And we're safely married still.
She began to wail and worry,
So we wedded in a hurry.
Well, it's quite all right that way—
We're all made of common clay,
And the grey-haired folk that bore us
Just as wanton were before us.

June, I hear, now lives in London
Where, I fear, she's sadly undone.
Jenny, still as virtuous
Missed the matrimonial bus.
Where our "first" set gossips buzzin'
Jill and I now have a dozen,
Ready in their turn to prove
There's no chastity in love.

June, so fickle and so fair,
Common was as barber's chair;
Jill provides me with good grub,
Lets me go nights to the pub.
Though her silver hairs are many,
One eve I might call on Jenny . . .
She may not need too much urging:
Must be hell to die a virgin.

VILLAGE DON JUAN

Lord, I'm grey, my race is run,
But by old Harry, I've had my fun;
And all about, I seem to see
Lads and lassies that look like me;
Ice-blue eyes on every hand,
Handsomest youngsters in the land.

"Old Stud Horse" they say of me,
But back of my beard I laugh with glee.
Far and wide have I sown my seed,
Yet by the gods I've improved the breed:
From byre and stable to joiner's bench,
From landlord's daughter to serving wench.

Ice-blue eyes and blade-straight nose,
Stamp of my virile youth are those;
Now you'll see them on every side,
Proof of my prowess, far and wide:
Even the Parson's handsome scamp,
And the Doctor's daughter have my stamp.

Many a matron cocks an eye
Of secret knowledge as I pass by;
As for the hubbies, what they don't know
Will never hurt them, so let them go:
The offspring most they seem to prize
Have blade-straight noses and ice-blue eyes.

Yet oh, I have a haunting dread
Brother and sister lust and bed;
The Parson's son and the Doctor's lass,
Yestreen in the moon I saw them pass;
The thought of them wed is like a knife. . . .
Brother and sister—man and wife.

DEATH AND LIFE

'Twas in the grave-yard's gruesome gloom
That May and I were mated;
We sneaked inside and on a tomb
Our love we consummated.
It's quite all right, no doubt we'll wed,
Our sin will go unchidden . . .
Ah! sweeter than the nuptial bed
Are ecstasies forbidden.

And as I held my sweetheart close,
And she was softly sighing,
I could not help but think of those
In peace below us lying.
Poor folks! No disrespect we meant,
And begs you'll be forgiving;
We hopes the dead will not resent
The rapture of the living.

And when in death I, too, shall lie,
And lost to those who love me,
I wish two sweethearts roving by
Will plight their troth above me.
Oh do not think that I will grieve
To hear the vows they're voicing,
And if their love new life conceive,
'Tis I will be rejoicing.

RESOLUTIONS

Each New Year's Eve I used to brood
On my misdoings of the past,
And vowed: "This year I'll be so good—
Well, haply better than the last."
My record of reforms I read
To Mum who listened sweetly to it:
"Why *plan* all this, my son?" she said;
    "Just do it."

Of her wise words I've often thought—
Aye, sometimes with a pang of pain,
When resolutions come to naught,
And high resolves are sadly vain;
The human heart from failure bleeds;
Hopes may be wrecked so that we rue them . . .
Don't let us dream of lovely deeds—
    Just do them.

And so, my son, uphold your pride.
Believe serenely in your soul.
Just take things in a steady stride,
Until behold! you've gained your goal.
But if, perchance, you frame a plan
Of conduct, let it be a free one:
Don't try to *make* yourself a man—
    Just *be* one.

STRIVING

Striving is life, yet life is striving;
I fight to live, yet live to fight;
The vital urge is in me driving,
Yet I must drive with all my might:
Each day a battle, and the fray
Stoutly renewed the coming day.

I am myself—yet when I strive
I build a self that's truer, higher;
I keep my bit of God alive
And forge me in heroic fire:
What if my goal I never gain—
Better to toil than to attain.

It is not what I do or make,
It is the travail of my trying;
The aim, the effort and the ache
Is in the end my glorifying:
Though triumph I may never see,
The will to win is victory.

Striving is strength: with all that's in me
I will not falter in the fray;
And though no shining crown it win me,
I'll fight unto my latest day:
Strive on!—and though I win no place,
Uphold the spirit of the race.

Behold yon peaks that mock my climbing. . . .
I peer from out the dusty plain;
Dark falls, the mission bells are chiming
As on to starry heights I strain;
Despite the night up, up I plod
To gain the golden meads of God.

AN OLIVE FIRE

An olive fire's a lovely thing;
Somehow it makes me think of Spring
As in my grate it over-spills
With dancing flames like daffodils.
They flirt and frolic, twist and twine,
The brassy fire-irons wink and shine. . . .
Leap gold, you flamelets! Laugh and sing:
An olive fire's a lovely thing.

An olive fire's a household shrine:
A crusty loaf, a jug of wine,
An apple and a chunk of cheese—
Oh I could be content with these.
But if my cruse of oil is there,
To fry a fresh-caught fish, I swear
I do not envy any king,
As sitting by my hearth I sing:
An olive fire's a lovely thing.

When old and worn, of life I tire,
I'll sit before an olive fire,
And watch the feather ash like snow
As softly as a rose heart glow;
The tawny roots will loose their hoard
Of sunbeams centuries have stored,
And flames like yellow chickens cheep,
Till in my heart Peace is so deep:
With hands prayer-clasped I sleep . . . and sleep.

MY INDIAN SUMMER

Here in the Autumn of my days
My life is mellowed in a haze.
Unpleasant sights are none too clear,
Discordant sounds I hardly hear.
Infirmities like buffers soft
Sustain me tranquilly aloft.
I'm deaf to duffers, blind to bores,
Peace seems to percolate my pores.
I fold my hands, keep quiet mind,
In dogs and children joy I find.
With temper tolerant and mild,
Myself you'd almost think a child.
Yea, I have come on pleasant ways
Here in the Autumn of my days.

Here in the Autumn of my days
I can allow myself to laze,
To rest and give myself to dreams:
Life never was so sweet, it seems.
I haven't lost my sense of smell,
My taste-buds never served so well.
I love to eat—delicious food
Has never seemed one half so good.
In tea and coffee I delight,
I smoke and sip my grog at night.
I have a softer sense of touch,
For comfort I enjoy so much.
My skies are far more blues than greys,
Here in the Autumn of my days.

177

Here in the Autumn of my days
My heart is full of peace and praise.
Yet though I know that Winter's near,
I'll meet and greet it with a cheer.
With friendly books, with cosy fires,
And few but favourite desires,
I'll live from strife and woe apart,
And make a Heaven in my heart.
For Goodness, I have learned, is best,
And should by Kindness be expressed.
And so December with a smile
I'll wait and welcome, but meanwhile,
Blest interlude! The Gods I praise,
For this, the Autumn of my days.

ADVENTURE

Out of the wood my White Knight came:
His eyes were bright with a bitter flame,
As I clung to his stirrup leather;
For I was only a dreaming lad,
Yet oh, what a wonderful faith I had!
And the song in my heart was never so glad,
As we took to the trail together.

"Friends and lovers, good-bye," I said;
Never once did I turn my head,
Though wickedly wild the weather.
Mine were the rover's rags and scars,
And the rover's bed beneath the stars,
But never the shadow of prison bars,
As we ranged the world together.

Dreary and darkling was the trail,
But my Knight was clad in a gleaming mail,
And he plucked from his plume a feather.
And oh how foolishly proud was I!
"I'll wear it," I told him, "till I die;
Freemen we'll be of sea and sky,
To the ends of the earth together."

. . . . .

Yet now I know by my failing breath
I'm ripe for the last adventure, Death,
And I've reached the end of my tether:
But my Knight of the shining mail is there,
And his eyes are bright and he bids me dare:
So into the Dark let's boldly fare,
Into the Dark . . . together.

ROSE LEAVES

When they shall close my careless eyes
And look their last upon my face,
I fear that some will say: "Here lies
    A man of deep disgrace;
His thoughts were bare, his words were brittle,
He dreamed so much, he did so little."

When they shall seal my coffin lid
And this worn mask I know as ME,
Shall from the sight of man be hid
    To all eternity—
Some one may say: "His sins were many.
His virtues—really, had he any?"

When I shall lie beneath my tomb,
Oh do not grave it with my name,
But let one rose-bush o'er me bloom,
    And heedless of my shame,
With velvet shade and loving laugh,
In petals write my epitaph.

LAST LOOK

What would I choose to see when I
To this bright earth shall bid good-bye?
When fades forever from my sight
The world I've loved with long delight?
What would I pray to look on last,
When Death shall draw the Curtain fast?

I've loved the farewell of the Sun,
Low-lapsing after work well done;
Or leaping from a sea forlorn,
Gold-glad to greet a day new born. . . .
Shall I elect to round my dream
The Sun I hail as Lord Supreme?

Ah no! Of Heaven's shining host,
It is the Moon I love the most;
And if, when I shall cease to be,
God lets me keep one memory
Of loveliness that held me thrall,
The Moon's the one I would recall.

. . . *The new Moon fine as pearly clip*
From Cleopatra's finger-tip;
. . . *The ripe Moon vaulting o'er the trees*
As ruddy as a Cheddar cheese;
. . . *The late Moon, frail and wanly fair,*
Relaxed on silver rocking chair. . . .

But most of all, the Moon intense
With radiant indifference;
So placid, glacid, pure, serene,
Of all perfection proudly Queen. . . .
O Mistress Mine, let me adore
Your beauty but one moment more!
One last look . . . Let the Curtain fall,
Then let me look no more at all.

THE END OF THE TRAIL

Life, you've been mighty good to me,
Yet here's the end of the trail;
No more mountain, moor and sea,
No more saddle and sail.
Waves a-leap in the laughing sun
Call to me as of yore. . . .
Alas! my errant days are done:
I'll rove no more, no more.

Life, you've cheered me all the way;
You've been my bosom friend;
But gayest dog will have his day,
And biggest binge must end.
Shorebound I watch and see afar
A wistful isle grow wan,
While over it a last lone star
Dims out in lilac dawn.

Life, you've been wonderful to me,
But fleetest foot must fail;
The hour must come when all will see
The last lap of the trail.
Yet holding in my heart a hymn
Of praise for gladness gone,
Serene I wait *my* star to dim
In the glow of the Greater Dawn.

FINALE

Here in this vale of sweet abiding,
My ultimate and dulcet home,
That gently dreams above the chiding
Of restless and impatient foam;
Beyond the hazards of hell weather,
The harceling of wind and sea,
With timbers morticed tight together
My old hulk havens happily.

The dawn exultantly discloses
My lawn lit with mimosa gold;
The joy of January roses
Is with me when rich lands are cold;
Serene with bells of beauty chiming,
This dream domain to me belongs,
By sweet conspiracy of rhyming,
And virtue of some idle songs.

I thank the gracious Lord of Living
Who gave me power and will to write:
May I be worthy of His giving
And win to merit in His sight. . . .
O merciful and mighty Master,
Though I have faltered in the past,
Your scribe I be. . . . Despite disaster
Let me be faithful to the last.

Provence, 1949

184

RHYMES OF A ROUGHNECK

TO FRANK DODD

Since four decades you've been to me
          Both Guide and Friend,
I fondly hope you'll always be,
          Right to the end;
And though my rhymes you rarely scan
          (Oh, small the blame!)
I joy that on this page I can
          Inscribe your name.

CONTENTS

LIBRARY LAYS

POEMS OF COMPASSION

RIBALD RHYMES

VIGNETTES IN VERSE

MORTUARY MUSE

PRELUDE

In youth I gnawed life's bitter rind
And shared the rugged lot
Of fellows rude and unrefined,
Frustrated and forgot;
And now alas! it is too late
My sorry ways to mend,
So sadly I accept my fate,
A Roughneck to the end.

Profanity is in my verse
And slang is in my rhyme,
For I have mucked with men who curse
And grovel in the grime;
My fingers were not formed, I fear,
To frame a pretty pen,
So please forgive me if I veer
From Virtue now and then.

For I would be the living voice,
Though raucous is its tone,
Of men who rarely may rejoice,
Yet barely ever moan:
The rovers of the raw-ribbed lands,
The lads of lowly worth,
The scallywags with scaley hands
Who weld the ends of earth.

LOW BROW LYRICS

MC'CLUSKY'S NELL

In Mike Maloney's Nugget Bar the hooch was flowin'
    free,
An' One-eyed Mike was shakin' dice wi' Montreal
    Maree,
An' roarin' rageful warning when the boys got overwild,
When peekin' through the double door he spied a tiny
    child.
Then Mike Maloney muttered: "Hell! Now ain't that
    jest too bad;
It's Dud McClusky's orphan Nell a-lookin' for her dad,
An' him in back, a-lushin' wine wi' Violet de Vere—
Three times I've told the lousy swine to keep away from
    here."
"Pore leetle sing! He leave her lone, so he go on ze spree:
I feex her yet, zat Violet," said Montreal Maree.

Now I'm accommodatin' when it comes to scented sin
But when I saw that innocent step in our drunken din,
I felt that I would like to crawl an' hide my head in
    shame.
An' judgin' by their features all them sourdoughs felt the
    same.
For there they stood like chunks o' wood, forgettin' how
    to swear,
An' every glass o' likker was suspended in the air.
For with her hair of sunny silk, and big, blue pansy eyes
She looked jest like an angel child stepped outa paradise.
So then Big Mike, paternal like, took her upon his knee.
"Ze pauv' petite! She ees so sweet," said Montreal
    Maree.

16

The kid was mighty scared, we saw, an' peaked an' pale
 an' sad;
She nestled up to One-eyed Mike jest like he was her
 dad.
Then he got strokin' of her hair an' she began to sob,
An' there was anger in the air of all that plastered mob,
When in a hush so stark an' strained it seemed to stab
 the ear,
We heard the lush, punk-parlour laugh o' Violet de Vere.
Then Montreal Maree arose an' vanished from our sight,
An' soon we heard the sound o' blows suggestin' female
 fight.
An' when she joined the gang again dishevelly was she:
"Jeezecrize! I feex zat Violet," said Montreal Maree.

Then Barman Bill came forward with what seemed a
 glass o' milk:
"It's jest an egg-nog Missy, but it's slick an' smooth as
 silk."
An' as the kiddy slowly sipped wi' gaze o' glad surprise,
Them fifty sozzled sourdoughs uttered fifty happy sighs.
Then Ragtime Joe swung on his stool an' soft began to
 play
A liltin' tune that made ye think o' daffydills in May;
An' Gumboot Jones in solemn tones said: "You should
 hear her sing;
They've got the cabin next to mine, an' like a bird in
 Spring,
She fills that tumble-down old shack wi' simple melo-
 dee."
"Maybe she sing a song for us," said Montreal Maree.

Now I don't hold wi' mushy stuff, tear-jerkin' ain't my
    line,
Yet somehow that kid's singin' sent the shivers down my
    spine;
An' all them salted sourdoughs sighed, an' every eye was
    dim
For what she sang upon the bar was just a simple hymn;
Somethin' about "Abide with me, fast falls the even-
    tide."
My Mother used to sing it—say, I listened bleary-eyed,
That childish treble was so sweet, so clear, so tender true,
It seemed to grip you by the heart an' did queer things
    to you.
It made me think o' childhood days from sin an' sorrow
    free:
"Zat child, she make me want to cry," said Montreal
    Maree.

Then up spoke One-eyed Mike: "We can't with us let
    her abide;
For her dear Mother's sake we gotta send that kid out-
    side.
Ye know this camp's a den o' sin, ye know that Dud's
    no dice—
Let's stake her to a convent school, an' have her brought
    up nice."
An' so them bearded sourdoughs crowded round an' one
    an' all,
Dug down an' flung upon the bar their nuggets great an'
    small.
"I guess we got a thousand bucks," exulted One-eyed
    Mike;

"You bastards are a credit to the camp of Lucky Strike."
"You see zis leetle silver cross my mozzaire give to me—
Look, boys, I hang it on zee *gosse,*" said Montreal Maree.

Time marches on; that little Nell is now a famous star,
An' yet she got her singin' start on Mike Maloney's bar.
Aye, it was back in ninety-eight she made her first day-
        boo,
An' of that audience to-day are left but only two.
For all them bibulous sourdoughs have bravely passed
        away,
An' Lucky Strike is jest another ghost town of to-day.
But Nell now sings in opera, we saw her in Boheem;
'Twas at a high-toned matinay, an' say! she was a dream.
So also thought the white-haired dame a-sittin' down by
        me—
My lovin' spouse that once was known as Montreal
        Maree.

DEATH'S WAY

Old Man Death's a lousy heel who will not play the
game:
Let graveyard yawn and doom down crash, he'll sneer and
turn away.
But when the sky with rapture rings and joy is like a
flame,
Then Old Man Death grins evilly, and swings around to
slay.

Jack Duval was my chosen pal in the ranks of the Reckless
Men.
Thick as thieves they used to say, and it may be that we
were:
Where the price of life is a naked knife and damned are
nine in ten,
It doesn't do to be curious in the *Legion Etrangère*.

So when it came to a hidden shame our mugs were zip-
pered tight;
He never asked me what I'd done, and he would never
tell;
But though like men we revelled, when it came to bloody
fight
I knew that I could bank on him clear to the hubs of
hell.

They still tell how we held the Fort back on the blasted
bled,
And blazed from out the shambles till the fagged relief
arrived.

"The garrison are slaughtered all," the Captain grimly
    said:
Piped Jack: "Give us a slug of hooch and say that two
    survived."

Then there was that time we were lost, canteen and car-
    case dry,
As on we staggered with the thought: "Here's where our
    story ends."
Ten desert days delirious, when black against the sky,
We saw a line of camels, and the Arabs were our friends.

And last of all, the lurid night we crashed the gates of hell
And stemmed the Teuton torrent as it roared on every
    side;
And we were left in blood and mud to rot on the
    Moselle—
Two lacerated Legionaires, whom all supposed had died.

Three times death thought to take us and three times he
    stayed his hand;
But when we left the Legion what a happy pair we were,
Then after reckless roving up and down the sunny land,
I found Jack eating *bouillabaisse* back on the Cannebière.

"Next week I wed," he gaily said, "the sweetest girl on
    earth."
I wonder why did Death pass by just then and turn to
    gloat?
"Oh I'm so happy! You must come and join us in our
    mirth." . . .
Death struck . . . Jack gasped and choked and—died:
                     A fishbone in his throat.

THE DUEL

In Pat Mahoney's booze bazaar the fun was fast and free,
And Ragtime Billy spanked the baby grand;
While carolling a saucy song was Montreal Maree,
With sozzled sourdoughs giving her a hand.
When suddenly erupting in the gay and gilded hall,
A stranger draped himself upon the bar;
As in a voice like bedrock grit he hollered: "Drinks for
    all,"
And casually lit a long cigar.

He bore a battered stetson on the grizzle of his dome,
And a bunch of inky whiskers on his jaw;
Then suddenly I knew the guy—'twas Black Moran
    from Nome,
A guinney like greased lightning on the draw.
But no one got his number in that wild and woolly
    throng,
As they hailed his invitation with *eclaw*,
And they crowded round the stranger, but I knew some-
    thing was wrong,
When in there stomped the Sheriff, Red McGraw.

Now Red McGraw from Arkansaw was noted for his
    spunk;
He had a dozen notches on his gun;
And whether he was sober or whether he was drunk,
He kept the lousy outlaws on the run.
So now he shouts: "Say, boys, there's been a hold-up
    Hunker way,
And by this poke I'm throwin' on the bar,

I bet I'll get the bastard braced before another day,
Or send him where a dozen others are."

He banged the bag of gold-dust on the bar for all to see,
When in a lazy drawl the stranger spoke:
"As I'm the man you're lookin' for an' feelin' mighty free,
I reckon, Sheriff, I'll jest take yer poke.
It's pleasant meetin' you like this, an' talkin' man to man,
For all the North has heard o' Red McGraw.
I'm glad to make ye eat yer words, since I am Black
    Moran,
An' no man livin' beats me on the draw."

And as they boldly bellied, each man's hand was on his
    rod,
Yet at that dreaded name the Sheriff knew
A single fumbling movement and he'd go to meet his
    God,
The which he had no great desire to do.
So there they stood like carven wood and hushed was
    every breath,
We watched them glaring, staring eye to eye;
But neither drew, for either knew a second split meant
    death—
And so a minute . . . two . . . then three went by.

The sweat pricked on the Sheriff's brow as suddenly he
    broke
And limp and weak he wilted to the floor;
And then the stranger's hand shot out and grabbed the
    heavy poke
As jeeringly he backed up to the door.

23

"Say, folks," he cried, "I'm off downstream; no more of
me you'll see,
But let me state the job was pretty raw. . . .
The guy that staged the robbery he thought to pin on me
Was your bastard of a Sheriff, Red McGraw."

TAKE IT EASY

When I was boxing in the ring
In 'Frisco back in ninety-seven,
I used to make five bucks a fling
To give as good as I was given.
But when I felt too fighting gay,
And tried to be a dinger-donger,
My second, Mike Muldoon, would say:
"Go easy, kid; you'll stay the longer."

When I was on the Yukon trail
The boys would warn, when things were bleakest,
The weakest link's the one to fail—
Said I: "By Gosh! I won't be weakest."
So I would strain with might and main,
Striving to prove I was the stronger,
Till Sourdough Sam would snap: "Goddam!
Go easy, son; you'll last the longer."

So all you lads of eighty odd
Take my advice—you'll never rue it:
Be quite prepared to meet your God,
But don't stampede yourselves to do it.
Just cultivate a sober gait;
Don't emulate the lively conger;
No need to race, slow down the pace,
Go easy, Pals—you'll linger longer.

COMPENSATION PETE

He used to say: "There ain't a doubt
Misfortune is a bitter pill,
But if you only pry it out
You'll find there's good in every ill.
There's comfort in the worst of woe,
There's consolation in defeat . . .
Oh what a solace-seeker! So
We called him Compensation Pete.

He lost his wealth—but was he pipped?
Why no—"That's fine," he used to say.
"I've got the government plumb gypped—
No more damn income tax to pay.
From cares of property set free,
And with no pesky social ties,
Why, even poverty may be
A benediction in disguise."

He lost his health: "Okay," he said;
"I'm getting on, may be it's best.
I've always loved to lie abed,
And now I have the *right* to rest.
Such heaps o' things I want to do,
I'll have no time to fret or brood.
I'll read the dam ol' Bible through:
Guess it'll do me plenty good."

He had that line of sunny shine
That makes a blessing of a curse,
And he would say: "Don't let's repine,
Though things are bad they might be worse."
And so he cherished to the end
Philosophy so sane and sweet
That everybody was his friend . . .
With optimism hard to beat—
God bless old Compensation Pete.

MAKING GOOD

No man can be a failure if he *thinks* he's a success;
He may not own his roof-tree overhead,
He may be on his uppers and have hocked his evening
       dress—
(Financially speaking—in the red.)
He may have chronic shortage to repay the old home
       mortgage,
And almost be a bankrupt in his biz.,
But though he skips his dinner,
And each day he's growing thinner,
If he thinks he is a winner,
              Then he is.

But when I say Success I mean the sublimated kind;
A man may gain it yet be on the dole.
To me it's music of the heart and sunshine of the mind,
Serenity and sweetness of the soul.
You may not have a brace of bucks to jingle in your jeans,
Far less the dough to buy a motor car;
But though the row you're hoeing
May be grim, ungodly going,
If you think the skies are glowing—
              Then they are.

For a poor man may be wealthy and a millionaire may
       fail,
It all depends upon the point of view.
It's the sterling of your spirit tips the balance of the scale,
It's optimism, and it's up to you.
For what I figure as success is simple Happiness,

The consummate contentment of your mood:
You may toil with brain and sinew,
And though little wealth it win you,
If there's health and hope within you—
                    You've made good.

THE GOD OF COMMON-SENSE

My Daddy used to wallop me for every small offence:
"It takes a hair-brush back," said he, "to teach kids com-
    mon-sense."
And still to-day I scarce can look a hair-brush in the face,
Without I want in sympathy to pat a tender place.
For Dad declared with unction: "Spare the brush and
    spoil the brat."
The dear old man! What e'er his faults he never did do
    that;
And though a score of years have gone since he departed
    hence,
I still revere his deity, the God of Common-sense.

How often I have played the ass (man's universal fate),
Yet always I have saved myself before it was too late;
How often tangled with a dame—you know how these
    things are,
Yet always had the gumption not to carry on too far;
Remembering that fancy skirts, however high they go,
Are not to be stacked up against a bunch of hard-earned
    dough;
And sentiment has little weight compared with pounds
    and pence,
According to the gospel of the God of Common-sense.

Oh blessings on that old hair-brush my Daddy used to
    whack
With such benign precision on the basement of my back.
Oh blessings on his wisdom, saying: "Son, don't play the
    fool,

Let prudence be your counsellor and reason be your rule.
Don't get romantic notions, always act with judgement
    calm,
Poetical emotions ain't in practice worth a damn.
Let solid comfort be your goal, self-interest your
    guide. . . ."
Then just as if to emphasize, whack! whack! the brush
    he plied.
And so I often wonder if my luck is Providence,
Or just my humble tribute to the God of Common-
    sense.

BROTHER JIM

My brother Jim's a millionaire,
While I have scarce a penny;
His face is creased with lines of care,
While my mug hasn't any.
With inwardness his eyes are dim,
While mine laugh out in glee,
And though I ought to envy him,
I think he envies me.

He has a chateau, I a shack,
And humble I should be
To see his stately Cadillac
Beside my jalopy.
With chain of gold his belly's girt,
His beard is barber trim;
Yet bristle-chinned with ragged shirt,
I do not envy Jim.

My brother is a man of weight;
For every civic plum
He grabs within the pie of state,
While I am just a bum.
Last Winter he was near to croak
With gastric ulcers grim. . . .
Ah no! although I'm stony broke
I will not envy Jim.

He gets the work, I get the fun;
He has no time for play;
Whereas with paddle, rod and gun
My life's a holiday.
As over crabbed script he pores
I scan the sky's blue rim. . . .
Oh boy! While I have God's outdoors
I'll never envy Jim.

OUR POTE

A pote is sure a goofy guy;
He ain't got guts like you or I
    To tell the score;
He ain't got gumption 'nuff to know
The game of life's to get the dough,
    Then get some more.
Take Brother Bill, he used to be
The big shot of the family,
    The first at school;
But since about a year ago,
Through readin' Longfeller and Poe,
    He's most a fool.

He mopes around with dimwit stare;
You might as well jest not be there,
    The way he looks;
You'd think he shuns the human race,
The how he buries down his face
    In highbrow books.
I've seen him stand for near an hour,
Jest starin' at a simple flower—
    Sich waste o' time;
Then scribblin' on an envelope . . .
Why, most of all his silly dope
    Don't even rhyme.

Now Brother Jim's an engineer,
And Brother Tim's a bank cashier,
        While I keep store;
Yet Bill, the brightest of the flock,
Might be a lawyer or a doc.
        And then some more.
But no, he moons and loafs about,
As if he tried to figger out
        Why skies are blue;
Instead o' gittin' down to grips
Wi' life an' stackin' up the chips
        Like me an' you.

*   *   *   *   *

Well, since them final lines I wrote,
We're mournin' for our Brother Pote:
        Bill crossed the sea
And solved his problem with the best,
For now he lies in peace and rest
        In Normandie.
He died the bravest of the brave,
And here I'm standin' by his grave
        So far from home;
With just a wooden cross to tell
How in the blaze of battle hell
As gloriously there he fell—
        Bill wrote his "pome".

ALIAS BILL

We bore him to his boneyard lot
One afternoon at three;
The clergyman was on the spot
To earn his modest fee.
We sprinkled on his coffin lid
The customary loam,
And so old Bill was snugly slid
> To his last home.

A lonesome celebate, we thought,
For close as clam was he;
We never guessed that he had got
A lawful family,
Till lo! we saw a gorgeous wreath
Reposing on his bier,
With on a scarlet scroll beneath:
> "To Father Dear."

He ordered it hisself, they said,
Before he had to go.
His folks don't know that he is dead—
Maybe they'll never know.
His step was frail, his hair was grey,
But though his sight was dim,
He liked to kid hisself that they
> Still thought of him.

Maybe they did: we never knew,
And he would never tell;
Perhaps their hearts were broken too—
His was, I think . . . Ah well,
We left him in his boneyard lot
With none to shed a tear,
And just a wreath, the one *he* bought:
        "To Father Dear."

JIM

He was a travelling tinker lad
And I was a gypsy jade,
Yet never were two so gay and glad,
And a perfect pair we made;
Bruises I've known since life began,
Blows and the love that smothers:
But I'd rather have the curse of my man,
Than the kisses of all the others.

When Black Mike called me a lousy bitch
Jim was so mad, like hell 'e
Flamed, and Mike lay there in the ditch
With a jack-knife in his belly.
Then came the cops and they put away
My bully behind the bars,
And he'll lose for a score of years, they say,
The light o' the larky stars.

And yet in spite o' his dismal doom
No garb of woe I'm wearing,
For the seed of him is in my womb,
And son for him I'm bearing;
And when they swing the prison gate,
And him like blind they're leading,
His boy and I with bliss will wait,
Although our hearts be bleeding.

Then we will take the wildwood track,
And he'll be wae and weary,
But when he gets his manhood back
And beats me I'll be cheery.
And maybe some fowl's neck I'll wring,
And maybe we'll get tipsy;
So by a thorn fire how we'll sing!
What heaven for a gypsy!

GRAVE-DIGGER

When I was young and full of sap
I had of many a maid my pleasure.
God's truth! I was a randy chap
And took of willing wench my measure;
Of Nell and Nan, of Bell and Bess,
But now I've got to life's November,
When I look back I must confess
One half of 'em I don't remember.

It seems right rum, for all are dead
And in fond memory respected.
Most honourably they were wed,
And none their strayfulness suspected.
And I have buried each sweet jade,
Ay, Jill and Jane and Maude and Mollie:
So now I lean upon my spade
And think of them with melancholy.

My sins have never found me out,
For I have covered up my traces;
Yet as I ramble all about,
I see so many childish faces,
The bairns of lassies I have loved,
Who have of me some strain indwelling . . .
Well, nothing ever can be proved:
God only knows, and he's not telling.

But now I'm burying the last,
The only one I truly cherished;
Not one love-look on me she cast,
Yet for her proudly I'd have perished.
I kissed the ground on which she trod,
And ere the gowans gay shall hide her,
I pray: O Understanding God!
May I be blest to rest beside her.

THE FRONT TOOTH

A-sittin' in the Bull and Pump
With double gins to keep us cheery,
Says she to me, says Polly Crump:
"What makes ye look so sweet, me dearie?
As if ye'd gotten back yer youth. . . ."
Says I: "It's just me new front tooth."

Says Polly Crump: "A gummy grin
Don't help to make one's business active;
We gels wot gains our bread by sin
Have got to make ourselves attractive.
I hope yer dentist was no rook?"
Says I: "A quid is what he took."

Says Polly Crump: "The shoes you wear
Are down at heel and need new soleing;
Why doncher buy a better pair?
The rain goes in and out the holeing.
They're squelchin' as ye walk yer beat. . . ."
Says I: "Blokes don't look at me feet."

Says Polly Crump: "You cough all day;
It just don't do in our perfession;
A girl's got to be pert and gay
To give a guy a good impression;
For if ye cough he's shy of you. . . ."
Says I: "An' wots a gel to do?"

Says Polly Crump: "I'm pink an' fat,
But you are bones an' pale as plaster;
At this dam' rate you're goin' at
You'll never live to be a laster.
You'll have the daisy roots for door. . . ."
Says I: "It's 'ell to be a 'ore.

"But I don't care now I can smile,
Smile, smile and not that gap-toothed grinning;
I'm wet and cold, but it's worth while
To once again look fairly winning,
And send ten bob or so to Mother. . . ."
Said Polly Crump: "Gawd! Have another?"

CONTENTMENT

An ancient gaffer once I knew,
Who puffed a pipe and tossed a tankard;
He claimed a hundred years and two,
And for a dozen more he hankered;
So o'er a pint I asked how he
Had kept his timbers tight together;
He grinned and answered: "It maun be
Because I likes all kinds o' weather.

"For every morn when I get up
I lights me clay pipe wi' a cinder,
And as me mug o' tea I sup
I looks from out the cottage winder;
And if it's shade or if it's shine
Or wind or snow befit to freeze me,
I always say: 'Well, now that's fine . . .
It's just the sorto' day to please me.'

"For I have found it wise in life
To take the luck the way it's coming;
A wake, a worry or a wife—
Just carry on and keep a-humming.
And so I lights me pipe o' clay,
And though the morn on blizzard borders,
I chuckle in me guts and say:
'It's just the day the doctor orders.' "

44

A mighty good philosophy
Thought I, and leads to longer living,
To make the best of things that be,
And take the weather of God's giving;
So though the sky be ashen grey,
And winds be edged and sleet be slanting,
Heap faggots on the fire and say:
"It's just the kind of day I'm wanting."

MY TWINS

Of twin daughters I'm the mother—
Lord! how I was proud of them;
Each the image of the other,
Like two lillies on one stem;
But while May, my first-born daughter,
Was angelic from the first,
Different as wine from water,
Maude, my second, seemed accurst.

I'm a tender-hearted dame,
Military is my bent;
Thus my pretty dears can claim
For their Pa the Regiment.
As they say: to err is human;
But though lots of love I've had,
I'm an ordinary woman,
Just as good as I am bad.

Good and bad should find their level,
So I often wonder why
May was angel, Maude was devil,
Yet between the two was I.
May, they say, has taken vows—
Sister Mary, pure and sweet;
Maudie's in a bawdy house,
Down in Mariposa Street.

It's not natural I'm thinking,
One should pray, the other curse;
I'm so worried I am drinking,
Which is making matters worse.
Yet my daughters love each other,
And I love them equal well;
Saint and sinner call me mother . . .
Ain't heredity just hell?

DAGO DITTIES

TOURIST

DAGO DITTIES

To Italy a random tour
I took to crown my education,
Returning relatively poor
In purse yet rich in conversation.
Old Rome put up a jolly show,
But I am not a classic purist,
Preferring to Mike Angelo
The slim stems of a lady tourist.

Venice, they say, was built on piles;
I used to muse, how did they do it?
I tramped the narrow streets for miles,
Religiously I gondoled through it.
But though to shrines I bowed my head,
My stomach's an aesthetic sinner,
For in St. Mark's I yawned and said:
"I hope we'll have *lasagne* for dinner."

Florence, I'll say, was mighty swell,
With heaps of statues stark and lusty;
I liked the Pitti Palace well,
The Offusi I found too fusty.
But though I "did" the best of it,
My taste, I fear, is low and nasty,
For in its bars I'd rather sit
Imbibing cups of sparkling Asti.

And so we go, a tourist host,
And pass art treasures little heeding,
While memories that haunt us most
Are those of rich and copious feeding.
In sooth I see no need to roam,
Since all I want this side of Hades,
I'll comfortably find at home—
Just eating, drinking and the Ladies.

FLORENTINE PILGRIM

"I'll do this old dump in a day,"
He told me in his brittle way.
"Two more, I guess, I'll give to Rome
Before I hit the trail for home;
But while I'm there I kindo' hope
To have an audience with the Pope."

We stood upon the terraced height
With sunny Florence in our sight.
I gazed and gazed, too moved to speak
Until he queried: "What's that creek?"
"The Arno, sir," I said surprised;
He stared at it with empty eyes.

"It is," said I, "the storied stream
Where Dante used to pace and dream,
And wait for Beatrice to pass."
(Oh how I felt a silly ass
Explaining this.) With eyes remote
He asked: "Was Beatrice a boat?"

Then tranced by far Fiesole
Softly I sought to steal away;
But his adhesiveness was grim,
I could not pry apart from him:
And so in our hotel-ward walk
Meekly I listened to his talk.

"*Bologna!* Say, the lunch was swell;
Them wops know how to feed you well.
Verona! There I met a blonde:
Oh how that baby could respond!
Siena! That's the old burg where
We soused on Asti in the square.

"Antiquity! Why, that's the bunk—
Statues and all that mouldy junk
Will never get you anywhere . . .
My line is ladies' underwear,
And better than a dozen Dantes
Is something cute in female scanties. . . .

"One day in Florence is too small
You think, maybe, to see it all.
Well, it don't matter what you've seen—
The thing is: you can say you've *been.*"

THE PIGEONS OF ST. MARKS

Something's wrong in Pigeon-land;
'Tisn't as it used to be,
When the pilgrim, corn in hand,
Courted us with laughing glee;
When we crooned with pinions furled,
Tamest pigeons in the world.

When we packed each arm and shoulder,
Never deeming man a menace;
Surely birds were never bolder
Than our dainty doves of Venice:
Who would have believed a pigeon
Could become wild as a widgeon.

Well, just blame it on the War,
When Venetians grew thinner,
And gaunt hands would grab us for
Succulence to serve a dinner . . .
How our numbers fast grew fewer,
As we perished on a skewer.

Pa and Mummie went like that,
So when tourist takes his stand,
On his Borsolino hat
Soft as whispered love I land;
Then with cooing liquid vowels
I . . . evacuate my bowels.

Something's wrong in Pigeon-land;
Mankind we no longer trust;
Shrinking from the tendered hand,
Pick we corn from out the dust;
While on guileless pilgrim pate,
Thinking that revenge is sweet,
Soft I croon my hymn of hate,
Drop my tribute and retreat.

RUINS

Ruins in Rome are four a penny,
And here along the Appian Way
I see the monuments of many
Esteemed almighty in their day. . . .
Or so he makes me understand—
My glib guide of the rubber bus,
And tells me with a gesture grand:
"Behold! the tomb of Romulus."

Whereat I stared with eyes of awe,
And yet a whit dismayed was I,
When on its crumbling wall I saw
A washing hanging out to dry;
Yea, that relict of slow decay,
With peristyle and gnarly frieze,
Was garnished with a daft display
Of bifurcation and chemise.

But as we went our Southward way
Another ruin soon I saw;
No antique tower, gaunt and grey,
But modern manor rubbled raw;
And on its sill a maiden sat,
And told me in a tone of rue:
"It was your allied bombs did that . . .
But do not think we're blaming you."

Thought I: Time is more kind than we
Who blot out beauty with a blow;
And truly it was sad to see
A gracious mansion levelled low . . .
While moulderings of ancient Rome
Still serve the peasants for their swine,
We do not leave a lovely home
A wall to hang a washing line.

THE LEANING TOWER

Having an aged hate of height
I forced myself to climb the Tower,
Yet paused at every second flight
Because my heart is scant of power;
Then when I gained the sloping summit
Earthward I stared, straight as a plummet.

When like a phantom by my side
I saw a man cadaverous;
At first I fancied him a guide,
For dimly he addressed me thus:
"Sir, where you stand, Oh long ago!
There also stood Galilleo.

"Proud Master of a mighty mind,
He worshipped truth and knew not fear;
Aye, though in age his eyes were blind,
Till death his brain was crystal clear;
And here he communed with the stars,
Where now you park your motor cars.

"This Pisa was a pleasant place,
Beloved by poets in their prime;
Yonder our Shelley used to pace,
And Byron *ottavas* would rhyme;
Till Shelley, from this fair environ,
Scrammed to escape egregious Byron.

"And you who with the horde have come,
I hate your guts, I say with candour;
Your wife wears slacks, and you chew gum,
So I, *the ghost of Savage Landor,*
Beg you, step closer to the edge,
That I may push you o'er the ledge."

But back I shrank, sped down the stair,
And sought the Baptistry where God is;
For I had no desire, I swear,
To prove the law of falling bodies. . . .
You're right—when one's nigh eighty he's a
Damphool to climb the Tower of Pisa.

APOLLO BELVEDERE

A-sittin' on a cracker box an' spittin' in the stove,
I took a sudden notion that I'd kindo' like to rove;
An' so I bought a ticket, jest as easy as could be,
From Pumpkinville in Idaho to Rome in Italy;
An' found myself in seven days of mostly atmosphere
A-starin' at a statoo called Apoller Belvydeer.

Now I'm a rum-soaked sinner, an' religion ain't my plan,
Yet I was flabbergasted by that gol-darned Vattyican;
An' when I seed Saint Peter's dome, all I could do was
    swear,
The which I reckon after all may be a form o' prayer;
But as I sought amid them sights bewildered-like to
    steer,
The king-pin was the one they called Apoller Belvydeer.

Say, I ain't got no culture an' I don't know any art,
But that there statoo got me, standin' in its room apart,
In an alcove draped wi' velvet, lookin' everlastin' bright,
Like the vision o' a poet, full o' beauty, grace an' light:
An' though I know them kind o' words sound sissy in the
    ear,
It's jest how I was struck by that Apoller Belvydeer.

I've gazed at them depictions in the glossy magazines,
Uv modern Art an' darned if I can make out what it
    means:
Will any jerk to-day outstand a thousand years of test?
Why, them old Pagans make us look like pikers at the
    best.

An' maybe, too, their minds was jest as luminous and
     clear
As that immortal statoo o' Apoller Belvydeer.

An' all yer march o' progress an' machinery an' such,
I wonder if, when all is said, they add up to so much?
An' were not these old fellers in their sweet an' simple
     way
Serener souled an' happier than we poor mugs to-day?
They have us licked, I thought, an' stood wi' mingled
     gloom an' cheer
Before that starry statoo o' Apoller Belvydeer.

So I'll go back to Pumpkinville an' to my humble home,
An' dream o' all the sights I saw in everlastin' Rome;
But I will never speak a word o' that enchanted land
That takes you bang into the Past—folks wouldn't un-
     derstand;
An' midmost in my memories I'll cherish close an' dear
That bit o' frozen music, that Apoller Belvydeer.

CANARIES CANNOT SING

"I am the Great Prestigio,
The world renowned illusionist.
I'm happy that you liked my show,
So glad the *clou* you haven't missed.
Please join me in a glass of wine;
We'll talk of that last trick of mine.

"You saw me strolling centre stage,
In tails, white gloves and black crush hat,
With in my hand a golden cage
In which a gold canary sat;
Or hopped about—they sometimes do,
Though one should scarce expect them to.

"On tripod stand I set my cage,
While over it I put my hat;
The music hushed, then as in rage
With fist I squashed my gibus flat;
I straightened it, searched everywhere . . .
No bird, no cage, just empty air.

"And now I'll tell you how it's done:
I touch a spring, the cage snaps small;
Of such fine wiring is it spun,
It contracts to a tiny ball.
I palm it, slip it up my sleeve,
So swiftly you could scarce believe.

"The audience, you saw, was thrilled;
I score a triumph every night.
Of course the little bird is killed,
(It can't be helped) but that's all right:
I buy them cheap—females are best,
Because their bones are fragilest.

"If only I could make them sing
A note or two 'twould help my Act,
A trill before I touch the spring
And make my golden cage contract
To crush them close from claw to beak—
You know, I use up nine a week.

"You've said it, sir, my Act is great,
'Tis fit to show before the King;
My birds are honoured by their fate,
But Oh if only they would sing!
. . . Why, must you go? The hour's not late;
Rome's so poetical in Spring."

GARDEN GLEES

MY GARDEN

The world is sadly sick, they say,
And plagued by woe and pain.
But look! How looms my garden gay,
With blooms in golden reign!
With lyric music in the air,
Of joy fulfilled in song,
I can't believe that anywhere
     Is hate and harm and wrong.

A paradise my garden is,
And there my day is spent;
I steep myself in sunny bliss,
Incredibly content.
Feeling that I am truly part
Of peace so rapt and still,
There's not a care within my heart . . .
     How can the world be ill?

Aye, though the land be sick, they say,
And naked unto pain,
My garden never was so gay,
So innocent, so sane.
My roses mock at misery,
My thrushes vie in song . . .
When only beauty I can see,
     How *can* the world be wrong?

BREAKFAST

Of all the meals that glad my day
My morning one's the best;
Purveyed me on a silver tray,
Immaculately dressed.
I rouse me when the dawn is bright;
I leap into the sea,
Returning with a rare delight
To honey, toast and tea.

My appetite was razor edged
When I was in my prime;
To eggs and bacon I was pledged ...
Alas! the March of Time;
For now a genial old gent
With journal on my knee,
I sip and take with vast content
My honey, toast and tea.

So set me up for my delight
The harvest of the bee;
Brown, crispy toast with butter bright,
Ceylon—two cups or three.
Let others lunch or dinner praise,
But I regale with glee,
As I regard with grateful gaze
Just honey, toast and tea.

NATURE'S WAY

To tribulations of mankind
Dame Nature is indifferent;
To human sorrow she is blind,
And deaf to human discontent.
Mid fear and fratricidal fray,
Mid woe and tyranny of toil,
She goes her unregarding way
    Of sky and sun and soil.

In leaf and blade, in bud and bloom
Exultantly her gladness glows,
And careless of Man's dreary doom
Around the palm she wreathes the rose;
Creating beauty everywhere,
With happy birds in holy song . . .
Please God, let us be unaware
    Like her of wrath and wrong.

Let us too be indifferent,
And in her hands our fate resign;
Aye, though the world with rage be rent
Let us be placid as the pine.
For if we turn from greed and guile
Maybe Dame Nature will relent,
And bless us with her lovely smile
    Of comfort and content.

68

SECURITY

Young man, gather gold and gear,
They will wear you well;
You can thumb your nose at fear,
Wish the horde in hell.
With the haughty you can be
Insolent and bold:
Young man, if you would be free
Gather gear and gold.

Mellow man of middle age,
Buy a little farm;
Then let revolution rage,
You will take no harm.
Cold and hunger, hand in hand
May red ruin spread;
With your little bit of land
You'll be warm and fed.

Old man, seek the smiling sun,
Wall yourself away;
Dream aloof from everyone
In a garden gay.
Let no grieving mar your mood,
Have no truck with tears;
Greet each day with gratitude—
Glean a hundred years.

THE SEARCH

Happiness, a-roving round
For a sweet abiding place,
In a stately palace found
Symmetry and gilded grace;
Courtliness and table cheer,
All that chimes with evening dress . . .
"I could never stick it here,"
Swift decided Happiness.

Happiness a-seeking still,
In a mansion of the town,
Comfort-crammed to overspill,
Sought in vain to settle down.
Every nook strained to express
Opulent prosperity . . .
But "Alas!" said Happiness,
"This is not my cup of tea."

In a cottage by the sea,
Most monastically bare,
Happiness peered wistfully,
And he spied me waiting there.
"Stay," said I; "No need to roam;
Though no riches I possess,
Squat and make yourself at home. . . ."
"Say, that's swell!" said Happiness.

POET'S PATH

My garden hath a slender path
With ivy overgrown,
A secret place where once would pace
A poet all alone;
I see him now with fretted brow,
Plunged fathoms deep in thought;
And sometimes he would write maybe,
And sometimes he would not.

A verse a day he used to say
Keeps worry from the door;
Without the stink of printer's ink
How life would be a bore!
And so from chime of breakfast time
To supper he would beat
The pathway flat, a mossy mat
For his poetic feet.

He wrote, I'm told, of gods of old
And mythologic men;
Far better he had sung, maybe,
Of plain folks now and then;
With bitterness he would confess
Too lofty was his aim. . . .
And then with woe I saw him throw
His poems to the flame.

He went away one bitter day
When death was in the sky;
No further word I ever heard
Beyond his last goodbye.
Did battle grim take toll of him
In heaven-rocking wrath?
Oh did he write in starry flight
His name in flame on hell-brewed night?
     . . . Well, there's my poet's path.

ANT HILL

Black ants have made a musty mound
My purple pine tree under,
And I am often to be found,
Regarding it with wonder.
Yet as I watch, somehow it's odd,
Above their busy striving
I feel like an ironic god
Surveying human striving.

Then one day came my serving maid,
And just in time I caught her,
For on each lusty arm she weighed
A pail of boiling water.
Said she with glee: "When this I spill,
Of life they'll soon be lacking."
Said I: "If even one you kill,
You bitch! I'll send you packing."

Just think—ten thousand eager lives
In that toil-won upcasting,
Their homes, their babies and their wives
Destroyed in one fell blasting!
Imagine that swift-scalding hell! . . .
And though, mayhap, it seem a
Fantastic, far-fetched parallel—
Remember . . . Hiroshima.

GREY GULL

'Twas on an iron, icy day
I saw a pirate gull down-plane,
And hover in a wistful way
Nigh where my chickens picked their grain.
An outcast gull, so grey and old,
Withered of leg I watched it hop,
By hunger goaded and by cold,
To where each fowl full-filled its crop.

They hospitably welcomed it,
And at the food rack gave it place;
It ate and ate; it preened a bit,
By way of gratitude and grace.
It parleyed with my barnyard cock,
Then resolutely winged away;
But I am fey in feather talk,
And this is what I heard it say:

"I know that you and all your tribe
Are shielded warm and fenced from fear;
With food and comfort you would bribe
My weary wings to linger here.
An outlaw scarred and leather-lean,
I battle with the winds of woe:
You think me scaly and unclean . . .
And yet my soul you do not know.

"I storm the golden gates of day,
I wing the silver lanes of night;
I plumb the deep for finny prey,
On wave I sleep in tempest height.
Conceived was I by sea and sky,
Their elements are fused in me;
Of brigand birds that float and fly
I am the freest of the free.

"From peak to plain, from palm to pine
I coast creation at my will;
The chartless solitudes are mine,
And no one seeks to do me ill.
Until some cauldron of the sea
Shall gulp for me and I shall cease . . .
Oh I have lived enormously
And I shall have prodigious peace."

With yellow bill and beady eye
Thus spoke, I think, that old grey gull;
And as I watched it Southward fly
Life seemed to be a-sudden dull.
For I have often held the thought—
If I could change this mouldy *me,*
By heaven! I would choose the lot,
Of all the gypsy birds, to be
A gull that spans the spacious sea.

MY PAL

To rouse me when the dawn is bright,
With eager and impatient wings
A-quiver in the morning light,
Exultantly a robin sings;
And in my garden all day long
He follows me from tree to tree,
With ardent and incessant song,
　　As if in love with me.

I feed him crumbs of cherry cake,
And when the garden loam I spade,
He hovers overhead to make
A dart on any worm displayed;
So perched upon an apple bough,
Possessively and without fear,
No other robin he'll allow
　　My presence to draw near.

I often watch him as he sings
So ardently, and wonder why?
Is it the joy he finds in things,
In sun and shade, in earth and sky?
The blackbird has a richer trill,
The thrush a more melodious tone,
But when my little robin's still,
　　How much I feel alone!

Ah, could I know what lies behind
That dauntless song, that spirit blest,
I think I'd be of all mankind
The wisest and the happiest!
Aye, though portends the winter blast,
And we are frail and soon must die,
Brave bird, be lyric to the last. . . .
        And so will I,
              And so will I.

THE CUCKOO

No lyric line I ever penned
The praise this parasitic bird;
And what is more, I don't intend
To write a laudatory word,
Since in my garden robins made
A nest with eggs of dainty spot,
And then a callous cuckoo laid
    A lone one on the lot.

Of course the sillies hatched it out
Along with their two tiny chicks,
And there it threw its weight about,
But with the others would not mix.
In fact, it seemed their guts to hate,
And crossly kicked them to the ground,
So that next morning, sorry fate!
    Two babes stone dead I found.

These stupid robins, how they strove
To gluttonize that young cuckoo!
And like a prodigy it throve,
And daily greedier it grew.
How it would snap and gulp and spit!
Till finally it came to pass,
Growing too big the nest to fit,
    It fell out on the grass.

So for a week they fed it there,
As in a nook of turf it lay;
But it was scornful of their care,
For it was twice as big as they.
When lo! one afternoon I heard
A flutelike call: Cuckoo! Cuckoo!
Then suddenly that foulsome bird
    Flapped to its feet and flew.

I'm sure it never said goodbye
To its fond foster Pa and Ma,
Though to their desolated sigh
It might have chirruped: "Au revoir."
But no, it went in wanton mood,
Flying the coop for climates new
And so I say: "Ingratitude,
    Thy name's Cuckoo."

DARK TRUTH

Birds have no consciousness of doom:
Yon thrush that serenades me daily
From scented snow of hawthorn bloom
Would not trill out his glee so gaily,
Could he foretell his songful breath
Would sadly soon be stilled in death.

Yon lambs that frolic on the lea
And incarnate the joy of life,
Would scarce disport them could they see
The shadow of the butcher's knife:
Oh Nature, with your loving ruth,
You spare them knowledge of Dark Truth.

To sad humanity alone,
(Creation's triumph ultimate)
The grimness of the grave is known,
The dusty destiny await. . . .
Oh bird and beast, with joy, elance
Effulgently your ignorance!
Oh Man, previsioning the hearse,
With fortitude accept your curse!

MY DOG

'Twas in a pub just off the Strand
When I was in my cups,
There passed a bloke with in his hand
Two tiny puling pups;
And one was on me with a bound,
Seeking to lick my face,
And so I bought him for a pound
And took him to my place.

Three acres by the shore I own,
A hut, a piney wood;
And there for fifteen years alone
He shared my solitude.
It was his own, his only world,
And when with hunting spent,
Each night beside my bed he curled,
And slept in sheer content.

My dog is dead. Though lone I be
I'll never have another;
For with his master-worship he
Was closer than a brother.
My foot is frail and I am old,
Yet how my heart can pity
Pups straining on a short leash-hold
And pent up in the city.

For from all thought of self above,
And purged of sex emotion,
I know no form of living love
So deep as dog devotion.
I have no hope at all of heaven,
I've lived in sin and strife;
But thank God! I at least have given
One dog a happy life.

MY PINEY WOOD

I have a tiny piney wood;
My trees are only fifty,
Yet give me shade and solitude
For they are thick and thrifty.
And every day to me they fling
With largess undenying,
Fat cones to make my kettle sing
And keep my pan a-frying.

Go buy yourself a piney wood
If you have gold for spending,
Where you can dream in mellow mood
With peace and joy unending;
Where you can cheerfully retreat
Beyond all churchly chiding,
And make yourself a temple sweet
Of rapturous abiding.

Oh Silence has a secret voice
That claims the soul for portal,
And those who hear it may rejoice
Since they are more than mortal.
So sitting in my piney wood
When soft the owl is winging,
As still as Druid stone I brood . . .
For hark! the *stars* are singing.

A LYRIC DAY

I deem that there are lyric days
So ripe with radiance and cheer,
So rich with gratitude and praise
That they enrapture all the year.
And if there is a God above,
(As they would tell me in the Kirk,)
How he must look with pride and love
Upon his perfect handiwork!

To-day has been a lyric day
I hope I shall remember long,
Of meadow dance and roundelay,
Of woodland glee, of glow and song.
Such joy I saw in maiden eyes,
In mother gaze such tender bliss . . .
How earth would rival paradise
If every day could be like this!

Why die, say I? Let us live on
In lyric world of song and shine,
With ecstasy from dawn to dawn,
Until we greet the Dawn Divine.
For I believe, with star and sun,
With peak and plain, with sea and sod,
Inextricably we are one,
Bound in the Wholeness—God.

TRANQUILISM

I call myself a Tranquilist;
With deep detachment I exist,
                From friction free;
While others court the gilded throng
And worship Woman, Wine and Song,
                I scorn the three.
For I have reached the sober age
When I prefer to turn a page
                Beside the fire,
And from the busy mart of men
To meditative book and pen
                With grace retire.

If you are craving peace of mind,
In Tranquilism you will find
                Philosophy;
Serenely fold your hands and wait
In cloistered calm whatever fate
                The Gods decree.
And though the world with rage be rent,
Hold it remote and claim content
                With quiet heart;
You can't do much to better it,
But your good-will may help a bit,
                Ere you depart.

So let us who are old and sere
To din of battle shut the ear,
And trumpet vain;
And though in no monastic mood
Accept the balm of solitude
And grace regain.
Let us be Tranquilists and try
In placid places to apply
Life's wisdom won;
In Nature's bounty we may bless
The Gods and wait with thankfulness
Our setting sun.

THE GREAT RECALL

I've wearied of so many things
Adored in youthful days;
Music no more my spirit wings,
E'en when a Master plays.
For stage and screen I have no heart,
Great paintings leave me cold;
Alas! I've lost the love of Art
That raptured me of old.

Only my love of books is left,
Yet that begins to pall;
And if of it I am bereft,
I'll read no more at all.
Then when I am too frail to walk
I'll sit out in the sun,
And there with Nature I will talk . . .
Last friend and dearest one.

For Nature's all in all to me;
My other loves are vain;
Her bosom brought me forth and she
Will take me back again.
So I will let her have her way,
For I've a feeling odd,
Whatever wiser men may say,
That she herself is GOD.

LIBRARY LAYS

FUTILITY

Dusting my books I spent a busy day:
Not ancient tomes, time-hallowed and unread,
But modern volumes, classics in their way,
Whose makers now are numbered with the dead;
Men of a generation more than mine,
With whom I tattled, battled and drank wine.

I worshipped them, rejoiced in their success,
Grudging them not the gold that goes with fame.
I thought them near-immortal, I confess,
And naught could dim the glory of each name.
How I perused their pages with delight! . . .
To-day I peer with sadness in my sight.

For, death has pricked each to a flat balloon.
A score of years have gone, they're clean forgot.
Who would have visioned such a dreary doom?
By God! I'd like to burn the blasted lot.
Only, old books are mighty hard to burn:
They char, they flicker and their pages turn.

And as you stand to poke them in the flame,
You see a living line that stabs the heart.
Brave writing that! It seems a cursed shame
That to a bonfire it should play it's part.
Poor book! You're crying, and you're not alone:
Some day someone will surely burn my own.

No, I will dust my books and put them by,
Yet never look into their leaves again;
For scarce a soul remembers them save I,
Re-reading them would only give me pain.
So I will sigh, and say with curling lip:
Futility! Thy name is authorship.

GOD'S SKALLYWAGS

The God of Scribes looked down and saw
The bitter band of seven,
Who had outraged his holy law
And lost their hope of Heaven:
Came Villon, petty thief and pimp,
And obscene Baudelaire,
And Byron with his letcher limp,
And Poe with starry stare.

And Wilde who lived his hell on earth,
And Burns, the baudy bard,
And Francis Thompson, from his birth
Malevolently starred. . . .
As like a line of livid ghosts
They stared to Paradise,
The galaxy of Heaven's hosts
Looked down in soft surmise.

Said God: "You bastards of my love,
You are my chosen sons;
Come, I will set you high above
These merely holy ones.
Your sins you've paid in gall and grief,
So to these radiant skies,
Seducer, drunkard, dopester, thief,
Immortally arise.

I am your Father, fond and just,
And all your folly see;
Your bestiality and lust
I also know in me.
You did the task I gave to you ...
Arise and sit beside
My Son, the best belovéd, who
Was also crucified.

HERO WORSHIP

Said he: "You saw the Master clear;
By Rushy Pond alone he sat,
Serene and silent as a seer,
In tweedy coat and seedy hat.
You tell me you did not intrude,
(Although his book was in your hand,)
Upon his melancholy mood . . .
            I do not understand.

"You did not tell him: 'I have come
From o'er the sea to speak to you.'
You did not dare, your lips were dumb . . .
You thought a little zephyr blew
From Rushy Pond a touch of him
You'll cherish to your dying day.
Perhaps with tears your eyes were dim . . .
            And then—you went away.

"And down the years you will proclaim:
'Oh call me dullard, dub me dunce!
But let this be my meed of fame:
I looked on Thomas Hardy once.
Aye, by a stile I stood a span
And with these eyes did plainly see
A little, shrinking, shabby man . . .
            But Oh a god to me!' "

Said I: " 'Tis true, I scarce dared look,
Yet he would have been kind, I'm sure;
But though I clutched his precious book
I feared to beg his signature.
Ah yes, my friend, I merit mirth.
You're bold, you have the right to laugh,
And if Christ came again to earth
                You'd cadge his autograph."

THE MOLE

Said he: "I'll dive deep in the Past,
And write a book of direful days
When summer skies were overcast
With smoke of humble hearths ablaze;
When War was rampant in the land,
And poor folk cowered in the night,
While ruin gaped on every hand—
Of ravishing and wrath I'll write."

Ten years he toiled to write his book,
Yet he was happy all the while;
The world he willingly forsook
To live alone in hermit style.
In garden sanctuaried sweet,
Full favoured by the steadfast sun,
Plunged in the Past, a life complete
He lived. . . . At last his work was done.

A worthy book that few would read
Yet all would praise—each precious page
Starred with some truth the rare would heed,
The vivid image of an age.
Then blinking, to the world again
He came, a sage, remote, austere . . .
When lo! his eyes were smote with flame,
The wail of war was in his ear.

He shrank and sighed: "Oh can it be
These old iniquities prevail!
That sons of men are still unfree
And time repeats her sorry tale!"
So with a long sad gaze and last,
Seeking his secret garden nook,
He slipped again into the Past
To *live*—and write another book.

FORGOTTEN MASTER

As you gaze beyond the bay
With such wanness in your eyes,
You who have out-stayed your day,
Seeing other stars arise,
Slender though your lifehold be,
Still you dream beside the sea.

We, alas! may live too long,
Know the best part of us die;
Echo of your even-song
Hushes down the darkling sky . . .
But your greatness would be less
If you cherished bitterness.

I am sure you do not care
Though the rabble turn thumbs down;
Their neglect you well can bear,
Knowing you have won your crown,
Proudly given of your best . . .
Maeterlinck, leave God the rest.

SHAKESPEARE AND CERVANTES
Obit 23rd April 1616

Is it not strange that on this common date,
Two titans of their age, aye of all Time,
Together should renounce this mortal state,
And rise like gods, unsullied and sublime?
Should mutually render up the ghost,
And hand in hand join Jove's celestial host?

What wondrous welcome from the scribes on high!
Homer and Virgil would be waiting there;
Plato and Aristotle standing nigh;
Petrarch and Dante greet the peerless pair:
And as in harmony they make their bow,
Horace might quip: "Great timing, you'll allow."

Imagine this transcendant team arrive
At some hilarious banquet of the gods!
Their nations battled when they were alive,
And they were bitter foes—but what's the odds?
Actor and soldier, happy hand in hand,
By death close-linked, like loving brothers stand.

But how diverse! Our Will had gold and gear,
Chattels and land, the starshine of success;
The bleak Castilian fought with casque and spear,
Passing his life in prisons—more or less.
The Bard of Avon was accounted rich;
Cervantes often bedded in a ditch.

Yet when I slough this flesh, if I could meet
By sweet, fantastic fate one of these two,
In languorous Elysian retreat,
Which would I choose? Fair reader, which would you?
Well, though our William more divinely wrote,
By gad! the lousy Spaniard has my vote.

AMATEUR POET

You see that sheaf of slender books
Upon the topmost shelf,
At which no browser ever looks,
Because they're by . . . myself;
They're neatly bound in navy blue,
But no one ever heeds;
Their print is clear and candid too,
Yet no one ever reads.

Poor wistful books! How much they cost
To me in time and gold!
I count them now as labour lost,
For none I ever sold;
No copy could I give away,
For all my friends would shrink,
And look at me as if to say:
"What waste of printer's ink!"

And as I gaze at them on high,
Although my eyes are sad,
I cannot help but breathe a sigh
To think what joy I had—
What ecstasy as I would seek
To make my rhyme come right,
And find at last the phrase unique
Flash fulgent in my sight.

Maybe that rapture was my gain
Far more than cheap success;
So I'll forget my striving vain,
And blot out bitterness.
Oh records of my radiant youth,
No broken heart I'll rue,
For all my best of love and truth
Is there, alive in you.

POEMS OF COMPASSION

SOMEONE'S MOTHER

Someone's Mother trails the street
Wrapt in rotted rags;
Broken slippers on her feet
Drearily she drags;
Drifting in the bitter night,
Gnawing gutter bread,
With a face of tallow white,
Listless as the dead.

Someone's Mother in the dim
Of the grey church wall
Hears within a Christmas hymn,
One she can recall
From the Oh so long ago,
When divinely fair,
In the holy altar glow
She would kneel in prayer.

Someone's Mother, huddled there,
Had so sweet a dream;
Seemed the sky was Heaven's stair,
Golden and agleam,
Robed in gown Communion bright,
Singingly she trod
Up and up the stair of light,
And there was waiting—God.

Someone's Mother cowers down
By the old church wall;
Soft above the sleeping town
Snow begins to fall;
Now her rags are lily fair,
But unproud is she:
Someone's Mother is not there . . .
Lo! she climbs the starry stair
Only angels see.

LOST SHEPHERD

Ah me! How hard is destiny!
If we could only know. . . .
I brought my son from Sicily
A score of years ago;
I haled him from our sunny vale
To streets of din and squalor,
And left it to professors pale
To make of him a scholar.

Had he remained a peasant lad,
A shepherd on the hill,
Like golden faun in goatskin clad
He might be singing still;
He would have made the flock his care
And leapt with gay reliance
On thymy heights, unwitting there
Was such a thing as science.

He would have crooned to his guitar,
Draughts of *chianti* drinking;
A better destiny by far
Than reading, writing, thinking.
So bent above his books was he,
His thirst for knowledge slaking,
He did not realize that we
Are worm-food in the making.

Ambition got him in its grip
And inched him to his doom;
Fate granted him a fellowship,
Then graved for him a tomb.
"Beneath my feet I can't allow
The grass to grow," he said;
And toiled so tirelessly that now
It grows above his head.

His honour scrolls shall feed the flame,
They mean no more to me;
His ashes I with bitter blame
Will take to Sicily.
And there I'll weep with heart bereft,
By groves and sunny rills,
And wish my laughing boy I'd left
A shepherd on the hills.

MY RIVAL

If she met him or he met her,
I knew that something must occur;
For they were just like flint and steel
To strike the spark of woe or weal;
Or like two splinters broken fine,
In perfect fitness to combine;
And so I kept them well apart,
For she was precious to my heart.

One time we all three met in church
I tried to give the lad the lurch,
But heard him say: "How like a rose!
It is your daughter, I suppose?"
"Why no," said I; "My wife she be,
And six months gone wi' child is she."
He looked astonished and distraught:
My boy, that's one for you, I thought.

The wife said: "What a handsome lad!
A sailor . . ." Somehow she looked sad;
And then his memory grew dim,
For nevermore she mentioned him.
And as I be nigh twice her age
I've always thought it mighty sage,
Lest she might one day go astray,
To keep her in the breeding way.

Oh did she ever dream of Jack?
The boy who nevermore came back,
And never will. I heard that he
Was drownded in the China Sea.
I told her not, lest she be sad.
And me? It's mean, but I was glad;
For if he'd come into my life
He would have robbed me of my wife.

But when at night by her I lie,
And in her sleep I hear her sigh,
I have a doubt if I did well
In separating Jack and Nell.
And though we have a brood of seven,
Yet marriage may be made in Heaven:
For Nell has cancer, Doctors state,
So maybe 'tis the way of fate
That in the end them two may mate.

EXPECTATION

My flask of wine was ruby red
And swift I ran my sweet to see;
With eyes that snapped delight I said:
"How mad with love a lad can be!"
The moon was laughing overhead;
I danced as nimbly as a flea.

Thought I: In two weeks time we'll **wed**;
No more a lonesome widow she;
For I have bought a double bed
And I will father children three.
So singing like a lark I sped
To her who ne'er expected me.

And then I went with wary tread,
Her sweet surprise to greet with glee;
To where her lamplit lattice shed
A rosy radiance on the lea:
. . . And then my heart sank low like lead,
Two shadows on the blind to see.

A man was sitting on the bed,
And she was nudely on his knee. . . .
I saw her face drain white with dread,
I saw her lover madly flee. . . .
Oh how her blood is ruby red,
And I await the gallows tree.

A HERO

Three times I had the lust to kill,
To clutch a throat so young and fair,
And squeeze with all my might until
No breath of being lingered there.
Three times I drove the demon out,
Though on my brow was evil sweat. . . .
And yet I know beyond a doubt
He'll get me yet, he'll get me yet.

I know I'm mad. I ought to tell
The doctors, let them care for me,
Confine me in a padded cell
And never, never set me free;
But Oh how cruel that would be!
For I am young—and comely too . . .
Yet dim my demon I can see,
And there is but one thing to do.

Three times I beat the foul fiend back;
The fourth, I know he will prevail,
And so I'll seek the railway track
And lay my head upon the rail,
And sight the dark and distant train,
And hear its thunder louder roll,
Coming to crush my cursed brain . . .
Oh God, have mercy on my soul!

SENTIMENTAL HANGMAN

'Tis hard to hang a husky lad
When larks are in the sky;
It hurts when daffydills are glad
To wring a neck awry.
When joy o' Spring is in the sap
And cheery is the sun,
'Tis sad to string aloft a chap,
No matter what he done.

And sittin' in the pub o' night
I hears that prison bell,
And wonders if it's reely right
To haste a man to hell,
For doin' what he *had* to do,
Through greed, or lust, or hate . . .
Aye, them seem rightful words to you,
But me, I calls it—Fate.

Lots more would flout the gallows tree,
But that they are afraid;
And so to save society,
I ply my grisly trade.
Yet as I throttle eager breath
And plunge to his hell-home
Some cringin' cove, to me his death
Seems more like martyrdom.

For most o' us have held betime
Foul murder in the heart;
And them sad blokes I swung for crime
Were doomed right from the start.
Of wilful choosing they had none,
For freedom's most a fraud,
And maybe in the end the one
Responsible is—God.

RETIRED SHOPMAN

He had the grocer's counter-stoop,
That little man so grey and neat;
His moustache had a doleful droop,
He hailed me in the slushy street.
"I've sold my shop," he said to me,
Cupping his hand behind his ear.
"My deafness got so bad, you see,
Folks had to shout to make me hear."

He sighed and sadly shook his head;
The hand he gave was chill as ice.
"I sold out far too soon," he said;
"To-day I'd get ten times the price.
But then how was a man to know,
(The War, the rising cost of life.)
We have to pinch to make things go:
It's tough—I'm sorry for the wife.

"She looks sometimes at me with tears.
'You worked so hard,' I hear her say.
'You had your shop for forty years,
And you were honest as the day.'
Ah yes, I loved my shop, it's true;
My customers I tried to please;
But when one's deaf and sixty-two
What can one do in times like these?

"My savings, that I fondly thought
Would keep me snug when we were old,
Are melting fast—what once I bought
For silver, now is sought with gold.
The cost of life goes up each day;
I wonder what will be the end?"
He sighed, I saw him drift away
And thought: Alas for you, my friend!

And every day I see him stop
And look and look with wistful eye
At what was once his little shop,
Whose goods he can no longer buy.
Then homeward wearily he goes
To where his wife bed-ridden lies,
A driblet dangling from his nose. . . .
But Oh the panic in his eyes!

LOST KITTEN

Two men I saw reel from a bar
And stumble down the street;
Coarse and uncouth as workmen are,
They walked with wobbly feet.
I watched them, thinking sadly as
I heard their hobnails clink,
The only joy a toiler has
Is to get drowned in drink.

A kitten cowered on a wall,
A skinny, starving stray;
It looked so pitifully small,
A fluff of silver grey.
One of the men came to a stand,
A kindly chap was he,
For with a huge and horny hand
He stroked it tenderly.

With wistful hope it gazed at him
And arched a spine of fur;
It licked his hand so grimy grim
And feebly tried to purr.
And then it climbed upon his chest,
And to his drunken glee,
Upon his shoulder came to rest,
Contented as could be.

The other fellow with a jeer
Made feint to dash it down,
But as it shrank with sudden fear
I saw the first one frown;
And then I heard him coarsely cry:
"Have care for what you do;
Just harm a hair of it and I
Will twist my knife in you."

So there they stood like brutes at bay,
Their blood at fighting heat;
And snarling at each other they
Went weaving down the street,
Leaving the kitten all alone
Upon its stony shelf . . .
And as I haven't heart of stone
I took it home myself.

CONTRAST

"Carry your suitcase, sir?" he said.
I turned away to hide a grin,
For he was shorter by a head
Than I and pitiably thin.
I could have made a pair of him,
So with my load I stoutly legged;
But his tenacity was grim:
"Please let me help you, sir," he begged.

I could not shake the fellow off,
So let him shoulder my valise;
He tottered, with a racking cough
That did not give him any peace.
He lagged so limply in my wake
I made him put the burden down,
Saying: "A taxi I will take,"
And grimly gave him half-a-crown.

Poor devil! I am sure he had
Not eaten anything that day;
His eyes so hungrily were glad,
Although his lips were ashen grey.
He vanished in the callous crowd,
Then when he was no more around,
I lugged my bag and thought aloud:
"I wish I'd given him a pound."

And strangely I felt sore ashamed,
As if somehow I had lost face;
And not only myself I blamed
But all the blasted human race;
And all this life of battle where
The poor are beaten to their knees,
And while the weak the burdens bear,
Fat fools like me can stroll at ease.

THE HOME-COMING

My boy's come back; he's here at last;
He came home on a special train.
My longing and my ache are past,
My only son is back again.
He's home with music, flags and flowers;
With peace and joy my heart's abrim;
He got here in the morning hours
With half the town to welcome him.

To hush my grief, night after night,
How I have digged my pillow deep,
And it would be the morning light
Before I sobbed myself to sleep.
And how I used to stare and stare
Across the harbour's yeasty foam,
Thinking he's fighting far out there . . .
But now with bells my boy's come home.

There's Mrs. Burke, she has her Ted,
But less the sight of his two eyes;
And Mrs. Smith—you know her Fred—
They took his legs off at the thighs.
How can these women happy be,
For all their bravery of talk,
One with a son who cannot see,
One with a boy who'll never walk.

I should be happier than they;
My lad came back without a scar,
And all the folks are proud, they say,
To greet their hero of the war.
So in the gentle eventide
I'll give God thanks my Bert's come home. . . .
As peacefully I sit beside
His tiny mound of new-turned loam.

THE RECORD

Fearing that she might go one day
With some fine fellow of her choice,
I called her from her childish play,
And made a record of her voice.
And now that she is truly gone,
I hear it sweet and crystal clear
From out my wheezy gramophone:
    "I love you, Daddy dear."

Indeed it's true she went away,
But Oh she went all, all alone;
Into the dark she went for aye,
Poor little mite! ere girlhood grown.
Ah that I could with her have gone!
But this is all I have to show—
A ghost voice on a gramophone:
    "Dear Dad, I love you so."

The saddest part of loss 'tis said,
Is that time tempers our regret;
But that is treason to the dead—
I'll not forget, I'll not forget.
Sole souvenir of golden years,
'Twere best to break this disc in two,
And spare myself a spate of tears . . .
    But that I cannot do.

So I will play it every day,
And it will seem that she is near,
And once again I'll hear her say:
"I love you so, Oh Daddy dear."
And then her kiss—a stab of woe.
The record ends . . . I breathe a plea:
"Oh God, speed me to where I know
       Wee lass, you wait for me."

SPINSTER

With him I loved I might have wed
And been a wonder wife,
But that blonde hussy turned his head
And cooked his goose for life;
So now I'm back at teaching school,
And sorry is my case:
Oh that a man should play the fool
Just for a pretty face!

He had the choice between us two,
The worthy and the fair;
Her every wile and guile he knew,
And yet he did not care.
I could have kept his hearth aglow,
A mother fond and brave,
But now unwedded I must go,
And barren to my grave.

And he a slattern has for keeps,
Who'll never bear him bairns,
Who drinks and dances as he sleeps
And squanders all he earns.
Yet Oh how many are like me,
Left loveless in the cold!
How blind as bats the men can be,
Mistaking gilt for gold!

THE SACRIFICES

Twin boys I bore, my joy, my care,
My hope, my life they were to me;
Their father, dashing, debonair,
Fell fighting at Gallipoli.
His daring gallantry, no doubt,
They 'herited in equal share:
So when the Second War broke out,
With eagerness they chose the air.

Said Dick: "The sea's too bally slow;
A flying ship's the one for me."
Said Peter: "Land! Foot-slogging—no!
The jolly sky's my cup of tea."
Well, Dick bailed out in Channel flight,
His foam-flailed body never found;
While Peter, with his plane alight,
Dashed down to death on Kentish ground.

Gay lads they were, and tall and fair,
And had they chosen land or sea,
Shirking the hazards of the air,
They might still have been left to me.
But nothing could I say or do
To move their scorn of sea and land;
Like eagles to the sun they flew—
Why? Only they could understand.

How day and night I prayed for them!
But knew that it was all in vain;
They measured with heroic men,
Yet . . . I will never pray again.
Though time may grieve my hair to grey,
My lips will never kiss the rod. . . .
Only in dying I may say
In pity—"I forgive you, God."

CINDERELLA

Cinderella in the street
In a ragged gown,
Sloven slippers on her feet,
Shames our tidy town;
Harsh her locks of ashen grey,
Vapour vague her stare,
By the curb this bitter day
Selling papers there.

Cinderella once was sweet,
Fine and lily fair,
Silver slippers on her feet,
Ribands in her hair;
Solid men besought her hand,
Tart was she as quince,
Living in a fairy land,
Waiting for a Prince.

Days went by and years went by,
Wistful wan was she;
Heedless of a mother's sigh,
Of a lover's plea;
On her lips a carol gay,
In her heart a dream—
Soon the Prince would come her way,
Gallant and agleam.

Then at last she learned the truth,
How her hope was vain;
Gone her beauty, gone her youth,
Leaving want and pain.
See! she's waiting all alone;
Hark! you hear her cry
Papers by the cold curb-stone,
Begging you to buy.

Winter winds are waxing chill,
Clouds rack overhead;
Cinderella will be ill,
Bye and bye be dead.
Yet she kept her vision clear,
To Romance was true,
Holding him forever dear
Whom she never knew.

*　　*　　*　　*　　*

Cinderellas of to-day
Take no chance of loss;
When a good guy comes your way,
Nail him to the cross.
Let some ordinary cuss
Your coy heart convince;
Never miss the nuptial bus
Waiting for a Prince.

DAYS

I am a Day . . .
My sky is grey,
My wind is wild,
My sea high-piled:
In year of days the first
In misery . . .
Oh pity me!
I am a Day
　　　Accurst.

"Sweet Day, not curst but blest:
Behold upon my breast
My baby born
Your early morn.
Safe in my arms alway . . .
Oh precious Day,
Let tempest be,
You are to me
In heart of mine
　　　Divine."

　　*　　*　　*　　*　　*

I am a Day . . .
From dawn's pure ray
Like to a peerless gem
In summer's diadem.
My sky so softly dreams,
My breeze is bland;
My sea is blue and creams
Upon the sand.
Behold! Of days the Queen
    I reign serene.

"Oh Day, not blest but curst!
Let savage storm-rack burst,
I will not care . . .
For lo! I bear
My baby's coffin to the height.
Ah! Would it were the foulest night
To match my mood's
Ingratitude.
I cannot pray . . .
Go your fell way,
      Accursed Day!"

MAN CHILD

All day he lay upon the sand
When summer sun was bright,
And let the grains sift through his hand
With infantile delight;
Just like a child, so soft and fair,
Though he was twenty-five—
An innocent, my mother-care
Had kept so long alive.

Oh it is hard to bear a cross
For five-and-twenty years;
A daft son and a husband's loss
Are woes out-weighing tears.
Yet bright and beautiful was he,
Though barely could he walk;
And when he signalled out to sea
His talk was baby talk.

The man I loved was drowned out there
When we were ten weeks wed.
'Tis bitter hard a boy to bear
That's fathered by the dead.
And now I give my life to him
Because he needs me so;
And as I look my sight is dim
With pity, love and woe. . . .

Then suddenly I see him rise,
Tall, stalwart and serene . . .
Lo! There he stands before my eyes,
The man he might have been.

"Dear Mother mine," I hear him say,
"The curse that bound me fast,
Some miracle has swept away,
And all your pain is past.
Now I am strong and sane and free,
And you shall have your due;
For as you loved and cherished me,
I'll love and cherish you."

His kisses sooth away my pain,
His clasp is paradise . . .
Then—then I look at him again
With terror in my eyes:
For down he sinks upon the sand,
And heavy droops his head;
The golden grains drift through his hand . . .
I know—my boy is dead.
                    —

THE UNDER-DOGS

What have we done, Oh Lord, that we
     Are evil starred?
How have we erred and sinned to be
     So scourged and scarred?
Lash us, Oh Lord, with scorpion whips,
     We can but run;
But harken to our piteous lips:
     What have we done?

How have we sinned to rouse your wrath,
     To earn your scorn?
Stony and steep has been our path
     Since we were born.
Oh for a sign, a hope, a word,
     A heaven glance;
Why is your hand against us, Lord?
     Give us a chance.

What shall we do, Oh God, to gain
     Your mercy seat?
Shall we live out our lives in pain
     And dark defeat?
Shall we in servitude bow low
     Unto the end?
How we would hope, could we but know
     You are our friend!

We are the disinherited,
                    The doomed, the lost.
For breath, with dust and ashes fed,
                    We pay the cost.
Dumb mouths! Yet though we bleed, with prayer
                    We kiss the sword;
Aye, even dying we forbear
                    To curse Thee, Lord.

RIBALD RHYMES

UNHOLY TRINITY

Though Virtue hurt you Vice is nice;
Aye, Parson says it's wrong,
Yet for my pleasing I'll suffice
With Woman, Wine and Song.
But though it be with jocund glee
My tavern voice is ringing,
Had I to chuck one of the three,
By gad! I'd give up singing.

But not the Vine. What draught divine
Could better souse my throttle?
God never meant that mellow wine
Should languish in the bottle.
So Cellerman, your best bring up;
Let silver cobwebs mist it;
When gold or ruby brims the cup,
Could even saint resist it?

I love the ladies, yes, I do,
I always did and will;
I like with dainty dames to coo,
And have been known to bill.
Yes, I agree it's wrong of me,
So call me grey rapscallion,
But when a lusty lass I see
I whinny like a stallion.

Oh let me be a reprobate,
Your canting care defying;
I'll court that gay triumvirate
Right to the day I'm dying.
So troll until the rafter rings,
And may my life be long
To praise the Lord for precious things
Like Woman, Wine and Song.

POLITENESS

The English and the French were met
Upon the field of future battle;
The foes were formidably set
And waiting for the guns to rattle;
When from the serried ranks of France
The English saw with woeful presage
Under a flaming flag advance
A trumpeter who bore a message.

'Twas from their Marshal, quite polite,
Yet made the English leader shiver.
"We're perched," said he, "upon the height,
While you're exposed beside the river.
We have the vantage, you'll agree,
And your look-out is melancholy;
But being famed for courtesy
We'll let you fire the starting volley."

The English General was moved,
In fact his eyes were almost tearful;
Then he too his politeness proved
By writing back: "We are not fearful.
Our England is too proud to take
The privilege you thrust upon her;
So let your guns in thunder break:
To you, M'sieu, shall be the honour."

Again a note the Marshal sent
By envoy from his battle station:
"Your spirit wins my compliment,
Your courage my appreciation.
Yet you are weak and we are strong,
And though your faith is most inspiring,
Don't let us linger all day long—
Mon General, *begin* the firing."

"How chivalrous the soul of France,"
The English General reflected.
"I hate to take this happy chance,
But I suppose it's what's expected.
Politeness is a platitude
In this fair land of gallant foemen."
So with a heart of gratitude
He primed his guns and cried: "Let's go, men!"

The General was puzzled when
No answer came; said he: "What is it?
Why don't they give us hell?" And then
The herald paid another visit.
The Marshal wrote: "To your salute
Please pardon us for not replying;
To shatter you we cannot shoot . . .
My men are dead and I am dying."

FEAR

I knew how father's strap would feel
If ever I were caught,
So mother's jam I did not steal,
Though theft was in my thought.
Then turned fourteen and full of pith,
Of love I was afraid,
And did not dare to dally with
Our pretty parlour maid.

And so it is and always was,
The path of rectitude
I've followed all my life because
The Parson said I should.
The dread of hell-fire held me straight
When I was wont to stray,
And though my guts I often hate,
I walk the narrow way.

I might have been a bandit or
A Casanovish blade,
But always I have prospered for
I've always been afraid;
Ay, fear's behind the best of us
And schools us for success,
And that is why I'm virtuous,
And happy—more or less.

So let me hail that mighty power
That goads me to be good,
And makes me cannily to cower
Amid foolhardihood;
Though I be criminal in grain,
My virtue a veneer,
I thank the God who keeps me sane,
And shields me from distress and pain,
And thrifts me on to golden gain,
     Almighty Fear.

PICTURE DEALER

There were twin artists A. and B.
Who painted pictures two,
And hung them in my gallery
For everyone to view;
The one exhibited by A.
The name "A Sphere" did bear,
While strangely brother B's display
Was catalogued: "A Square".

Now although A. (and this is queer)
Could squeeze a pretty tube,
The picture that he called a Sphere
Was blocky as a cube;
While B. (though no hint he disclosed
To pull the public leg)
The Square he placidly exposed
Was oval as an egg.

Thought I: To sell these pictures two
I never will be able;
There's only one thing I can do,
That's change around the label.
The rotund one I called a Sphere,
The cornered one a Square . . .
And yet, I thought: It's very queer,
Unbought they linger there.

142

Then strange as it may well appear,
Derision did I bare,
And blandly dubbed the Square a Sphere
And tabbed the Sphere a Square.
Behold the answer I had found,
For to my glad dismay
The curious came crowding round:
I sold the daubs next day.

Well, maybe A. and B. were right,
Not mugs like you and me,
With something missing in our sight
That only artists see.
So what it is and what it ain't
I'll never more discuss . . .
These guys believe in what they paint,
Or . . . are they spoofing us?

BIRTHDAYS

Let us have birthdays every day,
(I had the thought while I was shaving)
Because a birthday should be gay,
And full of grace and good behaving.
We can't have cakes and candles bright,
And presents are beyond our giving,
But let us cherish with delight
The birthday way of lovely living.

For I have passed three-score and ten
And I can count upon my fingers
The years I hope to bide with men,
(Though by God's grace one often lingers.)
So in the summers left to me,
Because I'm blest beyond my merit,
I hope with gratitude and glee
To sparkle with the birthday spirit.

Let me inform myself each day
Who's proudmost on the natal roster;
If Washington or Henry Clay,
Or Eugene Field or Stephen Foster.
Oh lots of famous folks I'll find
Who more than measure to my rating,
And so thanksgivingly inclined
Their birthdays I'll be celebrating.

For Oh I know the cheery glow
Of Anniversary rejoicing;
Let me reflect its radiance so
My daily gladness I'll be voicing.
And though I'm stooped and silver-haired,
Let me with laughter make the hearth gay,
So by the gods I may be spared
Each year to hear: "Pop, Happy Birthday."

DETACHMENT

As I go forth from fair to mart
With racket ringing,
Who would divine that in my heart
Mad larks are singing.
As I sweet sympathy express,
Lest I should pain them,
The money-mongers cannot guess
How I disdain them.

As I sit at some silly tea
And flirt and flatter
How I abhor society
And female chatter.
As I with wonderment survey
Their peacock dresses,
My mind is wafted far away
To wildernesses.

As I sit in some raucous pub,
Taboo to woman,
And treat myself to greasy grub
I feel quite human.
Yet there I dream, despite the din,
Of God's green spaces,
And sweetly dwell the peace within
Of sylvan graces.

And so I wear my daily mask
Of pleasant seeming,
And nobody takes me to task
For distant dreaming;
A happy hypocrite am I
Of ambiance inner,
Who smiling make the same reply
To saint and sinner.

KITTENS

A ray of sun strayed softly round,
For something to caress,
Until a resting place it found
Of joy and thankfulness;
'Twas Minette, our Angora cat,
With deep contented purr,
Relaxed in rapture on a mat,
Three kittens nuzzling her.

With tenderness the sunbeam kissed
Her fur of silver grey;
Her eyes held an ecstatic mist,
In boundless bliss she lay;
The sunny radiance seemed to hold
Her longer than it should,
As if it sought to shrine in gold
Such mystic motherhood.

The darling kittens grew and grew;
Then one day Mother Cat,
Back from their gambolling withdrew,
And glared at them and—spat.
Aye, though they toddled after her
With playful stratagem,
Instead of soft maternal purr
She snarled and clawed at them.

148

And now she goes her callous way
And never gives them heed;
You barely would believe that they
Were children of her breed.
Upon the roof we see her creep
And howl with fiendish tone,
While on the hearth-rug softly sleep
Three kittens on their own.

And such is nature's way, it seems,
And maybe right at that;
So Mother, drop your foolish dreams
And emulate the Cat.
And when your offspring well are grown,
And strong and swift and tall,
Just turn them out upon their own
And let them fight—or fall.

CAUSATION

Said darling daughter unto me:
"Oh Dad, how funny it would be
If you had gone to Mexico
A score or so of years ago.
Had not some whimsey changed your plan
I might have been a Mexican,
With lissome form and raven hair,
Instead of being fat and fair.

"Or if you'd sailed the Southern Seas
And mated with a Japanese
I might have been a squatty girl
With never golden locks to curl,
Who flirted with a painted fan,
And tinkled on a samisan,
And maybe slept upon a mat—
I'm very glad I don't do that.

"When I consider the romance
Of all your youth of change and chance
I might, I fancy, just as well
Have bloomed a bold Tahitian belle,
Or have been born . . . but there—ah no!
I draw the line—an Esquimeaux.
It scares me stiff to think of what
I might have been—thank God! I'm not."

Said I: "My dear, don't be absurd,
Since everything that has occurred,
Though seeming fickle in your eyes,
Could not a jot be otherwise.
For in this causal cosmic biz
The world can be but what it is;
And nobody can dare deny
Part of this world is you and I.

Oh call it fate or destiny
No other issue could there be.
Though half the world I've wandered through
Cause and effect have linked us two.
Aye, all the aeons of the Past
Conspired to bring us here at last,
And all I ever chanced to do
Inevitably led to you.

To you, to make you what you are,
A maiden in a Morris car,
In Harris tweeds, an airedale too,
But Anglo-Saxon through and through.
And all the good and ill I've done
In every land beneath the sun
Magnificently led to this—
A country cottage and . . . your kiss."

THE BLISS OF IGNORANCE

When Jack took Nell into his arms
He knew he acted ill,
And thought as he enjoyed her charms
Of his *fiancée* Jill.
"Poor dear," he sighed, "she dreams of me,
I shouldn't act like this;
But after all, she cannot see,
And ignorance is bliss."

Yet Jill at that same moment was
In Fred's embrace close caught,
And just a little sad because
Of sweetheart Jack she thought.
"Poor dear," she sighed, "he loves me so,
And what's a little kiss?
Or two or three—he'll never know,
And ignorance is bliss."

Now in fond wedlock all is well,
Though in their nuptial bed,
Jack's thought will sometimes stray to Nell,
And Jill's to handsome Fred.
Yet though in fancy they may flirt,
There's nothing much amiss:
What they don't know will never hurt—
Aye, Ignorance Is Bliss.

ANTI-PROFANITY

I do not swear because I am
A sweet and sober guy;
I cannot vent a single damn
However hard I try.
And in vituperative way,
Though I recall it well,
I never, never, never say
A naughty word like hell.

To rouse my wrath you need not try,
I'm milder than a lamb;
However you may rile me I
Refuse to say: Goddam!
In circumstances fury-fraught
My tongue is always civil,
And though you goad me I will not
Consign you to the divvle.

Ah no, I never, never swear;
Profanity don't pay;
To cuss won't get you anywhere,
(And neither will to pray.)
And so all blasphemy I stem.
When milk of kindness curds:
But though I never utter them—
Gosh! how I know the words.

ASPIRATION

When I was daft (as urchins are),
And full of fairy lore,
I aimed an arrow at a star
And hit—the barnyard door.

I've shot at heaps of stars since then,
But always it's the same—
A barnyard door has mocked me when
Uranus was my aim.

So, I'll shoot starward as of yore,
Though wide my arrows fall;
I'd rather hit a big barn door
Than never aim at all.

THE ARGUMENT

Said Jock McBrown to Tam McSmith,
"A little bet I'm game to take on,
That I can scotch this Shakespeare myth
And prove Will just a stoodge for Bacon."

Said Tam McSmith to Jock McBrown,
"Ye gyke, I canna let ye rave on.
See here, I put a shilling down:
My betting's on the Bard of Avon."

Said Jock McBrown to Tam McSmith,
"Come on, ye'll pay a braw wee dramlet;
Bacon's my bet—the proof herewith . . .
He called his greatest hero—HAMlet."

INCLUDE ME OUT

I grabbed the new *Who's Who* to see
        My name—but it was not.
Said I: "The form they posted me
        I filled and sent—so what?"

I searched the "essies," dour with doubt . . .
        Darn! It was plain as day
The scurvy knaves had left me out . . .
        Oh was I mad? I'll say.

Then all at once I sensed the clue;
        'Twas simple, you'll allow . . .
The book I held was *Who WAS Who*—
        Oh was I glad—and how!

THE SUPER

When I was with a Shakespeare show
I played the part of Guildenstern,
Or Rosenkrantz—at least I know
It wasn't difficult to learn;
But Reader, do not at me scoff,
For furthermore I should explain
I was the understudy of
The understudy of the Dane.

Oh how it crabbed me just to think
They barred me from that role divine;
And how I longed to have them drink
A cup of slightly poisoned wine!
As every night with struts and rants
I strove my quid a week to earn,
And put my soul in Rosenkrantz—
Or was it, haply, Guildenstern?

Alas! I might have spared my breath,
I never played the noble Dane;
And yet when Irving staged *Macbeth*
I bore a tree of Dunsinane,
And yearned for that barn-storming day,
Of hopes and dreams and patchy pants,
When Guildenstern I'd proudly play—
Or was it, maybe, Rosenkrantz?

MAZIE'S GHOST

In London City I evade
The charming Burlington Arcade—
For there in youth I met a maid
        By name of Mazie,
Who lost no time in telling me
The Ritz put up a topping tea,
But having only shillings three
        My smile was hazy.

"Instead," said I, "it might be sport
To take a bus to Hampton Court."
(Her manner, I remarked, was short,)
        But she assented.
We climbed on top, and all the way
I held her hand, I felt quite gay,
But Mazie, I regret to say,
        Seemed discontented.

In fact we almost had a tiff.
It's true it rained and she was stiff,
And all she did was sneeze and sniff
        And shudder coldly;
So I said: "Mazie, there's the maze;
Let's frolic in its leafy ways,"
And buying tickets where one pays
        I entered boldly.

Then, as the game is, we were lost;
We dashed and darted, crissed and crossed,
But Mazie she got vexed and sauced
   Me rather smartly;
There wasn't but us two about;
We hollered, no one heard our shout;
The rain poured down: "Oh let's get out,"
   Cried Mazie tartly.

"Keep cool," says I. "You fool," says she;
"I'm sopping wet, I want my tea,
Please take me home," she wailed to me
   In accents bitter.
Again we tried, this way and that,
Yet came to where we started at,
And Mazie acted like a cat,
   A champion spitter.

She stomped and romped till all was blue,
Then sought herself to find the clue,
And when I saw her next 'twas through
   A leafy screening;
"Come on," she cooed, "and join me here;
You'll take me to the Savoy, dear,
And Heidsieck shall our spirits cheer."
   I got her meaning.

And yet I sought her everywhere;
I hurried here, I scurried there,
I took each likely lane, I swear,
            As I surmised it:
Then suddenly I saw once more,
Confronting me, the exit door,
And I was dashing through before
            I realized it.

And there I spied a passing bus.
Thinks I: "It's mean to leave her thus,
But after all her fret and fuss
            I can't abide her.
So I sped back to London town
And grubbed alone for half-a-crown,
On steak and kidney pie washed down
            With sparkling cider.

But since I left that damsel fair,
The thought she may have perished there,
Of cold, starvation and dispair
            Nigh drives me crazy.
So, stranger, if you should invade
The charming Burlington Arcade,
Tell me if you behold a shade,
Ghost of a most unhappy maid
            By name of Mazie.

VIGNETTES IN VERSE

CAFÉ COMEDY

SHE

I'm waiting for the man I hope to wed.
I've never seen him—that's the funny part.
I promised I would wear a rose of red,
Pinned on my coat above my fluttered heart,
So that he'd know me—a precaution wise,
Because I wrote him I was twenty-three,
And Oh such heaps and heaps of silly lies . . .
So when we meet what will he think of me?

It's funny, but it has its sorry side;
I put an advert. in the evening Press:
"A lonely maiden fain would be a bride."
Oh it was shameless of me, I confess.
But I am thirty-nine and in despair,
Wanting a home and children ere too late,
And I forget I'm no more young and fair—
I'll hide my rose and run . . . No, no, I'll wait.

An hour has passed and I am waiting still.
I ought to feel relieved, but I'm so sad.
I would have liked to see him, just to thrill,
And sigh and say: "There goes my lovely lad!
My one romance!" Ah, Life's malign mishap!
"*Garçon, a café creme.*" I'll stay till nine . . .
The café's empty, just an oldish chap
Who's sitting at the table next to mine. . . .

HE

I'm waiting for the girl I mean to wed.
She was to come at eight and now it's nine.
She'd pin upon her coat a rose of red,
And I would wear a marguerite in mine.
No sign of her I see . . . It's true my eyes
Need stronger glasses than the ones I wear,
But Oh I feel my heart would recognize
Her face without the rose—she is so fair.

Ah! what deceivers are we aging men!
What vanity keeps youthful hope aglow!
Poor girl! I sent a photo taken when
I was a student, twenty years ago.
(Hers is so Springlike, Oh so blossom sweet!)
How she will shudder when she sees me now!
I think I'd better hide that marguerite—
How can I age and ugliness avow?

She does not come. It's after nine o'clock.
What fools we fogeys are! I'll try to laugh;
(*Garçon,* you might bring me another *bock*)
Falling in love, just from a photograph.
Well, that's the end. I'll go home and forget,
Then realizing I am over ripe
I'll throw away this silly cigarette
And philosophically light my pipe.

*　　*　　*　　*　　*

The waiter brought the coffee and the beer,
And there they sat, so woe-begone a pair,
And seemed to think: "Why do we linger here?"
When suddenly they turned, to start and stare.
She spied a marguerite, he glimpsed a rose;
Their eyes were joined and in a flash they knew . . .
The sleepy waiter saw, when time to close,
The sweet romance of those deceiving two,
Whose lips were joined, their hearts, their future too.

THE KEY OF THE STREET

"Miss Rosemary," I dourly said,
"Our balance verges on the red,
We must cut down our overhead.
One of the staff will have to go.
There's Mister Jones, he's mighty slow,
Although he does his best, I know.

"A dear old man; I like him well,
But age, alas! will always tell.
Miss Rosemary, please ring the bell
And tell old Jones to step this way . . .
Oh dear, oh dear, it isn't gay
To say the things I have to say.

"Come in and sit down, Mister Jones."
He thanks me in sepulchral tones.
Poor chap! I hear his creaking bones.
"Have a cigar? And how's your wife?
What's that! You're fearing for her life—
A cancer and the surgeon's knife. . . .

"Yes, operations are so dear,
But it's your comfort and your cheer
To know your job's so steady here."
These are his words; so meek, so mild,
He looks just like a simple child . . .
Gol darn it! Suddenly I'm riled.

And so I say: "That's just too bad.
But Mister Jones, it's very sad,
You know what losses we have had.
We must cut down in times like these,
So here's a cheque, Oh take it please—
'Twill help to pay your doctor's fees.

"And just to show how I appraise
Your work—despite these doleful days
I'm giving you . . . a little raise."

Said Rosemary: "Old Jones is crying."
Thought I: "Yes, each week I'll be sighing,
When from my pocket I am prying
Ten bucks to keep his wife from dying."

HUMILITY

I met upon a narrow way,
Dead weary from his toil,
A fellow warped and gnarled and grey,
Who reeked of sweat and soil.
His rags were readyful to rot,
His eyes were dreary dim;
Yet . . . yet I had the humble thought
To raise my hat to him.

For thinks I: "It's the likes of him
That make the likes of me;
With horny hand and lagging limb
He slaves to keep me free;
That I may have a golden time,
And praise the Lord on high,
Life grinds into the bloody grime
A better man than I.

Yet if in sheer humility
I yield this yokel place,
Will he not think it mockery
And spit into my face,
Saying: "How can you care a damn,
As now my way you bar,
When it's because of what I am,
You, Sir, are what you are?"

But no, he did not speak like that,
Nor homage did I pay;
I did not lift my bowler hat
To greet his common clay;
Instead, he made me feel an ass,
As most respectfully
He stepped aside to let *me* pass,
And raised his cap to ME.

MY FAVOURITE FAN

Being a writer I receive
Sweet screeds from folk of every land;
Some are so weird you'd scarce believe,
And some quite hard to understand:
But as a conscientious man
I type my thanks to all I can.

So when I got a foreign scrawl
That spider-webbed across the page,
Said I: "This is the worst of all;
No doubt a child of tender age
Has written it, so I'll be kind,
And send an answer to her mind.

Promptly I typed a nice reply
And thought that it would be the end,
But in due course confused was I
To get a letter signed: Your Friend;
And with it, full of girlish grace,
A snapshot of a winsome face.

"I am afraid," she wrote to me,
"That you must have been sure surprised
At my poor penmanship . . . You see,
My arms and legs are paralysed:
With pen held in a sort of sheath
I do my writing with my teeth."

Though sadness followed my amaze,
And pity too, I must confess
The look that lit her laughing gaze
Was one of sunny happiness. . . .
Oh spirit of a heroine!
Your smile so tender, so divine,
I pray, may never cease to shine.

MY CANCER CURE

"A year to live," the Doctor said;
"There is no cure," and shook his head.
Ah me! I felt as good as dead.
Yet quite resigned to fate was I,
Thinking: "Well, since I have to die
'Twill be beneath the open sky."

And so I sought a wildsome wood
Wherein a lonely cabin stood,
And doomed myself to solitude.
And there was no one I would see:
Each morn a farmer brought to me
My food and hung it on a tree.

Six eggs he brought, and milk a quart,
Enough for wretches of my sort
Whose life is fated to be short.
At night I laid me on the ground,
In robe of buffalo wrapped round . . .
'Twas strange that I should sleep so sound.

The farmer man I seldom saw;
I pierced my eggs and sucked them raw;
Sweet milk refreshed my ravaged maw.
So slowly days and weeks went by,
And always I would wonder why
I did not die . . . I did not die.

Thus brooding on my grievous lot
The world of men I fast forgot,
And in the wildwood friends I sought.
The brook bright melodies would sing,
The groves with feathered rapture ring,
And bring me strange, sweet comforting. . . .

Then all at once I knew that I
Miraculously would not die:
When doctors fail let Nature try.

MUNITION MAKER

I am the Cannon King, behold!
I perish on a throne of gold.
With forest far and turret high,
Renowned and rajah-rich am I.
My father was, and his before,
With wealth we owe to war on war;
But let no potentate be proud . . .
There are no pockets in a shroud.

By nature I am mild and kind,
To gentleness and ruth inclined;
And though the pheasants over-run
My woods I will not touch a gun.
Yet while each monster that I forge
Thunders destruction from its gorge.
Death's whisper is, I vow, more loud . . .
There are no pockets in a shroud.

My time is short, my ships at sea
Already seem like ghosts to me;
My millions mock me, I am poor
As any beggar at my door.
My vast dominion I resign,
Six feet of earth to claim as mine,
Brooding with shoulders bitter-bowed . . .
There are no pockets in a shroud.

Dear God, let me purge pure my heart,
And be of heaven's hope a part!
Flinging my fortune's foul increase
To fight for pity, love and peace.
Oh that I could with healing fare,
And pledged to poverty and prayer
Cry high above the cringing crowd:
"Ye fools! Be not by Mammon cowed . . .
There are no pockets in a shroud."

A SONG OF SUICIDE

Deeming that I were better dead,
"How shall I kill myself?" I said.
Thus mooning by the river Seine
I sought extinction without pain,
When on a bridge I saw a flash
Of *lingerie* and heard a splash . . .
So as I am a swimmer stout
I plunged and pulled the poor wretch out.

The female that I saved? Ah yes,
To yield the Morgue one corpse the less,
Apart from all heroic action,
Gave me a moral satisfaction.
Was she an old and withered hag,
Too tired of life to long to lag?
Ah no, she was so young and fair
I fell in love with her right there.

And when she took me to her attic
Her gratitude was most emphatic.
A sweet and simple girl she proved,
Distraught because the man she loved
In battle his life-blood had shed . . .
So I, too, told her of my dead,
The girl who in a garret grey
Had coughed and coughed her life away.

Thus as we sought our griefs to smother,
With kisses we consoled each other . . .
And there's the ending of my story;
It wasn't grim, it wasn't gory.
For comforted were hearts forlorn,
And from black sorrow joy was born:
So may our dead dears be forgiving,
And bless the rapture of the living.

BED SITTER

He stared at me with sad, hurt eyes,
That drab, untidy man;
And though my clients I despise
I do the best I can
To comfort them with cheerful chat;
(Quite *comme il faut*, of course)
And furnish evidence so that
Their wives may claim divorce.

But as this chap sobbed out his woes
I thought: How it's a shame!
His wife's a bitch and so he goes
And takes himself the blame.
And me behaving like a heel
To earn a filthy fee . . .
Said I: "You've had a dirty deal."
"What of yourself?" said he.

And so I told him how I was
A widow of the war,
And doing what I did because
Two sons I struggled for.
As I sat knitting through the night
He eyed me from the bed,
And in the rosy morning light
Impulsively he said:

"Though in this sordid game we play,
To cheat the law we plan,
I do believe you when you say
You hold aloof from man;
Unto the dead you have been true,
And on the day I'm free,
To prove how I have faith in you—
Please, will you marry me?"

That's how it was. Now we are wed,
And life's a list of joys.
The old unhappy past is dead;
He's father to my boys.
And I have told him just to-day,
(Though forty, I confess,)
A little sister's on the way
To crown our happiness.

TEA ON THE LAWN

It was foretold by sybils three
That in an air crash he would die.
"I'll fool their prophesy," said he;
"You won't get me to go on high.
Howe'er the need for haste and speed,
I'll never, never, never fly."

It's true he travelled everywhere,
Afar and near, by land and sea,
Yet he would never go by air
And chance an evil destiny.
Always by ship or rail he went—
For him no sky-plane accident.

Then one day walking on the heath
He watched a pilot chap on high,
And chuckled as he stood beneath
That lad a-looping in the sky.
Feeling so safe and full of glee
Serenely he went home to tea.

With buttered toast he told his wife:
"My dear, you can't say I've been rash;
Three fortune tellers said my life
Would end up in an air-plane crash.
But see! I'm here so safe and sound:
By gad! I'll never leave the ground.

"For me no baptism of air;
It's in my bed I mean to die.
Behold yon crazy fool up there,
A-cutting capers in the sky.
His motor makes a devilish din . . .
Look! Look! He's gone into a spin.

"He's dashing downward—*Oh my God!*" . . .
Alas! he never finished tea.
The motor ploughed the garden sod
And in the crash a corpse was he:
Proving that no man can frustrate
The merciless design of Fate.

DECADENCE

Before the florid portico
I watched the gamblers come and go,
While by me on a bench there sat
A female in a faded hat;
A shabby, shrinking, crumpled creature,
Of waxy tint, yet fine of feature,
Who looked casino-ward with eyes
Of lost soul seeking paradise.

Then from the Café de la Paix
There shambled forth a waiter fellow,
Clad dingily, down-stooped and grey,
With hollow face, careworn and yellow.
With furtive feet before our seat
He came to a respectful stand,
And bowed, my sorry crone to greet,
Saying: "Princess, I kiss your hand."

She gave him such a gracious smile,
And bade him linger by her side;
So there they talked a little while
Of kingly pomp and courtly pride;
Of Marquis This and Prince von That,
Of Old Vienna, glamour gay. . . .
Then sad he rose and raised his hat:
Saying: "My tables I must lay."

"Yes, you must go, dear Count," she said,
"For luncheon tables must be laid."
He sighed; from his alpaca jacket
He pressed into her hand a packet,
"Sorry, to-day it's all I'm rich in—
A chicken sandwich from the kitchen."
Then bowed and left her after she
Had thanked him with sweet dignity.

She pushed the package out of sight,
Within her bag and closed it tight;
But by and bye I saw her go
To where thick laurel bushes grow,
And there behind that leafy screen,
Thinking herself by all unseen,
That sandwich! How I saw her grab it,
And gulp it like a starving rabbit!

Thinks I: Is all that talk a bluff—
Their dukes and kings and courtly stuff:
The way she ate, why one would say
She hadn't broken fast all day.

THE DREAM

Said Will: "I'll stay and till the land."
Said Jack: "I'll sail the sea."
So one went forth kit-bag in hand,
The other ploughed the lea.

They met again at Christmas-tide,
And wistful were the two.
Said Jack: "You're lucky here to bide."
Said Will: "I envy you.

"For in your eyes a light I see
Of trophic shores agleam."
Said Jack: "You need not envy me,
For still you have the Dream.

"The Dream that lured me out to sea;
'Twas bright as paradise;
Far fairer than the memory
You see within my eyes.

So if my foolish urge you share
In foreign lands to roam,
Take up my kit-bag waiting there
And I will stay at home."

  * * * * *

Yet while the years have fated Will
To sow the sober loam,
The eyes of Jack are starry still,
High-riding hills of foam.

FREEDOM'S FOOL

To hell with Governments I say;
I'm sick of all the piddling pack.
I'd like to scram, get clean away,
And never, nevermore come back.
With heart of hope I long to go
To some lost island of the sea,
And there get drunk with joy to know
No one on earth is over me.

There will be none to say me nay,
So from my lexicon I can
Obliterate the word "obey",
And mock the meddling laws of man.
The laws of Nature and of God
Are good enough for guys like me,
Who scorn to kiss the scarlet rod
Of office and authority.

No Stars and Stripes nor Union Jack,
Nor tri-colour nor crimson rag
Shall claim my love, I'll turn my back
On every land, on every flag.
My banner shall be stainless white,
An emblem of the Golden Rule,
Yet for its freedom I will fight
And die—like any other fool.

Oh Government's a bitter pill!
No force or fear shall forge my fate;
I'll bow to no communal will,
For I myself shall be the State.
Uncurst by man-curb and control,
My Isle shall be emparadised,
And I will re-possess my soul . . .
Mad Anarchist!—*Well, wasn't Christ?*

POST OFFICE ROMANCE

The lady at the corner wicket
Sold me a stamp, I stooped to lick it,
And on an envelope to stick it;
A spinster lacking girlish grace,
Yet sweetly sensitive, her face
Seemed to en-star that stodgy place.

Said I: "I've come from o'er the sea
To ask you if you'll marry me—
That is to say, if you are free.
I see your gentle features freeze;
'I do not like such jokes as these,'
You seem to say . . . Have patience, please.

I saw you twenty years ago;
Just here you sold me stamps, and Oh
Your image seemed to haunt me so.
For you were lovely as a rose,
But I was poor, and I suppose
At me you tilted dainty nose.

Ah, well I knew love could not be,
So sought my fortune o'er the sea,
Deeming that you were lost to me.
Of sailing ships a mate was I,
From oriental ports to play . . .
Ten years went past of foreign sky

But always in the starry night
I steered my course with you in sight,
My dream of you a beacon light.
Then after a decade had sped
I came again: 'What luck?' I said,
'Will she be here and free to wed?'

Oh it was on a morn of Spring,
And I had in my purse a ring
I bought in Eastern voyaging,
With thought of you and only you;
For I to my love dream was true . . .
And here you were, your eyes as blue.

The same sun shining on your brow
Lustered your hair as it does now.
My heart was standing still, I vow.
I bought a stamp, my eyes were bent
Upon a ring you *wore*—I went
Away as if indifferent.

Again I sailed behind the mast,
And yet your image held me fast,
For once again ten years have passed.
And I am bronzed, with braid of gold;
The rank of Captain now I hold,
And fifty are my years all told.

Yet still I have that ruby ring
I bought for you that morn of Spring—
See, here it is, a pretty thing. . . .
But now you've *none* upon your finger;
Why? I don't know—but as I linger
I'm thinking: Oh what can I bring her,

Who all my life have ploughed the ocean,
A lonely man with one devotion—
Just you? Ah, if you'd take the notion
To try the ring. . . . Well, I declare
It's just the thing you *ought* to wear,
It fits so well. Do leave it there.

And here's a note addressed to you.
Ah yes, quite strangers are we two,
But—well, please answer soon . . . Adieu!"

*   *   *   *   *

Oh no, you never more will see
Her selling stamps at Wicket Three:
Queen of my home, she's pouring tea.

MORTUARY MUSE

CONQUEROR

Though I defy the howling horde
As bloody-browed I smite,
Back to the wall with shattered sword
When darkly dooms the night;
Though hoarse they cheer as I go down
Before their bitter odds,
'Tis I who win the victor's crown,
The guerdon of the gods.

For all who fall in fearless fight
Alight a deathless flame,
That glorifies the godless night
And fills the foe with shame.
'Tis they who triumph heaven-high,
And so in hell's despite,
Be mine the dauntless will to die
In battle for the right.

The rant and cant of futile folk
Break brittle in my ears;
Let me cast off the cursed yoke
And fall upon the spears.
Aye, though they mock my broken blade,
And stamp and spit on me,
Mine is the Shining Accolade,
The Star of Victory.

THE CHOICE

. . . And then I came to Three ways,
And each was mine to choose;
For all of them were free ways,
To take or to refuse.
"Now which shall be the best way,
East, West or South?" said I . . .
So then I went the West way—
I often wonder why.

. . . And then I came to Two ways,
And each was luring me;
For both of them were new ways,
And I was fancy free.
"Now which shall be the least way,"
Said I, "to gain my goal?"
And so I took the East way,
With freedom in my soul.

. . . And then I came to One way,
And to the South it ran;
Then lo! I saw this sun way
Was mine since time began:
My pitiless, my doom way;
No other could there be,
For at its end my tomb lay,
And it was waiting me. . . .
Poor fools! Who think you're free.

HATE

I had a bitter enemy,
His heart to hate he gave,
And when I died he swore that he
Would dance upon my grave;
That he would leap and laugh because
A livid corpse was I,
And that's the reason why I was
In no great haste to die.

And then—such is the quirk of fate,
One day with joy I read,
Despite his vitalizing hate
My enemy was dead.
Maybe the poison in his heart
Had helped to haste his doom:
He was not spared till I depart
To spit upon my tomb.

The other day I chanced to go
To where he lies alone.
'Tis easy to forgive a foe
When he is dead and gone. . . .
Poor devil! Now his day is done,
(Though bright it was and brave,)
Yet I am happy there is none
To dance upon my grave.

MY COFFIN

Deeming that I was due to die
I framed myself a coffin;
So full of graveyard zeal was I,
I set the folks a-laughing.
I made it snugly to my fit,
My joinering was honest;
And sometimes in it I would sit,
And fancy I was *non est*.

I stored it on my cabin shelf
Forever to remind me,
When I was tickled with myself,
That Death was close behind me.
Let's be prepared, I used to say,
E'er in the Dark we launch us:
And so with boding day by day
I kept me coffin-conscious.

Then came that winter dark as doom,
No firing wood had I;
My shack was icy as a tomb
And I was set to die.
But e'er the losing of my wits
I saw that coffin there,
So smashing the damned thing to bits
I made a gorgeous flare.

I never saw a flame so bright,
So goldenly divine,
As starred the blackness of the night
That boneyard box of mine.
And now I go forth coffin-shy,
With no more carnal fears,
For radiantly sure am I
I'll stack a hundred years.

THE HINTERLAND

You speak to me, but does your speech
With truest truth your thought convey?
I listen to your words and each
Is what I wait to hear you say.
The pattern that your lips reveal,
How does it measure with your mind?
What undertones do you conceal?
Your smile is sweet—but what's behind?

I speak to you, but do I tell
The secret working of my brain?
Frank honesty would make life hell,
And truth be tantamount to pain.
When deep into the mind one delves,
Appalling verities we view;
If we betrayed our inner selves,
Would you hate me and I hate you?

Are we not strangers each to each,
And all alone we live and die?
Deception is the stuff of speech,
And life a smug and glossy lie,
Where puppet-like our parts we play:
The first in public we rehearse,
The second when we shrink away
Into our private universe.

The soul has its grim hinterland
'Twere better never to explore;
Dark jungles where obscenely planned
Prowl monsters of primaeval lore;
With primal fear our lives are fraught,
And cravenly we cower behind
The silences of secret thought,
The murky mazes of the Mind.

REPENTANCE

"If you repent," the Parson said,
"Your sins will be forgiven.
Aye, even on your dying bed
You're not too late for Heaven."

That's just my cup of tea, I thought,
Though for my sins I sorrow;
Since salvation is easy bought
I will repent . . . to-morrow.

To-morrow and to-morrow went,
But though my youth was flying,
I was reluctant to repent,
Having no fear of dying.

'Tis plain, I mused, the more I sin,
(To Satan's jubilation)
When I repent the more I'll win
Celestial approbation.

So still I sin, and though I fail
To get snow-whitely shriven,
My timing's good: I hope to hail
The last bus up to Heaven.

MY HOUSE

I have a house I've lived in long:
I can't recall my going in.
'Twere better bartered for a song
Ere ruin, rot and rust begin.
When it was fresh and fine and fair,
I used it with neglect, I fear;
But now I husband it with care
And cherish it from year to year.

Oh do not put it to the flame
When I have gone, but let the dust,
The honest earth from which it came,
Reclaim it as is only just.
For when at last I close the door,
And turn the key and go away,
I deed my house forever more
To silence, sleep and slow decay.

My house is old beyond repair,
And soon I must abandon it,
A poor ghost, seeking everywhere
To find a home as fine and fit;
But if I win domain divine
Wherein eternally to dwell,
I'll not forget, O Body Mine!
Life home of Me, I've loved you well.

BRAVE NEW WORLD

One spoke: "Come, let us gaily go
With laughter, love and lust,
Since in a century or so
We'll all be boneyard dust.
When unborn shadows hold the screen,
(Our betters, I'll allow)
'Twill be as if we'd never been,
A hundred years from now.

When we have played life's lively gamme
Right royally we'll rot,
And not a soul will care a damn
The why or how we fought;
To grub for gold or grab for fame
Or raise a holy row,
It will be all the bloody same
A hundred years from now."

Said I: "Look! I have built a tower
Upon yon lonely hill,
Designed to be a daughter's dower,
Yet when my heart is still,
The stone I set with horny hand
And salty sweat of brow,
A record of my strength will stand
A hundred years from now.

"There's nothing lost and nothing vain
In all this world so wide;
The ocean hoards each drop of rain
To swell its sweeping tide;
The desert seeks each grain of sand
It's empire to endow,
And we a bright brave world have planned
A hundred years from now.

And all we are and all we do
Will bring that world to be;
Our strain and pain let us not rue,
Though other eyes shall see;
For other hearts will bravely beat
And lips will sing of how
We strove to make life sane and sweet
A hundred years from now.

BOON SOUL

Behold I'm old; my hair is white;
My eighty years are in the offing,
And sitting by the fire to-night
I sip a grog to ease my coughing.
It's true I'm raucous as a rook,
But feeling bibulously "bardy,"
These lines I'm scribbling in a book:
The verse complete of Thomas Hardy.

Although to-day he's read by few,
Him have I loved beyond all measure;
So here to-night I riffle through
His pages with the oldtime pleasure;
And with this book upon my knee,
(To-day so woefully neglected)
I muse and think how soon I'll be
Myself among the Great Rejected.

Yet as these lines with zest I write,
Although the hour for me is tardy,
I think: "Of all the world to-night
'Tis I alone am reading Hardy";
And now to me he seems so nigh
I feel I commune with his spirit,
And as none love him more than I,
Thereby I gain a modest merit.

Oh Brother Thomas, glad I'll be,
Though all the world may pass unheeding,
If some greybeard con over me,
As I to-night your rhymes are reading;
Saying: "Old Bastard, you and I
By sin are knit in mind and body. . . ."
So ere to hit the hay I hie
Your ghost I'll toast in midnight toddy.

THE HAND

Throughout my life I see
A guiding hand;
The pitfalls set for me
Were grimly planned.
But always when and where
They opened wide,
Someone who seemed to care
Stood by my side.

When up the pathway dark
I stumbled on,
Afar, ahead a spark
Of guidance shone.
When forked the tragic trail
And sad my plight,
My guardian without fail
Would lead me right.

How merciful a Mind
My life has planned!
Aye, though mine eyes were blind
I touched the Hand;
Though weary ways and wan
My feet have trod,
Always it led me on,
Starways to God.

THE OLD

Oh bear with me, for I am old
And count on fingers five
The years this pencil I may hold
And hope to be alive;
How sadly soon our dreaming ends!
How brief the sunset glow!
Be kindly to the old, my friends:
You'll miss them when they go.

I've seen so many disappear
That I can scarce forget,
For death has made them doubly dear
And ripened my regret.
How wistfully I've wished them back,
With cherishing to show
The gentleness I used to lack
In years of long ago.

You, young and fit, will falter too,
And when Time's load you bear,
'Twill help if others turn to you
With comforting and care;
With loving look and tender touch . . .
Aye, in their twilight wan
Revere the old—for Oh how much
You'll miss them when they've gone!

THE SUMMING UP

When you have sailed the seven seas
And looped the ends of earth,
You'll long at last for slippered ease
Beside a bonny hearth;
A cosy cottage in the sun,
A pleasant page to read—
You'll find when all is said and done,
That's nearly all you need.

You may have pow-wowed with the Great
And played a potent part
In serious affairs of state,
But now with quiet heart
You bide beside a rosy fire
And blether with a friend,
Discovering that you require
So little in the end.

And all your days of fevered fight
For glory, gold or gear
Will seem so futile when the Night
Draws dolorously near;
And you will only ask to be
With modest comfort blest,
With sweetness of symplicity,
With rich reward of rest.

RHYME
FOR MY
TOMB

Here lyeth one
Who loved the sun;
Who lived with zest,
Whose work was done.
Reward, dear Lord,
Thy weary son:
May he be blest
With peace and rest,
Nor wake again,
        Amen.

LYRICS OF A LOW BROW

PRELUDE

Ah yes, I know my brow is low
And often wished it high,
So that I might with rapture write
An epic of the sky;
A poem cast in contour vast,
Of fabled gods and fays;
A classic screed that few would read
Yet nearly all would praise.

Alas! Low-browed, to lure the crowd
With cap and bells I sing;
And some may cheer and some may jeer,
And some a farthing fling.
The lofty line will ne'er be mine,
To rude rhyme I belong,
And try to please the least of these
Who listen to my song.

Kind folk! excuse my moron muse
Whose earthiness I rue;
Of homespun class it is alas!
The best that I can do.
Of grosser grain I strive in vain
To scale the alps of Art . . .
A clown I go: Houp La!—*But Oh*
The hunger in my heart!

CONTENTS

DAWSON DITTIES

SPANISH SERENADE

RURAL RHYMES

VIGNETTES IN VERSE

RHYMES FOR RIPENESS

RHYMES FOR RUE

RHYMES FOR REVERENCE

DAWSON DITTIES

GHOSTS

DAWSON DITTIES

I to a crumpled cabin came
Upon a hillside high,
And with me was a withered dame
As weariful as I.
"It used to be our home," said she;
"How I remember well!
Oh that our happy hearth should be
Today an empty shell!"

The door was flailing in the storm
That deafed us with its din;
The roof that kept us once so warm
Now let the snow-drift in.
The floor sagged to the sod below,
The walls caved crazily;
We only heard the wind of woe
Where once was glow and glee.

So there we stood disconsolate
Beneath the Midnight Dome,
And ancient miner and his mate,
Before our wedded home,
Where we had known such love and cheer . .
I sighed, then soft she said:
"Do not regret—remember, dear,
                    We, too, are dead.

DANCE-HALL GIRLS

Where are the dames I used to know
In Dawson in the days of yore?
Alas, it's fifty years ago,
And most, I guess, have "gone before."
The swinging scythe is swift to mow
Alike the gallant and the fair;
And even I, with gouty toe,
Am glad to fill a rocking chair.

Ah me, I fear each gaysome girl
Who in champagne I used to toast,
Or cozen in the waltz's whirl,
Is now alas, a wistful ghost.
Oh where is Touch The Button Nell?
Or Minnie Dale or Rosa Lee,
Or Lorna Doone or Daisy Bell?
And where is Montreal Maree?

Fair ladies of my lusty youth,
I fear that you are dead and gone:
Where's Gertie of the Diamond Tooth,
And where the Mare of Oregon?
What's come of Violet de Vere,
Claw-fingered Kate and Gumboot Sue?
They've crossed the Great Divide, I fear;
Remembered now by just a few.

A few who like myself can see
Through half a century of haze
A heap of goodness in their glee
And kindness in their wanton ways.
Alas, my sourdough days are dead,
Yet let me toss a tankard down . . .
Here's hoping that you wed and bred,
And lives of circumspection led,
Gay dance-hall girls of Dawson Town!

ELDORADO

I pitched my tent beneath a pine
Upon a grassy mound,
And all that summer worked my mine,
Yet never wealth I found;
Each night I dreamed of fortune dear,
Of pokes of virgin gold:
Alas! what riches were so near,
The grass roots could have told.

So broke and burdened with despair,
Abandoning my "lay,"
Believing that no gold was there,
I upped and went away;
And then a Swede came to my mound;
With careless pick he struck,
And where I slept a fortune found,
For that's the way of Luck.

God save us all from sudden wealth
That makes the head to swell;
Champagne and women mined his health
And he went plumb to hell.
And me? To win my bread I drive
A heavy highway truck . . .
But he is dead and I'm alive,
—-And that's the way of Luck.

TWO MEN
(J. L. and R. B.)

In the Northland there were three
Pukka pliers of the pen;
Two of them had Fame in fee
And were loud and lusty men;
By them like a shrimp was I—
Yet alas! they had to die.

Jack was genius through and through.
Who his future could foretell?
What we sweated blood to do
He would deem a bagatelle.
Yet in youth he had to die,
And an ancient man am I.

Rex was rugged as an oak;
Story-teller born was he.
First of writing, fighting folk,
How he lived prodigiously!
Better man he was than I,
Yet forlorn he had to die.

Jack was made of god-like stuff,
Born to battle for the right;
Rex of fighting had enough
When the gods destroyed his sight . . .
Craven heart—I wonder why
Lingering alone am I?

6

They were men of valiant breed,
Fit and fearless in the fight,
Who in every thought and deed
Burned the flame of life too bright.
Cowards live, while heroes die . . .
They have gone and—here am I.

DUMB SWEDE

With barbwire hooch they filled him full,
Till he was drunker than all hell,
And then they peddled him the bull
About a claim they had to sell.
A thousand bucks they made him pay,
Knowing that he had nothing more,
And when he begged it back next day,
And wept!—they kicked him from the door.

They reckoned they were mighty slick,
Them two tinhorns from Idaho;
That poor dumb Swede could swing a pick,
But that was all he'd ever know.
So sitting in a poker game,
They lost the price for which they sold
To that bonehead a poor dud claim
That didn't have a speck of gold.

My story's true as gospel creed
Of these bright boys from Idaho;
They made a sucker of that Swede
And laughed to see the poor boob go,
And work like nigger on his ground,
Bucked by the courage of despair . . .
Till lo! A rich pay-streak he found,
That made him twice a millionaire.

So two smart Alecs, mighty sick,
Begged jobs at fifteen bucks a day.
Then said the Swede: "Give each a pick
And let them sweat to make their pay."
And though he don't know what it means,
Folks call that Swede "magnanimous"
—But picking nuggets big as beans,
You oughta' hear them fellers cuss!

MY BEAR

I never killed a bear because
I always thought them critters was
              So kindo' cute;
Though round my shack they often came,
I'd raise my rifle and take aim,
              But couldn't shoot.
Yet there was one full six-feet tall
Who came each night and gobbled all
              The grub in sight;
On my pet garden truck he'd feast,
Until I thought I must at least
              Give him a fright.

I put some corn mush in a pan;
He lapped it swiftly down and ran
              With bruin glee;
A second day I did the same,
Again with eagerness he came
              To gulp and flee.
The third day I mixed up a cross
Of mustard and tobasco sauce,
              And ginger too,
Well spiced with pepper of cayenne,
Topped it with treacled mush, and then
              Set out the brew.

He was a huge and husky chap;
I saw him shamble to the trap,
                    The dawn was dim.
He squatted down on his behind,
And through the cheese-cloth window-blind
                    I peeked at him.
I never saw a bear so glad;
A look of joy seraphic had
                    His visage brown;
He slavered, and without suspish-
—Ion hugged that horrid dish,
                    And swilled it down.

Just for a moment he was still,
Then he erupted loud and shrill
                    With frantic yell;
The picket fence he tried to vault;
He turned a double somersault,
                    And ran like hell.
I saw him leap into the lake,
As if a thirst of fire to slake,
                    And thrash up foam;
And then he sped along the shore,
And beat his breast with raucous roar,
                    And made for home.

I guess he told the folks back there
My homestead was taboo for bear,
                    For since that day,
Although my pumpkins star the ground,
No other bear has come around,
Nor trace of bruin have I found,
                    —Well, let me pray!

MIKE

My lead dog Mike was like a bear;
I reckon he was grizzly bred,
For when he reared up in the air
He over-topped me by a head.
He'd cuff me with his hefty paws,
Jest like a puppy actin' cute,
And I would swear: by Gosh! he was
The world's most mighty malemute.

But oh the grub that dog could eat!
Yet he was never belly-tight;
It almost broke me buying meat
To satisfy his appetite.
Then came a change I wondered at:
Returning when the dawn was dim,
He seemed mysteriously fat,
And scorned the bones I'd saved for him.

My shack was near the hospital,
Wherein there laboured Nurse Louise,
Who was to me a little pal
I planned in every way to please.
As books and sweets for her I bought,
My mug she seemed to kindo' like;
But Mike—he loved her quite a lot,
And she was very fond of Mike.

Strolling with her as moonlight gleamed,
I saw a strand of cotton trail
From Mike, the which unseemly seemed
To have its source behind his tail.
I trod on it with chagrin grim,
And with a kick his absence urged;
But as he ran, from out of him
Such yards and yards of lint emerged.

And then on me the truth did dawn
Beyond the shadow of a doubt:
That poor dam dog was gorged upon
The poultices Louise threw out. . . .
So "love my dog love me," I thought,
And seized the moment to propose . . .
Mike's dead, but in our garden lot
He's manure for a big dog-rose.

MY HUSKY TEAM

I met an ancient man who mushed
    With Peary to the Pole.
Said I: "In all that land so hushed
    What most inspired your soul?"
He looked at me with bleary eye,
    He scratched a hoary head:
"You know that Sourdoughs jest cain't lie,
    So here's the dope," he said.

"That hike was like a devil's dream,
    Jest blizzards, gales and fogs,
But I was leadin' wi' my team
    O' seven husky dogs.
Day after day I steered my sleigh,
    Yet spry o' heart was I,
And every night the Northern Light
    Danced ballys in the sky.

"Them dogs o' mine seemed to divine
    Their mighty destiny.
They howled with joy, and like a boy
    I jined them in their glee.
While like a spark from out the dark
    Fame spurred us to our goal,
On, on we sped, the winnin' sled
    To gain the *Pole,* the POLE.

"I saw it clear, I raised a cheer,
    I knowed the prize was won;
The huskies too, like wind they flew—
Them critters sure could run.
The light was dim, the site was grim,
    But sunshine swept my soul,
To see—each husky lift a limb
    And . . . *irrigate the Pole.*

MY CROSS

I wrote a poem to the Moon
    But no one noticed it;
Although I hoped that late or soon
    Someone would praise a bit
Its purity and grace forlorn,
    Its beauty tulip-cool . . .
But as my poem died still-born,
    I felt a fool.

I wrote a verse of vulgar trend
    Spiced with an oath or two;
I tacked a snapper at the end
    And called it *Dan McGrew*.
I spouted it to bar-room boys,
    Full fifty years away;
Yet still with rude and ribald noise
    It lives today.

'Tis bitter truth, but there you are—
    That's how a name is made;
Write of a rose, a lark, a star,
    You'll never make the grade.
But write of gutter and of grime,
    Of pimp and prostitute,
The multitude will read your rhyme,
    And pay to boot.

So what's the use to burn and bleed
    And strive for beauty's sake?
No one your poetry will read,
    Your heart will only break.
But set your song in vulgar pitch,
    If rhyme you will not rue,
And make your heroine a bitch . . .
      Like *Lady Lou*.

BLACK MORAN

The mule-skinner was Bill Jerome, the passengers were
 three;
Two tinhorns from the dives of Nome, and Father
 Tim McGee.
And as for sunny Southland bound, through weary
 woods they sped,
The solitude that ringed them round was silent as the
 dead.

Then where the trail crooked crazily, the frost-rimed
 horses reared,
And from behind a fallen tree a grim galoot appeared;
He wore a parki white as snow, a mask as black as
 soot,
And carelesslike weaved to and fro a gun as if to
 shoot.

"Stick up yer mitts an' freeze 'em there!" his raucous
 voice outrang,
And shaving them by just a hair a blazing rod went
 bang.
The sleigh jerked to a sharp stand-still: "Okay,"
 drawled Bill Jerome,
"Could be, this guy who aims to kill is Black Moran
 from Nome."

"You lousy crooks," the bandit cried; "You're slickly
    heeled, I know;
Come, make it snappy, dump outside your booty in
    the snow."
The gambling pair went putty pale; they crimped as if
    with cold.
    And heaved upon the icy trail two hefty pokes of
        gold.

Then softly stepping from the sleigh came Father Tim
    McGee,
And speaking in his gentle way: "Accept my Cross,"
    said he.
"For other treasure have I none, their guilty gold to
    swell . . .
Please take this crucifix, my son, and may it serve you
    well."

The bandit whispered in his ear: "Jeez-crize, you got
    me wrong.
I wouldn't rob you Father dear—to your *Church* I be-
    long."
Then swiftly striding to the sleigh he dumped the
    gold back in,
And hollered: "On your knees and pray, you lousy
    sons of sin!"

"Praise God," said Father Tim McGee, "he made you
    restitution,
And if he ever kneels to me I'll give him absolution."
"I'll have you guys to understand," said Driver Bill
    Jerome,
"The squarest gunman in the land is Black Moran
    from Nome."

SPANISH SERENADE

SPANISH PEASANT

We have no aspiration vain
For paradise Utopian,
And here in our sun-happy Spain,
Though man exploit his fellow man,
To high constraint we humbly yield,
And turn from politics to toil,
Content to till a kindly field
And bring forth bounty from the soil.

They tell us wars will never cease;
They say the world is out of joint.
How well we know! But peace is peace
Even imposed at pistol point.
And we have learnt our lesson well,
By many a death, by many a tear;
So let us live a feudal spell,—
The cost of freedom is too dear.

Let us be of the cattle kind,
Praying the goad be not a sword;
In servitude obeying blind
The tyrant ruling of our Lord.
His army can be swift to slay,
His Church teach us humility . . .
But never never will we pay
Again blood-price for Liberty.

WHITE-COLLAR SPANIARD

We have no heart for civil strife,
Our burdens we prefer to bear;
We long to live a peaceful life
And claim of happiness our share.
If only to be clothed and fed
And see our children laugh and play—
That means a lot when all is said,
In this grim treadmill of today.

The price of manhood is too high
When leap the sacrificial flames;
For Justice we refuse to die:
Honour and Pride are empty names.
We will not play the martyr's part,
We will not perish for a Cause;
Leave that to fools—with humble heart
We live according to the Laws.

For see! Comes up the city street,
Communion-clad a shining band
Of tiny children, angel-sweet,
Singing and holding hand in hand . . .
So let Might triumph over Right;
From sufferance content we take:
We fight because we do not fight,
And it is for our children's sake.

BARCELONA

The night before I left Milan
A mob jammed the Cathedral Square,
And high the tide of passion ran
As politics befouled the air.
A seething hell of human strife,
I shrank back from its evil core,
Seeing in this convulsive life
The living seeds of civil war.

To Barcelona then I came,
And oh the heavenly release!
From conflict and consuming flame
I knew the preciousness of peace.
Such veneration for the law!
How decorous was every one!
And then (significant) I saw
Each copper packed a tommy gun.

Well, maybe it is best that way.
Peace can mean more than liberty:
These people, state-directed, may
Be happier than those more free.
When politics wield evil grip,
And warring factions rise and fall,
Benevolent dictatorship
May be the answer, after all.

SPANISH MEN

The Men of Seville are, they say,
The laziest in Spain,
Consummate artists in delay,
Allergical to strain;
For if you have a job for them,
And beg them to be spry,
They only look at you with phlegm:
"*Mañana*," they reply.

The Men of gay Madrid, I'm told,
Siesta's law revere;
The custom is so ages old,
And to tradition dear;
So if you want a job done soon,
And shyly ask them: "When?"
They say: "Come back this afternoon:
We'll *hope* to do it then."

The Men of Barcelona are
Such mostly little chaps,
That when you see them from afar
They make you think of Japs;
Yet they can take life on the run,
Quite peppy, I'll allow,
For when there's something to be done,
They shout: "*We'll do it NOW.*"

25

SPANISH WOMEN

The Spanish women don't wear slacks
Because their hips are too enormous.
'Tis true each bulbous bosom lacks
No inspiration that should warm us;
But how our ardour seems to freeze
When we behold their bulgy knees!

Their starry eyes and dusky hair,
Their dazzling teeth in smile so gracious,
I love, but oh I wish they were
Not so confoundedly curvacious.
I'm sure I would prefer them willowy,
Instead of obviously pillowy.

It may be that they're plump because
The *caballeros* like them that way;
Since men are lean and Nature's laws
Of contrast sway them to the fat way:
For few their dames as much adore, as
The *señors* love their sleek *señoras*.

Well, each according to his taste.
The dons prefer their women lardy,
But me, I likes a tiny waist,
And breast that fits a hand that's hardy:
In short, my bottom money backs
The baby who looks well in slacks.

AT SAN SEBASTIAN

The Countess sprawled beside the sea
As naked as she well could be;
Indeed her only garments were
A "G" string and a *brassière*.
Her washerwoman was amazed,
And at the lady gazed and gazed,—
From billowy, bronze-bosom swell
To navel like a pink sea shell.

The Countess has of robes three score,
She doffs and leaves them on the floor;
She changes gowns ten times a day,
Her chambermaid puts them away.
"How funny!" thinks the washer-wife;
"I've moiled and toiled throughout my life,
And only have, to hide my skin,
This old rag that I'm standing in."

The Countess never toiled at all;
She begged for coin when she was small,
And later, in the ancient fashion,
In gay resorts she peddled passion.
But now to noble rank arrived,
(To wed the old Count she contrived)
Her youthful lover, lounging there,
Is hirsute as a teddy-bear.

The Countess will be honoured when
She dies past three-score years and ten.
The washer-woman will wear out
With labour fifty years about . . .
Yet as the two look at each other
The Countess thinks: "So was my mother;
And washer-wife to live and die,
But for God's grace so would be I."

TOLEDO

Three widows of the Middle West
Were grimly chewing gum;
The Lido *chef* a quail had dressed
With garlic and with rum,
And they were painfully oppressed
For they had eaten some.

Said One: "This famed El Greco guy
Gives me the blessed pip;
Them Saints look like they want to die—
Let's give our guide the slip,
And in some *bodega* close by
A glass of *vino* sip."

Said Two: "It's this Cathedral stuff
That fairly gets me down.
I think one church is quite enough
In any Spanish town;
But here there's four—that's pretty tough,
No matter their renown."

Said Three: "It's that Alcázar show
That simply knocked me out;
That dismal dungeon down below,
Them ruins all about;
That funny, fat old Moscardo
Who put the Reds to rout."

"Hey, Mister Guide!" implored the Three,
"Return to gay Madrid."
The guide was shocked, but trained was he
To do as he was bid.
So three dames of the Middle West,
Dyspeptically glum
Went back to town, and quite depressed
The guide was chewing gum.

THE MAN FROM COOK'S

"You're bloody right—I was a Red,"
The Man from Cook's morosely said.
And if our chaps had won the War
Today I'd be the Governor
Of all Madrid, and rule with pride,
Instead of just a lousy guide.

"For I could talk in Councils high
To draw down angels from the sky.
They put me seven years in gaol,—
You see how I am prison-pale . . .
Death sentence! Every dawn I thought
They'd drag me out and have me shot.

"Maybe far better if they had:
Suspense like that can make one mad.
Yet here I am serene and sane,
And at your service to explain
That gory battlefield out there,
The *Cité Universitaire.*

"See! Where the Marzanillo flows,
The women used to wash our clothes;
And often, even in its flood,
It would be purpled by our blood.
Contemptuous of shot and shell
Our women sang and—fought like hell.

"Deep trenches there ran up and down,
And linked us with the sightless town;
And every morn and every night
We sallied savagely to fight . . .
By yon ravine in bracken clad
I shot and killed a soldier lad.

"Such boys they were: methinks that one
Looked to me like my only son.
He might have been; they told my wife
Before Madrid he lost his life.
Sweet Mary! Oh if I but knew
It was not my own son I slew. . . ."

So spoke that man with eye remote
And stains of gravy on his coat;
I offered him a cigarette,
And as he sighed with vain regret,
Said he: "Don't change your dollars—wait:
I'll get you twice the market rate."

RAISING THE FLAG

Behold! the Spanish flag they're raising
Before the Palace courtyard gate;
To watch its progress bold and blazing
Two hundred patient people wait.
Though bandsmen play the anthem bravely
The silken emblem seems to lag;
Two hundred people watch it gravely—
But only *two* salute the flag.

Fine-clad and arrogant of manner
The twain are like dark dons of old,
And to that high and haughty banner
Uplifted palms they proudly hold.
The others watch them glumly, grimly;
No sullen proletariat these,
But middle-class, well clad though dimly,
Who seem to live in decent ease.

Then sadly they look at each other,
And sigh and shrug and turn away.
What is the feeling that they smother?
I wonder, but it's none too gay.
And as with puzzlement I bide me,
Beneath that rich, resplendent rag,
I hear a bitter voice beside me:
"It isn't ours—it's *Franco's flag*.

"I'm Right: I have no Left obsession.
I hate the Communists like hell,
But after ten years of oppression
I hate our Franco twice as well.
And hush! I keep (do not reprove me)
His portrait in a private place,
And every time my bowels move me
I—spit in El Caudillo's face."

These were the words I heard, I swear,
But when I turned around to stare,
Believe me—*there was no one there.*

MAD MARIA

Mad Maria in the Square
Sits upon a wicker chair.
When the keeper asks the price
Mad Maria counts her lice.
No *pesito* can she pay,
So he shrugs and goes away;
Hopes she'll pay him with her prayers,
Shabby keeper of the chairs.

Mad Maria counts her lice,
Cracks them once and cracks them twice,
Combs them from her sunny hair;
People stop to turn and stare.
Innocent in thought and deed
Mad Maria pays no heed,
And the Cross upon her breast
Proves her blessed of the blest.

So she sings a little song,
Happy as the day is long,
Hunting in her camisole
Shy partakers of her dole;
Thinking: Heaven please forgive—
Even lice have leave to live;
(But sweet Reader, do not blame,
For she kills them just the same.)

Mad Maria goes unchid,
Mildest maid in all Madrid;
While around in serried ranks
Rear the bold façades of Banks;
But when wrath of Heaven smites
Hosts of Mammon's parasites,
Mad Maria will not fall,
Being oh so very small.

Pariahs to God belong,
To be weak is to be strong;
Fools are richer than the wise,
And who see with shining eyes
Angels in the sordid street
Deem their happiness complete. . . .
Mad Maria counts her beads,
Cracks her lice and—Heaven heeds.

THE MISSAL MAKERS

To visit the Escurial
We took a motor bus,
And there a guide mercurial
                Took charge of us.
He showed us through room after room,
And talked hour after hour,
Of palace, crypt and royal tomb,
                Of pomp and power.

But in bewilderment of grace
What pleased me most of all
Were ancient missals proud in place
                In stately hall.
A thousand tomes there were at least,
All luminously bright,
That each a score of years some priest
                Had toiled to write.

Poor patient monk who brushed and penned
From rise to set of sun!
And when his book came to an end,
                His life was done.
With heart of love to God above
For guidance he would pray,
And here behold his art of gold
                Undimmed today.

And as our homeward way we took,
The thought occurred to me—
If scribes would only write *one* book,
How good 'twould be!
Or if our authors had to scroll
Their words on vellum fair,
Their output might be very small,
But oh how rare!

So writers of today take note,
If you your souls would save,
Let every line be one to quote
And to engrave.
Then though you dismally are dead,
You will be cheered to know
Your precious prose may still be read
—Ten years or so.

THE ALCÁZAR

The General now lives in town;
He's eighty odd, they say;
You'll see him strolling up and down
The Prada any day.
He goes to every football game,
The bull-ring knows his voice,
And when the people cheer his name
Moscardo must rejoice.

Yet does he, in the gaiety
Of opera and ball,
A dingy little cellar see,
A picture on a wall?
A portrait of a laughing boy
Of sixteen singing years . . .
Oh does his heart dilate with joy,
Or dim his eyes with tears?

And can he hear a wistful lad
Speak on the telephone?
"Hello! How is it with you, Dad?
That's right—I'm all alone.
They say they'll shoot me at the dawn
If you do not give in . . .
But never mind, Dad—carry on:
You know we've *got* to win."

And so they shot him at the dawn.
No bandage irked his eyes,
A lonely lad, so wistful wan,
He made his sacrifice.
He saw above the Citadel
His flag of glory fly,
And crying: "Long live Spain!" he fell
And died as heroes die.

THE CAT WITH WINGS

You never saw a cat with wings,
I'll bet a dollar—well, I did;
'Twas one of those fantastic things
One runs across in old Madrid.
A walloping big tom it was,
(Maybe of the Angora line),
With silken ears and velvet paws,
And silver hair, superbly fine.

It sprawled upon a crimson mat,
Yet though crowds came to gaze on it,
It was a supercilious cat,
And didn't seem to mind a bit.
It looked at us with dim disdain,
And indolently seemed to sigh:
"There's not another cat in Spain
One half so marvellous as I."

Its owner gently stroked its head,
And tickled it with fingers light.
"Ah no, it cannot fly," he said;
"But see—it has the *wings* all right."
Then tenderly from off its back
He raised, despite its feline fears,
Appendages that seemed to lack
Vitality—like rabbit's ears.

And then the vision that I had
Of Tabbie soaring through the night,
Quick vanished, and I felt so sad
For that poor pussy's piteous plight.
For though frustration has its stings,
Its mockeries in Hope's despite,
The hell of hells is to have wings
Yet be denied the bliss of flight.

KINGS MUST DIE

Alphonso Rex who died in Rome
Was quite a fistful as a kid;
For when I visited his home,
That gorgeous palace in Madrid,
The grinning guide-chap showed me where
He rode his bronco up the stair.

That stairway grand of marbled might,
The most majestic in the land,
In statured splendour, flight on flight,
He urged his steed with whip in hand.
No lackey could restrain him for
He gained the gilded corridor.

He burst into the Royal *suite,*
And like a cowboy whooped with glee;
Dodging the charger's flying feet
The Chamberlain was shocked to see:
Imagine how it must have been a
Great grief to Mother Queen Christina!

And so through sheer magnificence
I roamed from stately room to room,
Yet haunted ever by the sense
Of tragical dynastic doom.
The walls were wailing: Kings must die,
Being plain blokes like you and I.

Well, here's the moral to my rhyme:
When memories more worthy fade
We find that whimsically Time
Conserves some crazy escapade.
So as I left I stood to stare
With humorous enjoyment where
Alphonso crashed the Palace stair.

THE BULLS

Six bulls I saw as black as jet,
With crimsoned horns and amber eyes
That chewed their cud without a fret,
And swished to brush away the flies,
Unwitting their soon sacrifice.

It is the Corpus Christi *fête;*
Processions crowd the bannered ways;
Before the altars women wait,
While men unite in hymns of praise,
And children look with angel gaze.

The bulls know naught of holiness,
To pious pomp their eyes are blind;
Their brutish brains will never guess
The sordid passions of mankind:
Poor innocents, they wait resigned.

Till in a black room each is penned,
While from above with cruel aim
Two torturers with lances bend
To goad their fieriness to flame,
To devil them to play the game.

Then red with rage and mad with fear
They charge into the roaring ring;
Against the mockery most near
Of human might their hate they fling,
In futile, blind blood-boltering.

And so the day of unction ends;
Six bulls are dragged across the sand.
Ferocity and worship blends,
Religion and red thirst hold hand . . .
Dear Christ! 'Tis hard to understand!

SEVILLE

My Pa and Ma their honeymoon
Passed in an Andulasian June,
And though produced in Drury Lane,
I must have been *conceived* in Spain.
Now having lapsed from fair estate,
A coster's is my sorry fate;
Yet on my barrow lo! I wheel
The golden harvest of Seville.

"Sweet Spanish oranges!" I cry.
Ah! People deem not as they buy,
That in a dream a steel guitar
I strum beside the Alcázar,
And at the Miralda I meet
A signorita honey sweet,
And stroll beneath the silver moon
Like Pa and Ma that magic June.

Alack-a-day! I fear I'll never
Behold the golden Guadalquivir;
Yet here in Brixton how I feel
My spiritual home's Seville;
And hold the hope that some day I
Will visit there, if just to die;
Feeling I have not lived in vain
To crown my days in sunny Spain.

RHYMES FOR RIBALDRY

THE SEANCE

"The spirits do not like the light,"
The medium said, and turned the switch;
The little lady on my right
Clutched at my hand with nervous twitch.
(She seemed to be a pretty bitch.)

The moustached woman on my left,
With spirits on her heavy breath,
Lasciviously leaned her heft
On me as one who languisheth.
The sordid room was still as death.

"A shape I see," the medium cried,
Whose face and name I do not know . . ."
" 'Tis Robert Service," soft replied
A voice—"I passed a month ago,
And I've come back to let you know.

"The Other Side is gay and bright;
We are so happy there and free,
And Dan McGrew I oft recite,
And follow up with Sam McGee . . .
But now excuse me, I must flee."

The fat dame leaned to get my ear,
(Her breast was soft as feather bed.)
"I love his verses; oh dear, dear,
I didn't know that he was dead."
"No more did I," I sourly said.

The little lady grabbed me hard;
(She looked to me a "yesful" dear.)
Said she: "Don't you adore the Bard?"
Said I: "Before he fades, I fear
I'd like to kick his astral rear."

So then I bravely broke away
From spooks and ectoplasic gauze.
Yet in the brazen light of day
I had to pinch myself because
Really! I wondered if I *was*.

ODETTE

Along the Seine with empty belly
I wandered in the sunny morn;
My legs were wobbly as a jelly,
I wished that I had ne'er been born.
Of hope, alas! I hadn't any,
And I was weak from want of food;
When one has not a bloody penny,
Why, even suicide seems good.

I stumbled, seeking not to show it;
The quay was lined with bins of books,
But though I once had been a poet,
I gave them bleak and bitter looks.
Then shrinking in a faded cover,
Reminding me from musty shelf
Of days when I was life's gay lover,
I saw—a book I wrote myself.

The dealer watched me with suspicion;
My boots were cracked, my coat was old.
Oh sure it was a first edition,
For not a copy had I sold.
I opened to its dedication:
"To my adorable Odette."
Then . . . then I stared with consternation:
The pages were unsevered yet.

Yet she inspired its finest numbers . . .
And then a memory awoke
From half a century of slumbers—
A note, a *mille* did I not poke
Within it . . . There! Who would believe it?
As crisp and clean it was today,
And so I hastened to retrieve it,
Put back the book and walk away.

They say bread cast upon the waters
Returneth after many days.
Odette was one of Joy's fair daughters,
Yet sadly fickle in her ways.
Now I've wherewith for bread and butter,
And yet somehow my spirit grieves,
As paying garret rent I mutter:
"The trollop didn't cut the leaves."

CONFESSIONAL

A good priest, but from humble station,
Was little used to computation,
And often found himself amiss
In calculating penances;
With arithmetical discretion
He almost feared to take confession.

Then one day, spying through his grating,
He saw two worthy women waiting.
The first he bade to enter in
Was sorely conscious of her sin,
And meekly hanging down her head:
"My husband I've deceived," she said.

"How many times?" the Father sighed.
"Just eight," the downcast dame replied.
"Well," said the Priest, "I calculate
Of 'Hail Marys' just forty-eight,
And six 'Our Fathers' it will be—
In short, the blessed Rosary."

The second woman took her place
With penitence writ on her face.
"Father, I've sinned," she sorely grieved;
"My loving husband I've deceived."
"How many times?" the Father gravely
Asked her, and "Five" she told him bravely.

"It's kindo' hard to figger out
That penalty."—He sat in doubt
And scratched his head in worried thought,
Then gently said: "I tell you what—
Sin three times more and make it eight:
That's easier to calculate."

THE LOTTERY

"Young fellow, listen to a friend:
Beware of wedlock—'tis a gamble.
It's MAN who holds the losing end
In every matrimonial scramble."

"Young lady, marriage mostly is
A cruel cross of hope's concealing.
A rarity is wedded bliss
And WOMAN gets the dirty dealing."

. . . Such my advice to man and maid,
But though they harken few will take it.
The Parson plies his merry trade
The marriage seems much what you make it.

If Pa or Ma had counsel sought
Of me whose locks today are hoary,
And feared to tie the nuptial knot—
Would I be here to tell the story?

Nay, lad and lass, don't flout romance,
Nor heed this cynical old sinner;
Like bold Columbus take a chance,
And may your number be a winner.

Far be it from me to advise,
But in the marital relation
The safest bet is Compromise
And Mutual Consideration.

TWO HUSBANDS

Unpenitent, I grieve to state,
Two good men stood by heaven's gate,
Saint Peter's coming to await.

Then stooped the Keeper of the Keys,
Saying: "What suppliants are these,
Who wait me not on bended knees?

"To get my heavenly Okay
A man should have been used to pray,
Or suffered in some grievous way."

"Oh I have suffered," cried the first.
"Of wives I had the wicked worst,
Who made my life a plague accurst.

"Such martyrdom no tongue can tell;
In mercy's name it is not well
To doom me to another hell."

Saint Peter said: "I comprehend;
But tribulations have their end.
The gate is open,—go my friend."

Then said the second: "What of me?
More I deserve to pass than he,
For I've been wedded *twice*, you see."

Saint Peter looked at him a while,
And then he answered with a smile:
"Your application I will file.

"Yet twice in double yoke you've driven . . .
Though sinners with our Saints we leaven,
We don't take IMBECILES in heaven."

THE ENIGMA

The Sergeant of a Highland Reg-
-Iment was drilling of his men;
With temper notably on edge
He blest them every now and then.
A sweet old lady standing by,
Was looking on with fascination,
And then she dared this question shy,
That perturbates the Celtic nation.

"Oh gentle Sergeant do not scold;
Please tell me, though your tone so curt is:
These bare-legged boys look sadly cold—
Do they wear wool beneath their skirties?"
The Sergeant's face grew lobster red,
As one who sends a bloke to blazes. . . .
Then: "Round about turn, squad," he said;
"Now blast you! bend and *pick up daisies.*"

58

THE FARMER'S DAUGHTER

The Rector met a little lass
Who led a heifer by a rope.
Said he: "Why don't you go to Mass?
Do you not want to please the Pope?"

The village maiden made reply,
As on the rope she ceased to pull:
"My father said this morning I
Must take Paquerette to see the bull."

The Rector frowned. " 'Tis wrong, I wist
To leave your prayer-book on the shelf.
Your father has a stronger wrist;
Why can't he do the job himself?"

Then lovely in her innocence,
With gaze as pure as meadow pool,
The maid spoke in her sire's defence:
"But Daddy, please your Reverence,
Would rather *leave it to the bull.*"

HIGHLAND HOSPITALITY

Unto his housemaid spoke the Laird:
"Tonight the Bishop is our guest;
The spare room must be warmed and aired:
To please him we will do our best.
A worthy haggis you must make,
And serve a bowl of barley bree;
We must be hearty for the sake
Of Highland Hospitality.

The feast was set, the candles lit,
The Bishop came with modest mien,
And (one surmised) was glad to sit
And sup in this ancestral scene.
A noble haggis graced the board;
The Laird proposed a toast or two,
And ever and anon he poured
His guest a glass of Mountain Dew.

Then to his maid the Laird gave tongue:
"My sonsie Jean, my friend is old.
Comparatively you are young,
And not so sensitive to cold.
Poor chiel! His blood austerely beats,
Though it be sped by barley bree . . .
Slip half an hour between the sheets,
Brave lass, and warm his bed a wee.

Said she: "I'll do the best I can
So that his couch may cosy be,
And as a human warming pan
Prove Highland Hospitality."
So hearing sounds of mild carouse,
As in the down she pillowed deep:
"In half an hour I will arouse,"
She vowed, then soundly went to sleep.

So when the morn was amber-orbed
The Bishop from a dream awoke,
And as his parritch he absorbed,
Unto his host he slyly spoke:
"Your haggis, Laird, was nobly bred,
And braw your brew of barley bree—
But oh your thought to warm the bed!
That's Highland Hospitality.

DUELLO

A Frenchman and an Englishman
Resolved to fight a duel,
And hit upon a savage plan,
Because their hate was cruel.
They each would fire a single shot
In room of darkness pitchy,
And who was killed or who was not
Would hang on fingers twitchy.

The room was bare and dark as death,
And each ferocious fighter
Could hear his fierce opponent's breath
And clutched his pistol tighter.
Then Gaston fired—the bullet hissed
On its destructive mission . . .
"Thank God!" said John Bull. "He has missed."
The Frenchman cried: "Perdition!"

Then silence followed like a spell,
And as the Briton sought to
Reply he wondered where the hell
His Gallic foe had got to.
And then he thought: "I'll mercy show,
Since Hades is a dire place
To send a fellow to—and so
I'll blaze up through the fireplace."

So up the chimney he let fly,
Of grace a gallant henchman;
When lo! a sudden, sooty cry,
And down there crashed the Frenchman . . .
But if this yarn in France you tell,
Although its vein be skittish,
I think it might be just as well
To make your Frenchman—British.

JULIE CLAIRE

Oh Julie Claire was very fair,
Yet generous as well,
And many a lad of metal had
A saucy tale to tell
Of sultry squeeze beneath the trees
Or huggings in the hay . . .
Of love her share had Julie Claire
When life was lush and gay.

And then the village wealth to pillage
Came the Teuton horde;
The haughty Huns with naughty guns
And clattering of sword.
And Julie Claire had honey hair
With eyes of soft azure,
So she became the favoured flame
Of the Kommandatur.

But when at last the plague was past,
The bloody war well won,
We clipped the locks of every dox
Who dallied with the Hun.
Each wench with scorn was duly shorn;
Our Maire the shears would wield,
And Julie's head with ringlets shed
Was like a turnip peeled.

But of these days of wanton ways
No more the village talks,
For Julie Claire has wed the Maire
Who clipped her golden locks . . .
Nay, do not try to tell me I
Must suffer for my sins,
For all agree the *Maire* must be
The father of her twins.

ROMANCE

In Paris on a morn of May
I sent a radio transatlantic
To catch a steamer on the way,
But oh the postal fuss was frantic;
They sent me here, they sent me there,
They were so courteous yet so canny;
Then as I wilted in despair
A Frenchman flipped me on the fanny.

'Twas only just a gentle pat,
Yet oh what sympathy behind it!
I don't let anyone do that,
But somehow then I didn't mind it.
He seemed my worry to divine,
With kindly smile, that foreign mannie,
And as we stood in waiting line
With tender touch he tapped my fanny.

It brought a ripple of romance
Into that postal bureau dreary;
He gave me such a smiling glance
That somehow I felt gay and cheery.
For information on my case
The postal folk searched nook and cranny;
He gently tapped, with smiling face,
His reassurance on my fanny.

66

So I'll go back to Tennessee,
And they will ask: "How have you spent your
Brief holiday in gay Paree?"
But I'll not speak of my adventure.
Oh say I'm spectacled and grey,
Oh say I'm sixty and a grannie—
But say that in a morn of May
A Frenchman flipped me on the fanny!

THREE WIVES

Said Jones: "I'm glad my wife's not clever;
Her intellect is second-rate.
If she was witty she would never
Give *me* a chance to scintillate;
But cap my humorous endeavour,
And make me seem an addle-pate."

Said Smith: "I'm glad my wife's no beauty,
For if a siren's charms she had,
And stinted her domestic duty,
I fear that she would drive me mad:
For I am one of those sad fellows
Who are unreasonably jealous."

Said Brown: "I know my wife's not witty,
Nor is she very long in looks;
She's neither humorous nor pretty,
But oh how she divinely cooks!
You guys must come some night to dinner—
You'll see my little girl's a winner."

So it's important in our lives,
(Exaggerating more or less),
To be contented with our wives,
And prize the virtues they possess;
And with dispraise to turn one's back
On all the qualities they lack.

ARTIST

He gave a picture exhibition,
Hiring a little empty shop.
Above its window: FREE ADMISSION
Cajoled the passers-by to stop;
Just to admire—no need to purchase,
Although his price might have been low:
But no proud artist ever urges
Potential buyers at his show.

Of course he badly needed money,
But more he needed moral aid.
Some people thought his pictures funny,
Too ultra-modern, I'm afraid.
His painting was experimental,
Which no poor artist can afford—
That is, if he would pay the rental
And guarantee his roof and board.

And so some came and saw and sniggered,
And some a puzzled brow would crease;
And some objected: "Well, I'm jiggered!"
What price Picasso and Matisse?
The artist sensitively quivered,
And stifled many a bitter sigh,
But day by day his hopes were shivered
For no one ever sought to buy.

And then he had a brilliant notion:
Half of his daubs he labelled: SOLD.
And lo! he viewed with queer emotion
A public keen and far from cold.
Then (strange it is beyond the telling),
He saw the people round him press:
His paintings went—they still are selling . . .
Well, nothing succeeds like success.

ROSENSTEIN

"In all my life I've never read
A book," said Mister Rosenstein;
"I've never had the time, instead
I've concentrated on my line
Of ladies' fancy underwear,
So now I am a millionaire.

"My library is full of books;
My wife she says they're lots of fun;
But though I give them wiseful looks
I've never read a single one.
It takes me all my time, it seems,
To scan the fashion magazines.

"For now I'm toiling night and day
To make a million into more;
And keep my garments on display
In every town, in every store;
For quality and sheer design
Demand the mark of Rosenstein.

"Well maybe when I'm old and grey
I might turn publisher myself;
There's money in Romance, they say,
But my romance is piling pelf:
To me a healthy ledger looks
Far better than a thousand books.

"So each to his own job; and mine
Is making 'undies' for the dames,
To keep the firm of Rosenstein
High in the Trade's most famous names:
So on my tomb (if you should look)
See graved: *He never read a book.*"

DREAMS

I had a dream, a dream of dread:
I thought that horror held the house;
A burglar bent above my bed,
He moved as quiet as a mouse.
With hairy hand a naked knife
He poised to plunge a bloody stroke,
Until despairful of my life
I shrieked with terror—and awoke.

I had a dream of weary woes:
In weather that was fit to freeze,
I thought that I had lost my clothes,
And only wore a short chemise.
The wind was wild; to catch a train
I ran, but no advance did make;
My legs were pistoning in vain—
How I was happy to awake!

I had a dream: Upon a stair
I met a maid who kissed my lips;
A nightie was her only wear,
We almost came to loving grips.
And then she opened wide a door,
And pointed to a bonny bed . . .
Oh blast! I wakened up before
I could discover—were we wed?

Alas! Those dreams of broken bliss,
Of wakenings too sadly soon!
With memories of sticky kiss,
And limbs so languidly a-swoon!
Alas those nightmares devil driven!
Those pantless prowlings in Pall Mall!
Oh why should some dreams be like heaven
And others so resemble hell?

MY HERO

Of all the boys with whom I fought
In Africa and Sicily,
Bill was the bravest of the lot
In our dare-devil Company.
That lad would rather die than yield;
His gore he glorified to spill,
And so in every battlefield
A hero in my eyes was Bill.

Then when the bloody war was done,
He moseyed back to our home town,
And there, a loving mother's son,
Like other kids he settled down.
His old girl seemed a shade straight-laced,
For when I called my buddy "Bill,"
She looked at me with some distaste,
Suggesting that his name was "Will."

And then he had to get engaged,
And took unto himself a wife;
And so inevitably caged,
He settled down to wedded life.
He introduced me to his Missis,
But oh I thought her rather silly,
For in between their frequent kisses
She called my hard-boiled hero: "Willie."

Now he has long forgot the War,
The which he did a lot to win,
And feeling full of ginger for
He's happy Pop of cherubs twin.
Yet with his air: "Don't care a damn,"
On Main Street he's my hero still . . .
As proud he *wheels a double pram*
What guy has got the guts of Bill!

MY FUTURE

"Let's make him a sailor," said Father,
"And he will adventure the sea."
"A soldier," said Mother, "is rather
What I would prefer him to be."
"A lawyer," said Father, "would please me,
For then he could draw up my will."
"A doctor," said Mother, "would ease me;
Maybe he could give me a pill."

Said Father: "Let's make him a curate,
A Bishop in gaiters to be."
Said Mother: "I couldn't endure it
To have Willie preaching to *me*."
Said Father: "Let him be a poet;
So often he's gathering wool."
Said Mother with temper: "Oh stow it!
You know it, a poet's a fool."

Said Father: "Your son is a duffer,
A stupid and mischievous elf."
Said Mother, who's rather a huffer:
"That's right—he takes after yourself."
Controlling parental emotion
They turned to me, seeking a cue,
And sudden conceived the bright notion
To ask what I *wanted* to do.

Said I: "My ambition is modest:
A clown in a circus I'd be,
And turn somersaults in the sawdust
With audience laughing at me."
. . . Poor parents! they're dead and decaying,
But I am a clown as you see;
And though in no circus I'm playing,
How people are laughing at me!

AN EPICURE

Should you preserve white mice in honey
Don't use imported ones from China,
For though they cost you less in money
You'll find the Japanese ones finer.
But if Chinese, stuff them with spice,
Which certainly improves their savour,
And though the Canton mice are nice,
The Pekinese have finer flavour.

If you should pickle bracken shoots
The way the wily Japanese do,
Be sure to pluck them young—what suits
Our Eastern taste may fail to please you.
And as for nettles, cook them well;
To eat them raw may give you skin-itch;
But if you boil them for a spell
They taste almost as good as spinach.

So Reader, if you chance to be
Of Oriental food a lover,
And care to share a meal with me,
I'll add the addled eggs of plover;
And gaily I will welcome you
To lunch within an arbour sunny,
On nettle broth and bracken stew,
And nice white mice, conserved in honey.

OLD SWEETHEARTS

Oh Maggie, do you mind the day
 We went to school together,
And as we stoppit by the way
 I rolled you in the heather?
My! but you were the bonny lass
 And we were awfu' late for class.

Your locks are now as white as snow,
 And you are ripe and wrinkled,
A grandmother ten times or so,
 Yet how your blue eyes twinkled
At me above your spectacles,
 Recalling naughty neck-tickles!

It must be fifty years today
 I left you for the Yukon;
You haven't changed—you're just as gay
 And just as sweet to look on.
But can you see in this old fool
 The lad who made you late for school?

Oh Maggie, ask me in to tea
 And we can talk things over,
And contemplate the nuptial state,
 For I am still your lover:
And though the bell be slow to chime
 We'll no be grudgin' o' the time.

80

RURAL RHYMES

BIRD SANCTUARY

Between the cliff-rise and the beach
A slip of emerald I own;
With fig and olive, almond, peach,
Cherry and plum-tree overgrown;
Glad-watered by a crystal spring
That carols through the silver night,
And populous with birds who sing
Gay madrigals for my delight.

Some merchants fain would buy my land
To build a stately pleasure dome.
Poor fools! they cannot understand
How pricelessly it is my home!
So luminous with living wings,
So musical with feathered joy . . .
Not for all pleasure fortune brings,
Would I such ecstasy destroy.

A thousand birds are in my grove,
Melodious from morn to night;
My fruit trees are their treasure trove,
Their happiness is my delight.
And through the sweet and shining days
They know their lover and their friend;
So I will shield in peace and praise
My innocents unto the end.

POOR COCK ROBIN

My garden robin in the Spring
Was rapturous with glee,
And followed me with wistful wing
From pear to apple tree;
His melodies the summer long
He carolled with delight,
As if he could with jewelled song
Find favour in my sight.

And now that Autumn's in the air
He's singing, singing still,
And yet somehow I cannot bear
The frenzy of his bill;
The keen wind ruffs his ruddy breast
As to bare boughs he clings;
The sun is sullen in the West
Yet still he sings and sings.

Soon, soon the legions of the snow
Will pitch their tents again,
And round my window-sill I know
He'll call for crumbs in vain;
The pulsing passion of his throat
Has hint of Winter woe;
The piercing sweetness of his note
Entreats me not to go.

In vain, in vain, Oh valiant one,
You sing to bid me stay!
For all my life is in the sun
And I must flit away.
Yet by no gold of orange glow
Will I be comforted,
Seeing blood-bright in bitter snow—
                    A robin dead.

OLD BOY SCOUT

A bonny bird I found today
Mired in a melt of tar;
Its silky breast was silver-grey,
Its wings were cinnabar.
So still it lay right in the way
Of every passing car.

Yet as I gently sought to pry
It loose, it glared at me;
You would have thought its foe was I,
It pecked so viciously;
So fiercely fought, as soft I sought
From death to set it free.

Its pinions pitifully frail,
I wrested from the muck;
I feared the feathers of its tail
Would never come unstuck.
. . . Then jewel-bright it flashed in flight—
Oh how I wished it luck!

With happiness my heart was light,
To see how fair it flew;
To do my good deed I delight,
As grey-haired scouts should do;
Yet oh my bright reward's to write
This simple rhyme for you!

WHY DO BIRDS SING?

Let poets piece prismatic words,
Give me the jewelled joy of birds!

What ecstasy moves them to sing?
Is it the lyric glee of Spring,
The dewy rapture of the rose?
Is it the worship born in those
Who are of Nature's self a part,
The adoration of the heart?

Is it the mating mood in them
That makes each crystal note a gem?
Oh mocking bird and nightingale,
Oh mavis, lark and robin—hail!
Tell me what perfect passion glows
In your inspired arpeggios?

A thrush is thrilling as I write
Its obligato of delight;
And in its fervour, as in mine,
I fathom tenderness divine,
And pity those of earthy ear
Who cannot hear . . . who cannot hear.

Let poets pattern pretty words:
For lovely largesse—bless you, Birds!

86

CAPTIVITY

O meadow lark, so wild and free,
It cannot be, it cannot be,
That men to merchandise your spell
Do close you in a wicker hell!

O hedgerow thrush so mad with glee,
It cannot be, it cannot be,
They rape you from your hawthorn foam
To make a cell of steel your home!

O blackbird in the orchard tree,
It cannot be, it cannot be,
That devils in a narrow cage
Would prison your melodic rage!

O you who live for liberty,
Can you believe that it can be
That we of freedom's faith destroy
In dungeons, innocence and joy?

O decent folk who read this page,
If you should own a bird in cage,
Throw wide the door,—God gave it wings:
Then hear how in your *heart* it sings!

RED-TILED ROOF

Poets may praise a wattle thatch
Doubtfully waterproof;
Let me uplift my lowly latch
Beneath a rose-tiled roof.
Let it be gay and rich in hue,
Soft bleached by burning days,
Where skies ineffably are blue,
And seas a golden glaze.

But set me in the surly North
Beneath a roof of slate,
And as I sourly sally forth
My heart will hum with hate;
And I will brood beneath a pine
Where Nature seldom smiles,
Heart-longing for a starry vine
And roof of ruddy tiles.

For oh the South's a bonny clime
And sunshine is its life;
So there I'll finish up my time
A stranger unto strife.
And smoke my pipe and sit aloof
From care by miles and miles,
Sagaciously beneath a roof,
Geranium-gay and panic proof,
Of ruby tinted tiles.

RICH POOR MAN

We pitied him because
He lived alone;
His tiny cottage was
His only own.
His little garden had
A wall around;
Yet never was so glad
A bit of ground.

It seemed to fair rejoice
With flowers and fruit;
With blooms it found a voice
When ours was mute.
It smiled without a pause
In gracious glow:
I think it was because
He loved it so.

He had no news to read,
No rent to pay;
His vegetable need
He plucked each day.
His grateful garden gave
Him ample fare;
He lived without a crave,
Without a care.

His bread and milk and tea
Were all he bought;
To us he seemed to be
A sorry lot . . .
But when we're dead and gone,
With all our fuss,
I guess he'll carry on,
And laugh at us.

MY WHITE MOUSE

At dusk I saw a craintive mouse
That sneaked and stole around the house;
At first I took it for a ghost,
For it was snowy white—almost.

I've seen them in captivity,
But this white mouse was wild and free,
And every eve with stealth it stole
And foraged in the garbage hole.

I told the folks, yet wondered why
No one could see the mouse but I;
For it was really, truly white,
And not just silvered by moonlight.

And then there came a big black cat,
And though I said: "Get out of that!"
It stared at me with savage eyes,
As big and yellow as moonrise.

And often times I wonder whether
They didn't just go off together,
In the bright moonlight, paw in paw,
For never more my mouse I saw.

FLOWER GARDENER

Gas got me in the first World War,
And all my mates at rest are laid.
I felt I might survive them for
I am a gardener by trade.
My life is in the open air,
And kindly is the work I do,
Since flowers are my joy and care,
    And comfort too.

My flowers are a fairy sight,
Yet I'm an ugly, warped old man,
For I have lived in Fate's despite
A year beyond one's mortal span;
And owe my health to gentle toil
From dawn to dark, contented hours,
Of loving kinship with the soil,
    A friend of flowers.

My dahlias are my pride today,
And many my creations be.
They're worth a fortune, people say,
But what does money mean to me?
Their glory is my rich reward,
And as their radiant heads they raise,
I dedicate them to the Lord,
    With love and praise.

I grieve to think that sullen Powers
On bombs and guns their might depend;
If man had heart for growing flowers
Then would we all be friend and friend.
The glory of the world is his
Who seeks salvation in the sod,
And finds that golden sunshine is
                    The laugh of God.

JALOPPY JOY

Past ashcans and alley cats,
Fetid, overflowing gutters,
Leprous lines of rancid flats
Where the frowsy linen flutters;
With a rattle and a jar,
Hark! I sing a happy ditty,
As I speed my Master far
From the poison of the City.

Speed him to the sportive sea,
Watch him walloping the briny,
Light his pipe and brew his tea
In a little wood that's piny;
Haven him to peace of mind,
Drowsy dreams in pleasant places,
Where the woman's eyes are kind,
And the men have ruddy faces.

Just a jaloppy am I,
But he's always been my lover,
So each Sunday morn I try
Youthful joy to re-discover.
For he loves the wild and free,
And though he would never know it,
Nature thrills him with the glee
And the rapture of a poet.

He's a little invoice clerk,
I'm a worn and ancient flivver;
I have an asthmatic spark,
He an alcoholic liver;
Yet with clatter, clang and creak
We are lyrical for one day;
Then another loathly week,
Living for another Sunday.

FALLEN LEAVES

Why should I be the *first* to fall
Of all the leaves on this old tree?
Though sadly soon I know that all
Will lose their hold and follow me.
While my birth-brothers bravely blow,
Why should I be the first to go?

Why should I be the *last* to cling
Of all the leaves on this bleak bough?
I've fluttered since the fire of Spring
And I am worn and withered now.
I would escape the Winter gale
And sleep soft-silvered by a snail.

When swoop the legions of the snow
To pitch their tents in roaring weather
We fallen leaves will lie below
And rot rejoicingly together;
And from our rich and dark decay
Will laugh our brothers of the May.

DYSPEPTIC CLERK

I think I'll buy a little field,
Though scant am I of pelf,
And hold the hope that it may yield
A living for myself;
For I have toiled ten thousand days
With ledger and with pen,
And I am sick of city ways
And soured with city men.

So I will plant my little plot
With lettuce, beans and peas;
Potatoes too—oh quite a lot,
And pear and apple trees.
My carrots will be coral pink,
My turnips ivory;
And I'll forget my pen and ink,
And office slavery.

My hut shall have a single room
Monastically bare;
A faggot fire for winter gloom,
A table and a chair.
A Frugalist I call myself,
My needs are oh so small;
My luxury a classic shelf
Of poets on the wall.

Here as I dream, how grey and cold
The City seems to me;
Another world of green and gold
Incessantly I see.
So I will fling my pen away,
And learn a hoe to wield:
A cashbook and a stool today . . .
Soon, soon a Little Field.

INNOCENCE

By open window all night long
I sleep and drink the air like wine,
Rousing to glee of garden song,
With leaves a-shimmer, lawn a-shine;
Glitter and gladness everywhere,
A lyric world without a care.

Without a care, and none have I,
No more than has my rosebud thrush,
That seeks melodious reply
From some blythe brother in the bush;
Echo on echo, song on song,
And all to innocence belong.

For innocence is happiness:
Let little children tell you this;
Let purity of heart express
Its joy of sunny benefice . . .
Please, Garden God, ere I go hence
Grant me your gift of innocence.

VIGNETTES IN VERSE

DECORATIONS

My only medals are the scars
I've won in weary, peacetime wars,
A-fighting for my little brood,
To win them shelter, shoon and food;
But most of all to give them faith
In God's good mercy unto death.

My sons have medals gleaming bright,
Proud trophies won in foreign fight;
But though their crosses bravely shine,
My boys can show no wounds like mine—
Grim gashes dolorously healed,
And inner ailings unrevealed.

Life-lasting has my battle been,
My enemy a fierce machine;
And I am marked by many a blow
In conflict with a tireless foe,
Till warped and bent beneath the beat
Of life's unruth I own defeat.

Yet strip me bare and you will see
A worthy warrior I be;
Although no uniform I've worn,
By wounds of labour I am torn;
Leave them their ribbands and their stars . . .
Behold! I proudly prize my scars.

TWO BLIND MEN

Two blind men met. Said one: "This earth
Has been a blackout from my birth.
Through darkness I have groped my way,
Forlorn, unknowing night from day.
But you—though War destroyed your sight,
Still have your memories of Light,
And to allay your present pain
Can live your golden youth again."

Then said the second: "Aye, it's true,
It must seem magical to you
To know the shape of things that are,
A woman's lips, a rose, a star.
But therein lies the hell of it;
Better my eyes had never lit
To love of bluebells in a wood,
Or daffodils in dancing mood.

"You do not know what you have lost,
But I, alas! can count the cost—
Than memories that goad and gall,
Far better not to see at all.
And as for love, you know it not,
For pity is our sorry lot.
So there you see my point of view:
'Tis I, my friend, who envy you."

And which was right still puzzles me:
Perhaps one should be blind to see.

BRITANNICA

Sheer knowledge was the goal he sought;
He did not wed, and being thrifty,
A new *Britannica* he bought,
And settled down, though nearing fifty,
Its sturdy volumes twenty-four
To ponder o'er and o'er and o'er.

He started with the letter A,
And read with ardour undiminished,
Nor hesitated by the way
Until the letter Z he finished;
And though some subjects rather irked,
Not even the most dull he shirked.

So every year he made the trip
From A to Z and back returning;
He never once relaxed his grip
Although his midnight oil was burning;
Till grey professors straight from college
Would compliment him on his knowledge.

Yet he was happy all the while
Though little lucre he was earning,
And he would tell you with a smile:
"Life's truest treasure lies in learning.
What satisfaction it can bring
To know something of everything!"

And so he read and read and read
To slake his thirst for information;
But when they told me he was dead
How I was filled with consternation!
To think his store of learned lore
Was lost, alas! for evermore.

So his *Britannica* I bought,
Of knowledge to acquire a smatter.
Alas! it gathers dust a lot,
But I reflect—what does it matter?
On brain of scholar, sot and swine,
(On his replete, and arid mine)
With equal zest the worm doth dine.

MUGUET

'Twas on the sacred First of May
I made a sentimental sally
To buy myself a slender spray
Of pearly lily of the valley;
And setting it beside my bed,
Dream back the smile of one now dead.

But when I asked how much a spray?
The figure seemed so astronomic
I rather fear that my dismay
Must have appeared a little comic.
The price, the shopgirl gravely said,
Alas! was fifteen francs a head.

However, I said: "Give me three,
And wrap them in a silver paper,
And I will take them home with me,
And light an 'in memoriam' taper,
To one whose smile, so heaven bright,
Was wont to make my darkness light."

Then lo! I saw beside me stand
A woman shabby, old and grey,
Who pointed with a trembling hand
And shyly asked: "How much are they?"
But when I told her, sadly said:
"I'll save my francs for milk and bread."

"Yet I've a daughter just sixteen,
Long sick abed and oh so sad.
I thought—well, how they would have been
A gift, maybe, to make her glad . . ."
And then I saw her eyes caress
My blossoms with such wistfulness.

I gave them: sought my garret bare,
Knowing that she whom I had loved,
Although no blooms I brought her there,
Would have so tenderly approved . . .
And in the dark I lay awhile,
Seeing again her radiant smile.

MAY MIRACLE

On this festive first of May,
Wending wistfully my way
Three sad sights I saw today.

The first was such a lovely lad
He lit with grace the sordid street;
Yet in a monk's robe he was clad,
With tonsured head and sandalled feet.
Though handsome as a movie star
His eyes had holiness in them,
As if he saw afaint, afar
A stable-stall in Bethlehem.

The second was a crippled maid
Who gazed and gazed with eager glance
Into a window that displayed
The picture of a ballet dance.
And as she leaned on crutches twain,
Before that poster garland-gay
She looked so longingly and vain
I thought she'd never go away.

The last one was a sightless man
Who to the tune of a guitar
Caught coppers in a dingy can,
Patient and sad as blind men are.
So old and grey and grimy too,
His fingers fumbled on the strings,
As emptily he looked at you,
And sang as only sorrow sings.

Then I went home and had a dream
That seemed fantastical to me . . .
I saw the youth with eye agleam
Put off his robe and dance with glee.
The maid her crutches threw away;
Her withered limbs seemed shapely fine;
And there the two with radiance gay
Divinely danced in soft entwine:
While the blind man, his sight restored,
Guitared the Glory of the Lord.

WINNIE

When I went by the meadow gate
The chestnut mare would trot to meet me,
And as her coming I would wait,
She'd whinney high as if to greet me.
And I would kiss her silky nose,
And stroke her neck until it glistened,
And speak soft words: I don't suppose
She understood—but how she listened!

Then in the war-net I was caught,
Returning three black winters older;
And when the little mare I sought
The farmer told me he had sold her.
And so time passed—when in the street
One day I heard a plaintive whinney
That roused a recollection sweet,
So then I turned and there was Winnie.

I vow she knew me, mooning there.
She raised her nose for me to fondle,
And though I'd lost an arm I'll swear
She kissed the empty sleeve a-dangle.
But oh it cut me to the heart,
Though I was awful glad to meet her,
For lo! she dragged a tinker's cart
And stumbled weakly as he beat her.

Just skin and bone, a sorry hack!
Say, fellows, you may think it funny:
I made a deal and bought her back,
Though it took all my bonus money.
And she'll be in the meadow there,
As long as I have dough for spending . . .
Gee! I'll take care of that old mare—
"Sweetheart! you'll have a happy ending."

PAVEMENT POET

God's truth! these be the bitter times.
In vain I sing my sheaf of rhymes,
And hold my battered hat for dimes.

And then a copper collars me,
Barking: "It's begging that you be;
Come on, dad; you're in custody."

And then the Beak looks down and says:
"Sheer doggerel I deem your lays:
I send you down for seven days."

So for a week I won't disturb
The peace by singing at the curb.
I don't mind that, but oh it's hell
To have my verse called doggerel.

MY HUSBANDS

My first I wed when just sixteen
And he was sixty-five.
He treated me like any queen
The years he was alive.
Oh I betrayed him on the sly,
Like any other bitch,
And how I longed for him to die
And leave me young and rich!

My second is a gigolo
I took when I was old;
That he deceives me well I know,
And hungers for my gold.
While I adore each silken hair
That crowns his handsome head,
I'm everlastingly aware
He wishes I were dead.

How I would love my *vieux* if he
Today were by my side;
My gig would have been daft for me
When I was first a bride.
But for his mother I can pass,
Although I am his wife;
Like father was my first—alas!
The irony of life.

SELF-MADE MAN

A hundred people I employed,
But when they struck for higher pay,
I was so damnably annoyed
I told them they could stay away.
I simply shut my business down;
I closed my doors and locked them out,
And now you'll find all round the town
A lot of idle men about.

Of course I know it is my loss,
And I their point of view can see,
But I must show them I'm the boss,
And any raise must come from ME.
But when they claim it as a right,
And send their Union leaders round,
Why then, by God, I'm out to fight,
Or burn my workshop to the ground.

I've risen from the ranks myself;
By brawn and brain I've made my way.
Had I bet, beered and blown my pelf,
I would have been as poor as they.
Had I wed young to thrift's unheed,
I might have been a toiler now,
With rent to pay and kids to feed,
And bloody sweat upon my brow.

Ah there's the point! *"I might have been."*
I might have been as peeved as they,
And know what misery can mean,
And ask like them a raise of pay.
I see myself. . . . *"The telephone!"*
. . . Had I not been so bloody wise—
(A poor old rich man all alone) . . .
"Hullo! Strike's off. I grant the rise."

114

THE PIGEON SHOOTING

They say that Monte Carlo is
A sunny place for shady people;
But I'm not in the gambling biz,
And sober as a parish steeple.
So though this paradisal spot
The devil's playground of the rich is,
I love it and I love it not,
As men may sometimes fall for bitches.

I lazed beneath the sky's blue bliss,
The sea swooned with a sequin glimmer;
The breeze was shy as maiden kiss,
The palms sashayed in silken shimmer.
The peace I soaked in every pore
Did me more good than ten religions . . .
And then: *Bang! Bang!* my joy was o'er;
Says I: "There goes them poor dam pigeons."

I see them bob from out their traps,
The swarded green around them ringing;
Bewildered, full of joy perhaps,
With sudden hope of skyey winging.
They blink a moment at the sun,
They flutter free of earthy tether . . .
A fat man holds a smoking gun,
A boy collects some blood and feather.

And so through all the sainted day,
Bang! Bang! a bunch of plumage gory.
Five hundred francs they cost to slay,
And few there live to tell the story . . .
Yet look! there's one so swift to fly,
Despite the shots a course he's steering . . .
Brave little bird! he's winging high,
He's gained the trees—I feel like cheering.

In Monte Carlo's garden glades
With dreamful bliss one softly lingers,
And lazily in leafy shades
The doves pick breadcrumbs from one's fingers . . .
Bang! Bang! Farewell, oh sylvan courts!
Where peace and joy are sweetly blended . . .
God curse these lousy Latin sports!
My pigeons scat, my dream is ended.

ROULETTE

I'll wait until my money's gone
Before I take the sleeping pills;
Then when they find me in the dawn,
Remote from earthly ails and ills
They'll say: "She's broke, the foreign bitch!"
And dump me in the common ditch.

So thought I, of all hope bereft,
And by my evil fate obsessed;
A thousand francs was all I'd left
Of that fair fortune I possessed.
. . . I throw it on the table there,
And wait, with on my lips a prayer.

I fear my very life's at stake;
My note is lying on the Red . . .
I know I'll lose it, then I'll take
My pills and sleep until I'm dead . . .
Oh God of mercy, understand!
In pity guide the croupier's hand.

My heart beats hard, my lips are dry;
I feel I cannot bear to look.
I dread to hear the croupier's cry,
I'll sit down in this quiet nook.
The lights go dim, my senses reel . . .
See! *Jesus Christ is at the wheel.*

*   *   *   *   *

Kind folks arouse me from my trance.
"The Red has come ten times," they say.
"Oh do not risk another chance;
Please, Lady, take your gains away,
And to the Lord of Luck give thanks—
You've won nigh half a million francs."

Aye, call me just a daft old dame;
I knit and sew to make my bread,
And nevermore I'll play that game,
For I've a glory in my head. . . .
Ah well I know, to stay my fall,
'Twas our dear Lord who spun the ball.

ROOM GHOST

Though elegance I ill afford,
My living-room is green and gold;
The former tenant was a lord
Who died of drinking, I am told.
I fancy he was rather bored;
I don't think he was over old.

And where on books I dully browse,
And gaze in rapture at the sea,
My predecessor would carouse
In lavish infidelity
With ladies amoral as cows;
But interesting, you'll agree.

I'm dull as water in a ditch,
Making these silly bits of rhyme;
My Lord, I'm told, was passing rich
And must have had a lovely time;
With champagne and a pretty bitch,
No need to heed the church-bell chime.

My living-room is marble floored,
And on its ceiling cherubs play;
But like my lord I'm often bored
And put my sullen books away;
And though my people say I snored,
I dream of indiscretions gay.

And often in the niggard night,
When in sweet sleep I fail to drown,
I seem to see that noble sprite
In monocle and dressing-gown:
A glass of brandy to the light
He holds and winks and drinks it down.

When life's so beautifully planned,
Dear Reader, can you understand
Why men should die by their own hand?

RHYMES FOR RIPENESS

BINDLE STIFF

When I was brash and gallant-gay
Just fifty years ago,
I hit the ties and beat my way
From Maine to Mexico;
For though to Glasgow gutter bred
A hobo heart had I,
And followed where adventure led,
Beneath a brazen sky.

And as I tramped the railway track
I owned a single shirt;
Like canny Scot I bought it black
So's not to show the dirt;
A handkerchief held all my gear,
My razor and my comb;
I was a feckless lad, I fear,
With all the world for home.

Yet oh I thought the life was grand
And loved my liberty!
Romance was my bed-fellow and
The stars my company.
And I would think, each diamond dawn,
"How I have forged my fate!
Where are the Gorbals and the Tron,
And where the Gallowgate?"

Oh daft was I to wander wild,
And seek the Trouble Trail,
As weakly as a wayward child,
And darkly doomed to fail . . .
Aye, bindle-stiff I hit the track
Just fifty years ago . . .
Yet now . . . *I drive my Cadillac*
From Maine to Mexico.

THE OLD ARMCHAIR

In all the pubs from Troon to Ayr
Grandfather's father would repair
With Bobby Burns, a drouthy pair,
      The glass to clink;
And oftenwhiles, when not too "fou,"
They'd roar a bawdy stave or two,
From midnight murk to morning dew,
      And drink and drink.

And Grandfather, with eye aglow
And proper pride, would often show
An old armchair where long ago
      The Bard would sit;
Reciting there with pawky glee
"The Lass that Made the Bed for Me;"
Or whiles a rhyme about a flea
      That ne'er was writ.

Then I would seek the Poet's chair
And plant my kilted buttocks there,
And read with joy the Bard of Ayr
      In my own tongue;
The Diel, the Daisy and the Louse
The Hare, the Haggis and the Mouse,
(What fornication and carouse!)
      When I was young.

Though Kipling, Hardy, Stevenson
Have each my admiration won,
Today, my rhyme-race almost run,
        My fancy turns
To him who did Pegasus prod
For me, Bard of my native sod,
The sinner best beloved of God—
        Rare Robbie Burns.

PORTRAIT

Painter, would you make my picture?
Just forget the moral stricture,
           Let me sit
With my belly to the table,
Swilling all the wine I'm able,
           Pipe a-lit;
Not a stiff and stuffy croaker
In a frock coat and a choker
           Let me be;
But a rollicking old fellow
With a visage ripe and mellow
           As you see.

Just a twinkle-eyed old codger,
And of death an artful dodger,
           Such I am;
I defy the Doc's advising
And I don't for sermonising
           Care a damn.
Though Bill Shakespeare had in his dome
Both——I'd rather wit than wisdom
           For my choice;
In the *glug glug* of the bottle,
As I tip it down my throttle,
           I rejoice.

Paint me neither sour nor soulful,
For I would not have folks doleful
                    When I go;
So if to my shade you're quaffing
I would rather see you laughing,
                    As you know.
In Life's Great Experiment
I'll have heaps of merriment
                    E're I pass;
And though devil beckon me,
And I've many a speck on me,
Maybe some will reckon me—
                    Worth a glass.

MY CENTENARIAN

A hundred years is a lot of living
I've often thought, and I'll know, maybe,
Some day if the gods are good in giving,
And grant me to turn the century.
Yet in all my eighty years of being
I've never known but one ancient man,
Who actively feeling, hearing, seeing,
Survived to beyond the hundred span.

Thinking? No, I don't guess he pondered;
He had the brains of a tiny tot,
And in his mind he so often wandered,
I doubted him capable of thought.
He hadn't much to think of anyway,
There in the village of his birth,
Painfully poor in a pinching penny-way,
And grimed with the soiling of Mother Earth.

Then one day motoring past his cottage,
The hovel in which he had been born,
I saw him supping a mess of pottage,
On the sill of the door, so frail forlorn.
Thinks I: I'll give him a joy that's thrilling,
A spin in my open Cadillac;
And so I asked him, and he was willing,
And I installed him there in the back.

Then I put the big bus through its paces,
A hundred miles an hour or more;
And he clutched at me with queer grimaces,
(He'd never been in a car before.)
The motor roared and the road was level,
The old chap laughed like an impish boy,
And as I drove like the very devil,
Darn him! he peed his pants with joy.

And so I crowned his long existence
By showing him how our modern speed
Easily can annihilate distance,
And answer to all our modern need.
And I went on my way but little caring,
Until I heard to my mild dismay,
His drive had thrilled him beyond all bearing . . .
The poor old devil!—*He died next day.*

WISTFUL

Oh how I'd be gay and glad
If a little house I had,
Snuggled in a shady lot,
With behind, a garden plot;
Simple grub, old duds to wear,
A book, a pipe, a rocking-chair . . .
You would never hear me grouse
If I had a little house.

Oh if I had just enough
Dough to buy the needful stuff;
Milk and porridge, toast and tea,
How contented I would be!
You could have your cake and wine,
I on cabbage soup would dine,
Joking to the journey's end—
Had I just enough to spend.

Oh had I no boss to please
I'd give thanks on bended knees;
Could I to myself belong,
I would fill the day with song.
Freedom's crust is sweeter far
Than control and caviare;
How my ragged hat I'd toss
If I didn't have a boss.

So you see my point of view,
But there's nothing I can do;
Oh the weariness of work,
Duties that I may not shirk.
Though simplicity I crave
I must go down to my grave,
Bossed by bullion, crossed by care—
Just a poor damn millionaire.

REFORMATION

I vowed my vices to give up
Ere I attained senility;
To much indulgence in the cup,
Or violent virility.
My appetite I would restrain
From everything I think that nice is:
In short, although it gave me pain
I'd jettison my favourite vices.

Alas! Deploringly I find,
Though I have run to eighty winters,
To toss the tankard I've no mind,
And closed my credit at the vintners.
A female leg is just a stem,
And with astringent eyes I see
Instead of me renouncing them,
My vices have deserted me.

And yet I make the pretty bluff
That I'm a most sagacious man,
Who knows when I have had enough
Of things that old folks ought to ban.
And looking at my shrivelled shanks
That led me off on many a spree,
I give my guardian angel thanks
My vices have abandoned *me*.

RETIRED

I used to sing, when I was young,
The joy of idleness;
But now I'm grey I hold my tongue,
For frankly I confess
If I had not some job to do
I would be bored to death;
So I must toil until I'm through
With this asthmatic breath.

Where others slothfully would brood
I beg for little chores,
To peel potatoes, chop the wood,
And even scrub the floors.
When slightly useful I can be,
I'm happy as a boy;
Dish-washing is a boon to me,
And brushing boots a joy.

The young folks tell me: "Grandpa, please,
Don't be so manual;
You certainly have earned your ease—
Why don't you rest a spell?"
Say I: "I'll have a heap of rest
On my sepulchral shelf;
So now please let me do my best
        To justify myself."

For one must strive or one will die,
And work's our dearest friend;
God meant it so, and that is why
I'll toil unto the end.
I thank the Lord I'm full of beans,
So let me heft a hoe,
And I will don my garden jeans
And help the beans to grow.

GRUMPY GRANDPA

Grand-daughter of the Painted Nails,
As if they had been dipped in gore,
I'd like to set you lugging pails
And make you scrub the kitchen floor.
I'm old and crotchety of course,
And on this point my patience fails;
I'd sue my old girl for divorce
If she showed up with painted nails.

Grand-daughter of the Painted Nails,
Like to a Jezebel are you;
Do you expect to snare the males
With talons of such bloody hue?
I could forgive your smudging lips,
Your scarlet cheek that powder veils,
But not your sanguine finger-tips . . .
Don't paw *me* with your painted nails.

Grand-daughter of the Painted Nails,
Were I the sire of maidens ten,
I'd curse them over hills and dales,
And hold them to the scorn of men
If they had claws of crimson dye;
Aye, though they sang like nightingales,
Unto the welkin I would cry:
"Avaunt, ye hags with Painted Nails!

WINDING WOOL

She'd bring to me a skein of wool
And beg me to hold out my hands;
So on my pipe I'd cease to pull
And watch her twine the shining strands
Into a ball so snug and neat,
Perchance a pair of socks to knit
To comfort my unworthy feet,
Or pullover my girth to fit.

As to the winding I would sway,
A poem in my head would sing,
And I would watch in dreamy way
The bright yarn swiftly slendering.
The best I liked were coloured strands;
I let my pensive pipe grow cool . . .
Two active and two passive hands,
So busy twining shining wool.

Alas! Two of those hands are cold,
And in these days of wrath and wrong,
I am so wearyful and old,
I wonder if I've lived too long.
So in my loneliness I sit
And dream of sweet domestic rule . . .
When gentle women used to knit,
And men were happy winding wool.

UNANIMOUS

They call me Old Unanimous
Because I never disagree;
In any argumentive fuss
I side with the majority;
Feeling I'm overage to fight
I find conciliation best,
And in the choice of left and right
I take the way that's easiest.

They see my enigmatic smile,
My folded hands, my face serene;
They little know that all the while
My mind incredibly is mean.
My heart's revolt they cannot guess,
As in my secret soul I cuss—
And yet I always answer: "Yes,
Consider me unanimous."

So when it comes to Yea and Nay
I'm always ready to agree;
It's so much simpler to obey
Than buck the family decree.
"Old Grandpa is so sweet," they say,
"So quick to click with all of us;
We love him well"—I grin: "Okay!
I reckon it's Unanimous."

A BUSY MAN

This crowded life of God's good giving
No man has relished more than I;
I've been so goldarned busy living
I've never had the time to die.
So busy fishing, hunting, roving,
Up on my toes and fighting fit;
So busy singing, laughing, loving,
I've never had the time to quit.

I've never been a one for thinking,
I've always been an action guy;
I've done my share of feasting, drinking,
And lots of wenching on the sly.
What all the blasted cosmic show meant,
I've never tried to understand;
I've always lived just for the moment,
And done the thing that came to hand.

And now I'll toddle to the garden
And light a good old Henry Clay.
I'm ninety odd, so Lord, please pardon
My frequent lapses by the way.
I'm getting tired; the sunset lingers;
The evening star serenes the sky;
The damn cigar burns to my fingers . . .
I guess . . . I'll take . . . time off . . . *to die.*

THE THINKER

Of all the men I ever knew
The thinkingest was Uncle Jim;
If there were any chores to do
We couldn't figure much on him.
He'd have a *thinking* job on hand,
And on the rocking-chair he'd sit,
And think and think to beat the band,
And snap his galuses and spit.

We kids regarded him with awe—
His beard browned by tobacco stains,
His hayseed hat of faded straw
That covered such a bunch of brains.
When some big problem claimed his mind
He'd wrestle with it for a fall;
But some solution he would find,
To be on hand for supper call.

A mute, inglorious Einstein he,
A rocking-chair philosopher;
I often wondered what, maybe,
His mighty meditations were.
No weighty work he left behind,
No words of wisdom or of wit;
Yet how I see him in my mind
Snap on his galuses and spit.

GROWING OLD

Somehow skies don't seem so blue
    As they used to be;
Blossoms have a fainter hue,
    Grass less green I see.
There's no twinkle in a star,
    Dawns don't seem so gold . . .
Yet, of course, I know they are:
    Guess I'm growing old.

Somehow sunshine seems less bright,
    Birds less gladly sing;
Moons don't thrill me with delight,
    There's no kick in Spring.
Hills are steeper now and I'm
    Sensitive to cold;
Lines are not so keen to rhyme . . .
    Gosh! I'm growing old.

Yet in spite of failing things
    I've no cause to grieve;
Age with all its ailing brings
    Blessings, I believe:
Kindo' gentles up the mind
    As the hope we hold
That with loving we will find
Friendliness in human kind,
    Grace in growing old.

RHYMES FOR RUE

DOMESTIC SCENE

The meal was o'er, the lamp was lit,
The family sat in its glow;
The Mother never ceased to knit,
The Daughter never slacked to sew;
The Father read his evening news,
The Son was playing *solitaire:*
If peace a happy home could choose
I'm sure you'd swear that it was there.

BUT

The Mother:

"Ah me! this hard lump in my breast . . .
Old Doctor Brown I went to see;
Because it don't give me no rest,
He fears it may malignant be.
To operate it might be well,
And keep the evil off awhile;
But oh the folks I dare not tell,
And so I sit and knit and smile."

The Father:

"The mortgage on the house is due,
My bank account is overdrawn;
I'm at my wit's end what to do—
I've plunged, but now my hope is gone.
For coverage my brokers call,
But I'm so deeply in the red . . .
If ever I should lose my all,
I'll put a bullet in my head."

The Daughter:

"To smile I do the best I can,
But it's so hard to act up gay.
My lover is a married man,
And now his child is on the way.
My plight I cannot long conceal,
And though I bear their bitter blame,
Unto my dears I must reveal
My sin, my sorrow and my shame."

The Son:

"Being a teller in a Bank
I'd no right in a blackjack game.
But for my ruin I must thank
My folly for a floozie dame.
To face the Manager I quail;
If he should check my cash I'm sunk . . .
Before they throw me into gaol
I guess I'd better do a bunk."

So sat they in the Winter eve
In sweet serenity becalmed,
So peaceful you could scarce believe
They shared the torments of the damned . . .
Yet there the Mother smiles and knits;
The Daughter sews white underwear;
The Father reads and smokes and spits,
While Sonny Boy plays *solitaire.*

MY SUICIDE

I've often wondered why
Old chaps who choose to die
In evil passes,
Before themselves they slay,
Invariably they
Take off their glasses?

As I strolled by the Castle cliff
An oldish chap I set my eyes on,
Who stood so singularly stiff
And stark against the blue horizon:
A poet fashioning a sonnet,
I thought—how rapt he labours on it!

And then I blinked and stood astare,
And questioned at my sight condition,
For I was seeing empty air—
He must have been an apparition.
Amazed I gazed . . . no one was there:
My sanity roused my suspicion.

I strode to where I saw him stand
So solitary in the sun—
Nothing! just empty sea and land,
No smallest sign of anyone.
While down below I heard the roar
Of waves, five hundred feet or more.

I had been drinking, I confess;
There was confusion in my brain,
And I was feeling more or less
The fumes of overnight champagne.
So standing on that dizzy shelf:
"You saw no one," I told myself.

"No need to call the local law,
For after all it's not your business.
You just imagined what you saw . . ."
Then I was seized with sudden dizziness:
For at my feet, beyond denying,
A pair of spectacles were lying.

And so I simply let them lie,
And sped from that accursed spot.
No lover of the police am I,
And sooner would be drunk than not.
"I'll scram," said I, "and leave the locals
To find and trace them dam bi-focals."

PRETENDERS

The Doctor thought, when David's health was failing,
Of duodenal ulcers he was ailing;
And so they opened him and found the answer:
His trouble was a case of kidney cancer;
And seeing operation would be vain,
The surgeon simply sewed him up again.

And so once more my husband's heart is stout,
For he believes they cut the evil out,
And pretty soon he will be fit and well.
I watch him tenderly, yet dare not tell
The truth to him, although I am his wife,—
That he has just a few more months of life.

A few more months of agony and sweat,
Of wistful wonder why he doesn't get
A little better with each passing day,
And why the gnawing pains won't go away.
It's only morphine gives him brief relief:
I smile and smile,—yet oh my heart of grief!

He makes believe that he is not so bad,
And plans a future sunshiny and glad;
But I can hear him sigh and sigh again:
"True happiness is not to suffer pain."
And so he tries to smile and act up brave,
The poor soul with one foot well in the grave.

I dare not tell, for if he only knew
The blackness of the rat that gnaws him through,
I know he'd mix some poison in a cup
And in his desperation drink it up . . .
Well, maybe if that brought him peace and rest,
It could be, yes it *would* be for the best.

I might prepare a deadly draught myself,
And leave it careless on the bedside shelf . . .
But no, though anguish may my bosom rend,
I'll watch him agonize unto the end.
So pity us, a poor pretending pair,
He with a heart of terror, I—despair.

THE WEDDING RING

I pawned my sick wife's wedding ring,
To drink and make myself a beast.
I got the most that it would bring,
Of golden coins the very least.
With stealth into her room I crept
And stole it from her as she slept.

I do not think that she will know,
As in its place I left a band
Of brass that has a brighter glow
And gleamed upon her withered hand.
I do not think that she can tell
The change—she does not see too well.

Pray God, she doesn't find me out.
I'd rather far I would be dead.
Yet yesterday she seemed to doubt,
And looking at me long she said:
"My finger must have shrunk, because
My ring seems bigger than it was."

She gazed at it so wistfully,
And one big tear rolled down her cheek.
Said she: "You'll bury it with me . . ."
I was so moved I could not speak.
Oh wretched me! How whisky can
Bring out the devil in a man!

And yet I know she loves me still,
As on the morn that we were wed;
And darkly guess I also will
Be doomed the day that she is dead.
And yet I swear, before she's gone,
I will retrieve her ring from pawn.

I'll get it though I have to steal,
Then when to ease her bitter pain
They give her sleep oh I will feel
Her hand and slip it on again;
Through tears her wasted face I'll see,
And pray to God: "Oh pity me!"

MURDERERS

He was my best and oldest friend.
I'd known him all my life.
And yet I'm sure towards the end
He knew I loved his wife,
And wonder, wonder if it's why
He came so dreadfully to die.

He drove his car at racing speed
And crashed into a tree.
How could he have so little heed?
A skilful driver he.
I think he must have found that day
Some love-letters that went astray.

I looked into the Woman's eyes
And there I saw she knew.
There was no shadow of surmise,—
For *her* himself he slew:
That he might leave her free to wed
The "me" she worshipped in his stead.

She whispered as she bade me go:
"I think he found us out."
And in her face the hate and woe
Was his revenge, no doubt.
Life cannot link us . . . though glad-green
His grave—*he stands between.*

BRETON WIFE

A Wintertide we had been wed
When Jan went off to sea;
And now the laurel rose is red
And I wait on the quay.
His berthing boat I watch with dread,
For where, oh where is he?

"Weep not, brave lass," the Skipper said;
"Return to you he will;
In hospital he lies abed
In Rio in Brazil;
But though I know he is not dead,
I do not know his ill."

The Seaman's Hospital I wrote,
And soon there came reply.
The nurse's very words I quote:
"Your husband will not die;
But you must wait a weary boat—
I cannot tell you why."

The months of sun went snailing by.
I wrote by every mail,
Yet ever came the same reply:
"Your patience must not fail.
But though your good lad will not die,
We cannot tell his ail."

*   *   *   *   *

Ten months have gone—he's back again,
But aged by years a score,
And tells me with a look of pain
He'll never voyage more;
And at the tide, with longing vain,
He stares from out the door.

And in his sleep he turns from me
And moans with bitter blame
Of Spanish jades beyond the sea
Who wrought him evil shame,
So ever in him bleak will be
The Ill That Has No Name.

LOBSTER FOR LUNCH

His face was like a lobster red,
His legs were white as *mayonnaise;*
"I've had a jolly lunch," he said,
That Englishman of pleasant ways.
"They do us well at our hotel:
In England food is dull these days."

"We had a big *langouste* for lunch.
I almost ate the whole of it.
And now I'll smoke and read my *Punch,*
And maybe siesta a bit;
And then I'll plunge into the sea
And get an appetite for tea."

We saw him plunge into the sea,
With jolly laugh, his wife and I.
"George does enjoy his food," said she;
"In Leeds lobsters are hard to buy.
How lucky we to have a chance
To spend our holidays in France!"

And so we watched him swim and swim
So far and far we scarce could see,
Until his balding head grew dim;
And then there came his children three,
And we all waited there for him,—
Ah yes, a little anxiously.

But George, alas! came never back.
Of him they failed to find a trace;
His wife and kids are wearing black,
And miss a lot his jolly face . . .
But oh how all the lobsters laugh,
And write in wrack his epitaph.

ALPINE HOLIDAY

He took the grade in second—quite a climb,
Dizzy and dangerous, yet how sublime!
The road went up and up; it curved around
The mountain and the gorge grew more profound.
He drove serenely, with no hint of haste;
And then she felt his arm go round her waist.

She shrank: she did not know him very well,
Being like her a guest at the hotel.
Nice, but a Frenchman. On his driving hand
He wore like benedicks a golden band . . .
Well, how could she with grace refuse a drive
So grand it made one glad to be alive?

Yet now she heard him whisper in her ear:
"Don't be afraid. With one hand I can steer,
With one arm hold you . . . Oh what perfect bliss!
Darling, please don't refuse me just one kiss.
Here, nigh to Heaven, let us rest awhile . . .
Nay, don't resist—give me your lips, your smile . . ."

So there in that remote and dizzy place
He wrestled with her for a moment's space,
Hearing her cry: "Oh please, please let me go!
Let me get out . . . You brute, release me! No, *no,*
    NO!"
. . . In the ravine was found their burnt-out car—
Their bodies trapped and crisped into a char.

BEAK-BASHING BOY

But yesterday I banked on fistic fame,
Figgerin' I'd be a champion of the Ring.
Today I've half a mind to quit the Game,
For all them rosy dreams have taken wing,
Since last night in a secondary bout
I let a goddam nigger knock me out.

It must have been that T-bone steak I ate;
They might have doped it, them smart gambling guys,
For round my heart I felt a heavy weight,
A stab of pain that should have put me wise.
But oh the cheering of the fans was sweet,
And never once I reckoned on defeat.

I had the nigger licked—twice he went down,
And there was just another round to go.
I played with him, I made him look a clown,
Yet he was game, and traded blow for blow.
And then that piston pain, the dark of doom . . .
Like meat they lugged me to my dressing-room.

So that's the pay-off to my bid for fame.
But yesterday my head was in the sky,
And now I slink and sag in sorry shame,
And hate to look my backers in the eye.
They think I threw the fight; I sorto' feel
The ringworms rate me for a lousy heel.

Oh sure I could go on—but gee! it's tough
To be a pork-and-beaner at the best;
To beg for bouts, yet getting not enough
To keep a decent feed inside my vest;
To go on canvas-kissing till I come
To cadge for drinks just like a Bowery bum.

Hell no! I'll slug my guts out till I die.
I'll be no bouncer in a cheap saloon.
I'll give them swatatorium scribes the lie,
I'll make a come-back, aye and pretty soon.
I'll show them tinhorn sports; I'll train and train,
I'll hear them cheer—oh Christ! the *pain*, the
      PAIN . . .

Stable-Boss:
"Poor punk! you're sunk—you'll never scrap again."

THE WIDOWER

Oh I have worn my mourning out,
And on her grave the green grass grows;
So I will hang each sorry clout
High in the corn to scare the crows.

And I will buy a peacock tie,
And coat of cloth of Donegal;
Then to the Farmer's Fair I'll hie
And peek in at the Barley Ball.

But though the fiddlers saw a jig
I used to foot when I was wed,
I'll walk me home and feed the pig,
And go a lonesome man to bed.

So I will wait another year,
As any decent chap would do,
Till I can think without a tear
Of her whose eyes were cornflower blue.

Then to the Harvest Ball I'll hie,
And I will wear a flower-sprigged vest;
For Maggie has a nut-brown eye,
And we will foot it with the best.

And if kind-minded she should be
To wife me—'tis the will of God . . .
But Oh the broken heart of me
For Her who lies below the sod!

158

SEA CHANGE

I saw a Priest in beetle black
Come to our golden beach,
And I was taken sore aback
Lest he should choose to preach
And chide me for my only wear,
A "Gee" string and a *brassière*.

And then I saw him shyly doff
And fold his grim *soutane,*
And one by one his clothes take off,
Until like any man
He stood in bathing trunks, a sight
To thrill a maiden with delight.

For he was framed and fashioned like
Apollo Belvedere;
I felt my heart like cymbal strike
Beneath my *brassière.*
And then the flounce of foam he broke,
And disappeared with flashing stroke.

We met. 'Twas in the billows roll.
Oh how he sang with joy;
But not a hymn,—a merry troll
With gusto of a boy.
I looked, and lo! the Priest was gone,
And in his place a laughing faun. . . .

Today confession I have made.
The Father's face was stern,
And I was glad that in the shade
Mine he could not discern . . .
He gave me grace—but oh the bliss,
The salty passion of his kiss!

THE HAT

In city shop a hat I saw
That so my fancy seemed to strike,
I gave my wage to buy the straw,
And make myself a one the like.

I wore it to the village fair;
Oh proud I was, though poor was I.
The maids looked at me with a stare,
The lads looked at me with a sigh.

I wore it Sunday to the Mass.
The other girls wore handkerchiefs.
I saw them darkly watch and pass,
With sullen smiles, with hidden griefs.

And then with sobbing fear I fled,
But they waylayed me on the street,
And tore the hat from off my head,
And trampled it beneath their feet.

I sought the Church; my grief was wild,
And by my mother's grave I sat:
. . . I've never cried for clay-cold child,
As I wept for that ruined hat.

MY PICTURE

I made a picture; all my heart
I put in it, and all I knew
Of canvas-cunning and of Art,
Of tenderness and passion true.
A worshipped Master came to see;
Oh he was kind and gentle, too.
He studied it with sympathy,
And sensed what I had sought to do.

Said he: "Your paint is fresh and fair,
And I can praise it without cease;
And yet a touch just here and there
Would make of it a masterpiece."
He took the brush from out my hand;
He touched it here, he touched it there.
So well he seemed to understand,
And momently it grew more fair.

Oh there was nothing I could say,
And there was nothing I could do.
I thanked him, and he went his way,
And then——I slashed my picture through.
For though his brush with soft caress
Had made my daub a thing divine,
Oh God! I wept with bitterness,
. . . It wasn't mine, it wasn't mine.

TWO GRAVES

First Ghost

To sepulchre my mouldy bones
I bought a pile of noble stones,
And half a year a sculptor spent
To hew my marble monument,
The stateliest to rear its head
In all this city of the dead.

And generations passing through
Will gape, and ask: What did he do
To earn this tomb so rich and rare,
In Attic grace beyond compare?
How was his life in honour spent,
To worthy this proud monument?

What did I do? Well, nothing much.
'Tis true I had the Midas touch.
A million pounds I made, wherewith
To glorify the name: John Smith;
Yet not a soul wept for me when
Death reft me from my fellow men.
My sculptor wins undying fame,
While I, who paid, am just a name.

Second Ghost

A wooden cross surveys my bones,
With on it stencilled: Peter Jones.
And round it are five hundred more;
(A proper job did old man War!)
So young they were, so fresh, so fit,
So hopeful—that's the hell of it.

The old are sapped and ripe to die,
But in the flush of Spring was I.
I might have fathered children ten,
To come to grips with sterling men;
And now a cross in weeds to rot,
Is all to show how fierce I fought.

The old default, the young must pay;
My life was wasted, thrown away.
While people gladden, to forget
The bitterness of vain regret,
With not a soul to mourn for me
My skull grins up in mockery.
. . . Pale crosses greet the grieving stars,
And always will be—War and Wars.

RHYMES FOR REVERENCE

SUPPOSE?

It's mighty nice at shut of day
With weariness to hit the hay,
To close your eyes, tired through and through,
And just forget that "you are you."

It's mighty sweet to wake again
When sunshine floods the window pane;
I love in cosy couch to lie,
And re-discover "I am I."

It would be grand could we conceive
A heaven in which to believe,
And in a better life to be,
Find out with joy "we still are we."

Though we assume with lapsing breath
Eternal is the sleep of death,
Would it not be divinely odd
To wake and find that—"God is God."

A LITTLE PRAYER

Let us be thankful, Lord, for little things—
The song of birds, the rapture of the rose;
Cloud-dappled skies, the laugh of limpid springs,
Drowned sunbeams and the perfume April blows;
Bronze wheat a-shimmer, purple shade of trees—
Let us be thankful, Lord of Life, for these!

Let us be praiseful, Sire, for simple sights;—
The blue smoke curling from a fire of peat;
Keen stars a-frolicking on frosty nights,
Prismatic pigeons strutting in a street;
Daisies dew-diamonded in smiling sward—
For simple sights let us be praiseful, Lord!

Let us be grateful, God, for health serene,
The hope to do a kindly deed each day;
The faith of fellowship, a conscience clean,
The will to worship and the gift to pray;
For all of worth in us, of You a part,
Let us be grateful, God, with humble heart.

WEARY

Some praise the Lord for Light,
    The living spark;
I thank God for the Night
    The healing dark.
When wearily I lie,
    With aching sight,
With what thanksgiving I
    Turn out the light!

When to night's drowsy deep
    Serene I sink,
How glad am I to sleep,
    To cease to think!
From care and fret set free,
    In sweet respite,
With joy I peacefully
    Turn out the light.

Lie down thou weary one,
    And sink to rest;
Nay, grieve not for the sun,
    The dark is best.
So greet with grateful breath
    Eternal Night,
When soft the hand of Death
    Turns out the light.

THE APE AND GOD

Son put a poser up to me
That made me scratch my head:
"God made the whole wide world," quoth he;
"That's right, my boy," I said.
Said Son: "He made the mountains soar,
And all the plains lie flat;
But Dad, what did he do before
                He did all that?"

Said I: "Creation was his biz;
He set the stars to shine;
The sun and moon and all that is
Were His unique design.
The Cosmos is his concrete thought,
The Universe his chore. . . ."
Said Son: "I understand, but what
                Did He before?"

I gave it up; I could not cope
With his enquiring prod,
And must admit I've little hope
Of understanding God.
Indeed I find more to my mind
The monkey in the tree
In whose crude form Nature defined
                Our human destiny.

Thought I: "Why search for Deity
In visionary shape?
'Twould better be if we could see
The angel in the ape.
Let mystic seek a God above:
Far wiser he who delves,
To find in kindliness and love
                    God in ourselves."

THE ANSWER

Bill has left his house of clay,
Slammed the door and gone away:
How he laughed but yesterday!

I had two new jokes to tell,
Salty, but he loved them well:
Now I see his empty shell.

Poker-faced he looks at me;
Peeved to miss them jokes—how he
Would have belly-laughed with glee!

He gives me the pip, I swear;
Seems just like he isn't there:
Flown the coop—I wonder where?

Bill had no belief in "soul";
Thought the body was the whole,
And the grave the final goal.

Didn't reckon, when we pass,
This old carcase maybe has
Spirit that sneaks out like gas.

"Look here, Bill, I'm asking you
What's the Answer? Tell me true:
Is death the end of all we do?

"Hand me out the dope—are we
No more than monkeys on a tree?"
. . . And then I swear to God I see
Bill bat an eye and—wink at me.

THANKFULNESS

"God is so good to me," I said,
As with the golden dawn I rose.
"How can poor people lie abed
When all the land with gladness glows?"
Then drinking deep of air like wine,
And listening to winged delight,
And gazing wide with eyes ashine
On beauty that bewitched my sight,
I thanked the Lord who granted me
His gift of loveliness to see.

I give thanks for my daily bread
And appetite to savour it,
The cosy roof above my head,
My body marvellously fit.
I give thanks for the sea and sky,
And stars and trees and linnet wings;
I bless the Lord that I am I,
And part of all the sum of things.
I'm thankful for the boon of breath,
And will be to the door of death.

So let me hold the bright belief,
Despite the blight of greying days,
And pain and poverty and grief,
That Gratitude is prayer and praise.
And though I love and cherish them,
Of all the virtues I possess,
(Alas! too few)—I count the gem,
The crown of all is Thankfulness.
So let my last lip-falter be:
"Dear God, how you've been good to me!"

NEGRESS IN NOTRE DAME

When I attended Mass today
A coloured maid sat down by me,
And as I watched her kneel and pray,
Her reverence was good to see.
For whether there may be or no'
A merciful and mighty God,
The love for Him is like a glow
That glorifies the meanest clod.

And then a starched and snotty dame
Who sat the other side of me
Said: "Monsieur, is it not a shame
Such things should be allowed to be?
In my homeland, I'm proud to say,
We know to handle niggers right,
And wouldn't let a black wench pray
And worship God beside a white."

Her tone so tart bewildered me,
For I am just a simple man.
A friend in every one I see,
Though yellow, brown or black and tan.
For I would father children five
With any comely coloured maid,
And lush with any man alive,
Of any race, of any shade.

Religion may be false or true,
The Churches may be wrong or right,
But if there be the Faith in you
It can be like a shining light.
And though I lack not piety
And pray my best, I'm sure that God
To that black wench and not to me
Would give his most approving nod.

Aye, you may scrub him day and night,
You'll never change a nigger's hide;
But maybe he is just as white,
(Or even more) than you . . . inside.

MY GUARDIAN ANGEL

When looking back I dimly see
The trails my feet have trod,
Some hand divine, it seems to me,
Has pulled the strings with God;
Some angel form has lifeward leaned
When hope for me was past;
Some love sublime has intervened
To save me at the last.

For look you! I was born a fool,
Damnation was my fate;
My lot to drivel and to drool,
Egregious and frustrate.
But in the deep of my despair,
When dark my doom was writ,
Some saving hand was always there
To pull me from the Pit.

A Guardian Angel—how absurd!
I scoff at Power Divine.
And yet . . . a someone spoke the word
That willed me from the swine.
And yet, despite my scorn of prayer,
My lack of love or friend,
I know a Presence will be there,
To save me at the end.

FREETHINKER

Although the Preacher be a bore,
The Atheist is even more.

I ain't religious worth a damn;
My views are reckoned to be broad;
And yet I shut up like a clam
When folks get figgerin' on God;
I'd hate my kids to think like me,
And though they leave me in the lurch,
I'm always mighty glad to see
    My fam'ly trot to Church.

Although of books I have a shelf
Of sceptic stuff, I must confess
I keep their knowledge to myself:
Doubt doesn't help to happiness.
I never scoff at Holy Writ,
But envy those who hold it true,
And though I've never been in it
    I'm proud to own a pew.

I always was a doubting Tom;
I guess some lads are born that way.
I couldn't stick religion from
The time I broke the Sabbath Day.
Yet unbelief's a bitter brew,
And this in arid ways I've learned;
If you *believe a thing,* it's true
    As far as you're concerned.

I'm sentimental, I agree,
For how it always makes me glad
To turn from Ingersoll and see
My little girls Communion-clad.
And as to church my people plod
I cry to them with simple glee:
"Say, folks, if you should talk to God,
Put in a word for me."

DIVINE DETACHMENT

One day the Great Designer sought
His Clerk of Birth and Death.
Said he: "Two souls are in my thought,
To whom I gave life-breath.
I deemed my work was fitly done,
But yester-eve I saw
That in the finished brain of one
There was a tiny flaw.

"It worried me, and I would know,
Since I am all to blame,
What happened to them down below,
Of honour or of shame;
For if the latter did befall,
My sorrow will be grave . . ."
Then numbers astronomical
Unto the Clerk he gave.

The Keeper of the Rolls replied:
"Of them I've little trace;
But one he was a Prince of Pride,
And one of lowly race.
One was a Holy Saint proclaimed;
For one no hell sufficed. . . .
Let's see—the last was Nero named,
The other . . . Jesus Christ."

OUR DAILY BREAD

"Give me my daily bread."
It seems so odd,
When all is done and said,
This plea to God.
To pray for cake might be
The thing to do;
But bread, it seems to me,
Is just our due.

"Give me my daily toil,"
I ought to say—
(If from life's cursed coil
I'd time to pray.)
Give me my daily sweat,
My body sore,
So that bread I may get
To toil for more.

"Give me my daily *breath*,"
Though half a sob,
Until untimely death
Shall end my job.
A crust for my award,
I cry in dread:
"Grant unto me, Oh Lord,
My daily bread!"

L'ENVOI

"Alas! my songs have ceased to sell,"
Bemoaned a brother bard;
To me his words were like a knell,
Inexorably hard.
For well I know the day is nigh
When Time will toll the bell,
And people will no longer buy
The songs I have to sell.

To barter books for bread, thought I,
I have no pressing need;
I do not care if folks will buy,
So long as they will read.
No more, I said, I'll fash my head
With dollars or with pence;
But I would go before I know
Mankind's indifference.

For O I've loved my puny pen
Beyond all human tie!
My life I give to it and when
It fails me I will die.
So like a child, each precious night,
Indulgence I implore;
Praying: "O God! please let me write
                    Just one book more."

RHYMES OF A REBEL

CONTENTS

SYLVAN SONGS

WHIMSICALITIES

POEMS OF PEOPLE

PRELUDE

I've little time to talk with men,
  For I must talk to trees;
Or blades of grass, or blossoms when
  They frolic in the breeze.
I worship sun and sea and sky,
  And with a simple mind,
I've so much love for Nature I
  Have little for mankind.

The radio I rarely hear,
  To tell me noisome things;
For I am more concerned, I fear,
  With brooks and linnet wings.
I try to make myself believe
  Delight is everywhere;
And garden-walled I little grieve
  Man-made despair.

I must confess I'm worry-shy,
  Content with gentle joy;
With books and dogs and roses I
  My borrowed time employ.
No social worth have I to give;
  To Nature I belong . . .
So Friends, forget!—Please let me live
          Life out in Song.

RHYMES FOR REBELS

A FRENCHMAN SPEAKS

In World War One my father died;
A famous patriot was he.
"I fall that France may rise!" he cried,
Or some such imbecility.
He went keyed up to battle pitch;
We waited till a comrade said
He saw Dad lying in a ditch,
     And minus was his head.

I had to fight in World War Two,
And went like all with heavy heart;
For our unfitness well we knew,
And we were beaten from the start.
I was a prisoner of war,
But though I live I do not bless
The country of my fathers for
     I have a leg the less.

My son will fight in World War Three;
(Oh! Could I only take his place!)
A butchered victim he may be
Of lust for power and hate of race.
They're training him for battle now,
And as my boy is all to me,
To dictature I'd sooner bow
     Than him blood-boltered see.

For in an age of sordid shames,
When tyrants throw the devil's dice,
Honour and glory are but names,
And we poor *bougres* pay the price.
No longer patriots are we;
The days of sacrifice are sped;
Slaughter is worse than slavery:
How cheap a hero—dead!

NORMANDY PEASANT

They've taken all my fields of corn
  To make them strips of strife;
They've razed the house where I was born
  And lived in all my life.
Where once I jolted with content
  Along deep rutted lanes,
They've straddled runways of cement
  To ground their aeroplanes.

They've made me sell my bit of land
  And paid me with their gold.
Alas, they could not understand
  It was my heart I sold.
From my beloved soil bereft
  It was my soul I gave,
And now I know there's nothing left
  Between me and the grave.

They say that progress must go on
  Though darkly glooms the Pit.
Ah well, my life is nearly gone
  And I am glad of it.
They buy my land and millions spend
  To sponsor war's red woe,
And what will be the awful end
  Thank God! I'll never know.

4

For oh the world is in a mess,
   And day by day grows worse;
I've had my bid of happiness
   And now I know the Curse
Of monstrous might and speed that's blind,
   And see, as fails my breath,
The doom of martyred humankind,
   When Science mates with Death.

VOLUNTEER

Upon a rimed and rocky road
  Beneath an evil sky
I met a lilting lad who strode
  With laughter in his eye.
Said I: "My boy, why do you sing
  When birds bide under wing?"

Said he: "I sing because I go
  To palms and golden sun,
To subjugate a rebel foe
  With bayonet and gun.
Tomorrow I'll be on the sea—
  That's why I sing," quoth he.

Said I: "I know that silver land,
  Its skies of blinding blue,
Its maidens waiting wreath in hand
  To give their lips to you."
Said he: "Their kisses I'll forego
  Until we rout the foe."

Said I: "You may meet up with doom:
  Far better linger here."
He laughed: "I leave a sky of gloom
  For one of love and cheer.
Besides, in wars not one in ten
  Are killed of fighting men."

And now this morning in the Press
  His laughing face I see.
It gives me pain, I must confess—
  Just "*Mort pour la Patrie.*"
. . . No kiss for him beneath the sun:
  From ten Death chose the ONE.

EUROPEAN CONSCRIPT

I am not patriotic worth a damn;
Most governments I think a bloody mess.
My country I detest, yet here I am,
Entrapped and togged up in her warrior dress;
Supposed to be a killer, more or less.

The swine who rule us claim they have the right
To take our lives and use them at their need;
To force us for invested funds to fight,
To sacrifice us to imperial greed:
In name of nationality to bleed.

Hell! I believe my life is mine alone,
My property to do with as I will.
No Power shall seize it and no State shall own
Me mind and soul, and send me forth to kill:
No so-called enemy my blood shall spill.

I do not love my native land of fog
And cold and damp and wind and ruthless rain,
Where I have played the part of underdog,
Trying three times to emigrate—in vain:
To break away from poverty and pain.

My life's my own, I say; none have the right
To rive it from me, barter it for death.
I know I'm trapped, but if in foreign fight
I fall in "glory"—canting shibboleth!
I'll curse my country with my dying breath.

8

THE MARSHAL
(1951)

The Marshal now is very old,
Wellnigh a hundred, I am told.
Gallieni, Joffre, Foch have gone,
Yet stubbornly he lingers on,
Writing his Memoirs, so they say. . . .
Oh! Will he tell us of the day,
With all our love at his command
      He shook a felon's hand!

Let History appraise his blame,
Judge if he played a traitor's game—
My mind goes back to that dark day
I fought in Verdun's bloody fray
And saw the cannon-fodder tossed
Into its hideous holocaust;
Until one regiment went red
      And from the battle fled.

They say that from a thousand men
The Marshal picked out one in ten,
And ruthlessly, upon the spot,
He lined them up and had them shot;
And then to certain doom he sent
The remnant of the regiment. . . .
Well, maybe what he did was right,
      For soldiers have to fight.

The Marshal, with a single breath,
Could launch ten thousand men to death,
And for some questionable gain
Would carpet sunny fields with slain.
And now a dotard in his cell,
Undaunted by no earthly hell,
Maybe he sees, when memory jogs,
    The boys he shot like dogs.

Yet not the Marshal's be the blame
For all the shambles and the shame;
Let us all share the blood guilt for
In greed and jealousy is War;
And let us dream a golden time
When pride of race be held a crime,
And freedom's flag in peace unfurled
    Proclaim ONE WORLD.

THE PADRE

Oh! I'll remember till I die
That lad upon the battle field;
He lay stark staring at the sky,
And though I was to slaughter steeled,
Sadly I stooped and closed his eyes,
So blue, so blinded with surprise.

Of bloody wound I saw no trace;
His rifle he was holding tense;
There was no horror in his face,
Just terrible indifference.
So waxen white and cold it was,
A marble peace in battle pause.

And beautiful! I never knew
A lad with such bright hair of gold,
With eyes so utter in their blue,
A face so cast in classic mould.
I've buried many, but that one
Haunts me—he might have been my son.

I was to horror calloused then,
And battle memories are dim,
Yet 'mid a host of martyred men
Somehow I most remember him:
A father's pride, a mother's joy,
A poor, bewildered, butchered boy.

Well, bone is brittle, blood is red;
A flag's a rag when all is said.

LET US BELIEVE
(1950)

Let us thank God for this translucent time,
This chrystal tide of peace beyond two wars,
When we can hear the bells of beauty chime,
And build our homes anew and lick our scars.
Let us give praise for each dawn-birth of joy,
Each day in sunniness serenely spent;
Let no dark boding grievously annoy
Our quietude and trouble our content.

Let us not seek to weigh our happiness,
But take the moment for its passing worth;
Let no dark memories of strain and stress
Come now between us and our easy mirth.
Let us be one with happy, heedless things,
With lisping leaves and singing mountain rills,
Green fire of ferns, and lilting linnet wings,
Delight in children's eyes—and daffodils.

Let us forget our memories of War,
And in this gentling interlude of peace
Take hope and comfort from the joys that are,
And hold the humble hope of their increase.
Let no fear of the future bring dismay;
Let no pain of the past our gladness grieve,
But with our hearts high-heavened let us say:
"There will be no more wars—*believe, BELIEVE.*"

I BELIEVE

It's my belief that every man
    Should do his share of work,
And in our economic plan
    No citizen should shirk.
That in return each one should get
    His meed of fold and food,
And feel that all his toil and sweat
    Is for the common good.

It's my belief that every chap
    Should have an equal start,
And there should be no handicap
    To hinder his depart;
That there be fairness in the fight,
    And justice in the race,
And every lad should have the right
    To win his proper place.

It's my belief that people should
    Be neither rich nor poor;
That none should suffer servitude,
    And all should be secure.
That wealth is loot, and rank is rot,
    And foul is class and clan;
That to succeed a man may not
    Exploit his brother man.

It's my belief that heritage
  And usury are wrong;
That each should win a worthy wage
  And sing an honest song. . . .
Not one like this—for though I rue
  The wrong of life, I flout it.
Alas! I'm not prepared to do
  A goddam thing about it.

PATERNITY

When I was very young and gay
    And raffish life I led,
I put Jill in the family way,
    And so we had to wed.
But now my life's a fear and fret
    For we've a brood of five,
And I will have to toil and sweat
    So long as I'm alive.

And that's the way we lads are caught
    And nevermore win free;
'Twere better far to toss the pot
    And leave the lassies be.
There may be in a lush of ale
    A headache for a day,
But matrimony can entail
    An aching head for aye.

The hell of it's they hold your heart,
    Them kiddies you gave breath;
To let them have a decent start
    You slave yourself to death.
And are they grateful? I'll say no:
    To hearth-fires of their own
With haste self-seekingly they go
    And leave you all alone.

So Sons of Sweat, forbear to breed;
　　Just leave it to the Rich;
Your boy in brutal war may bleed,
　　Your girl may be a bitch.
And though like other stiffs you mate,
　　Thank Heaven for its grace,
You've no need to perpetuate
　　This lousy human race.

HIS POINT OF VIEW

It is the fate of man to fight,
It is the doom of man to die.
Let heroes battle for the Right—
I'm just an ordinary guy;
I battle for my daily bread,
I fight for shelter overhead.

You can't expect a bloke to bleed
On foreign soil—or croak at worst.
I have a wife and kids to feed,
And to my thinking they come first:
If it breaks up my home I'm not—
Blast me! a bloody patriot.

For flag and freedom! Common coves
Like us scarce know what freedom means.
That's okay for the High Aboves
Who push us round and grab the beans.
They've got us haltered, muzzled too:
There ain't a thing that we can do.

For home and country! After all
It's just an accident of birth
That makes a Teuton or a Gaul—
We're all made up of common earth;
With common virtues, common sins,
We're all the same beneath our skins.

A fitter in an engine shop
With oily hands is all I am;
And yet I'll toil until I drop
To buy my kids their lick of jam;
And I'm as happy as can be
To tinker with machinery.

And so to me it don't seem right
To send us working stiffs to fight;
When governments get in a mess—
To clean the muck up, more or less. . . .
Thank God I'll soon be fifty for
I'll be too old to die in War.

THE PRINCE

In uniform they deck me out,
    Pin medals on my chest;
With braid of gold beyond a doubt
    I shine above the best.
They set me on a splendid steed,
    Salute me as they pass,
Who never did a gallant deed,
    And should bestride an ass.

Today an Admiral I am;
    Tomorrow I will be
A General, a sorry sham
    Whom thousands cheer to see.
Although a plane I never flew,
    Bright wings of flight I wear,
And radiant pilots I review
    As Marshal of the Air.

I spout the speeches that they write,
    As if from my own pen;
And though I don't know how to fight
    I rant to fighting men
And yet, perhaps, I too am brave
    In my submissive way,
And personally do not crave
    The role I play.

Of pageantry I am a part,
  And to its pattern fit;
Yet oh how in my humble heart
  I loathe the farce of it!
A Royal Varlet, I obey,
  And may no choice evince . . .
Yet how I curse the bitter day
  That I was born—a Prince.

LABOUR LEADER

Bill Smith came cadging for our vote and swore he'd
    treat us fair,
And standin' in a pub he stood the drinks:
But now he's William Smith, M.P., he gives us
    blokes the air;
He's just another windbag and he stinks.
He's just another stuffed shirt in a lousy bunch of
    bums,
A-sticken' out his tummy like a toff;
But let the blighter wait until the next election comes,
We'll show him ruddy well where he gets off.

What suckers are we working stiffs, to hoist a man
    on high,
So that we're just a door-mat for his feet;
But yesterday Bill palled with us, but now he's labour
    shy
And hates ter reckernize us in the street.
And that's the way wi' most o' em when once they
    gets the job
To represent us in the Parliament.
They do not care a tinker's cuss—Bill wouldn't spare
    a bob
To save me bein' chucked out for the rent.

To hell wi' governments, say I, and all the cantin'
    crew
Wot seeks to steer the leaky ship o' state.
They push us round like cattle an' there's nuthin'
    we can do,
We've handed them our freedom on a plate.
By Cripes! I'll never vote again and play the silly
    fool;
I'll give no man the right to master *me*.
We'll have no need for rulers when we hail the Golden
    Rule
In the universal reign of liberty. . . .
Ha! Ha! Oh when, if ever, it will be.

GOD'S GRACE

"The poor," you say, "are so uncouth".
    Well, many of them are.
They did not, like you, live their youth
    Beneath a kindly star.
They were not gently born and bred,
    From families refined. . . .
Yet e'en as yours their blood is red,
    Their hearts are kind.

You say that they are coarse and crude;
    They eat peas with a knife,
Inhale their soup, their ways are rude,
    You shudder from their life.
Yet but for accident of birth
    You might have been as they,
Your porcelain of common earth,
    Your china—clay.

Is it not that by God's good grace
    You were not hovel born?
You might have grovelled in the place
    Of grimy men you scorn;
You might have worn a singlet torn
    And scratched a lousy itch,
And swung a pick with hands of horn
    Deep in a ditch.

You might have . . . Well, I saw today
    My drain-digger do that;
And to him, bent and badger-grey,
    I doffed my Homburg hat;
For though I have no pride of race
    Like hell it haunted me
To think that—but for heaven's grace
    I might be he.

OPPORTUNITY

Because I ply a pawky pen
　　And rhyme's a bonny trade,
I pity brother minstrel men
　　Who fail to make the grade.
Because a lucky lot I drew
　　And live in lyric France,
I'm sorry for the fellows who
　　Have never had a chance.

A pasty shambler of the slums
　　I might as well have been,
My lips of music stricken dumb
　　By duties dark and mean.
E'en had I been a Burns or Keats,
　　With pallid brats to cling,
How could I from the sordid streets
　　Have had the heart to sing?

They say that Opportunity
　　Knocks once on every door:
I question it—although for me
　　It's tapped a-many more.
It oft' forgets, and that is why
　　I cry: "For pity's sake,
God help the guys as good as I
　　Who never—get a—break".

REBEL ANGEL

If ever I am angel bright
　　With golden wings to fit,
I'll pluck from one a feather light
　　And make a pen of it;
And write a verse of nobler worth
　　Than I composed on earth.

What shall it be? I do not know—
　　But not of radiant Heaven;
Rather of weariness and woe,
　　Of earth-folk downward driven;
Of ruthless martyrdom of man,
　　Since human life began.

Of those first children of the night
　　In caves of bitter bale,
Who fought their way up to the Light,
　　Through filth and cold and ail;
Whose depth of pain was all their measure,
　　And lack of pain their pleasure.

Our ancestors who knew not tears
　　And had no heart for grief;
Who thought old age was thirty years,
　　And bore beyond belief
A suffering that men today
　　Seek morphine to allay.

And unto HIM who rules on high,
    Whose face I may not see,
With indignation I would cry:
    "Why had this blight to be?
Aeons of agony to pass
    Till champagne brim the glass!"

Then would the Lord of Heaven say:
    "Why should this bard rebel?"
And send me downward straight away
    To plumb the depths of hell.
But I would rather languish there
    Than know in Paradise despair
For all the darkness and the dearth,
    The Hell of sons of Earth.

WAGE SLAVE

Somehow he irritated me,
That shabby chap so old and grey,
Who threw plump pebbles in the sea,
Hour after hour, day after day,
Throughout the fortnight of his stay.

So wistfully he sought my eye,
And then one morn he spoke to me:
"Mister, no doubt you wonder why
I throw them pebbles in the sea?
It makes me feel a boy," says he.

"I've dreamed o' this through all my life;
A mucky collier lad I be;
Living in sweat and slummy strife,
I've never stood beside the sea . . .
God! but it's clean and fresh and free."

He left next day. How he was sad!
And now 'tis I with boyish glee,
Who pitch round pebbles—oh so glad
To end my days beside the sea;
And wonder if that pitman shy
Was not a poet more than I?

RESENTMENT

A man's a mug to slog away
   And stint himself of ease,
When bureaucrats take half his pay
   To glut their treasuries.
A guy's a dope to work like hell
   To make one dollar two,
When most of it will go to swell
   The fiscal revenue.

So you who gripe at super-tax
   Of sixty-five per cent,
Why don't you blissfully relax,
   And beat the government?
Cut down to half the work you do,
   Contrive on less to live:
Go easy on the job and you
   Will have less gain to give.

Just plumb refuse to slave and sweat;
   Forbear to do your best,
When only half your wage you get
   And taxes claim the rest.
Although your talents go to rust,
   Your usefulness abate. . . .
Why make an extra dollar just
   To give it to the State?

If I possessed a million I
   Would change it all to gold,
And in a safe my bedside nigh
   My treasure I would hold.
And though a tenth each year I spent,
   I'd live in leisure lax
On capital—Oh! So content
   To bilk the income tax!

NINETEEN NINETY-NINE

Dire New Year's Eve—a Century is near
Its agonizing, unlamented death;
A hundred years of fortitude and fear,
Of devastation and distressful breath,
Racked by world wars, the last four-fold the worst:
'Tis passing now—a Century accurst.

And sitting by my dying fire tonight
I think: O what a woeful world this is!
I've seen the rise and fall of Russian might,
The crash of dictatures and dynasties:
When each new moon was millioning the dead
I've borne the Teuton terror and the Red.

Yet no salvation for mankind I see;
The devil-men have swayed this world too long;
Mankind will ever struggle to be free,
And right will never triumph over wrong.
(How I recall with nauseating shock
The horror of the Nazi midnight knock!)

Nature is beautiful and mostly kind,
And yet with war a curt decade away
I see a rancid race, embittered, blind,
In lands of desolation and decay;
I see a Century that dies in pain
From languishing of anarchy's red reign.

Life is a mystery and will always be;
The destiny of Man is dawnless death.
No hope of human brotherhood I see,
One world, one race, one rule—waste not your breath!
We have unleashed dark demons of unruth:
We die of too much knowledge, too much truth.

In ignorance is happiness, a cot
Is richer than the palace of a king;
The brutish peasant in his lowly lot
Should be the object of our envying:
Back to the soil—our pride shall end in this:
The path of progress leads to the abyss.

The span from fruitfulness to frightfulness
Is just the echo of a tyrant's word.
Tonight a *siécle* of dark distress
Is dying—O have mercy on us, Lord!
Be Peace Thy very name, if God Thou be,
And in our hearts, this new-born Century
May there reign Justice, Love, Humility!

SONGS FROM SEVILLE

THE FOUNTAIN

Alphonzo Rex a fountain grand
   Set in his garden rare;
But round it secret jets he planned
   To spout into the air.
And while his guests about it stood
   In raiment gay and rich,
Alphonzo Rex in festive mood
   Would turn a switch.

And then each jet of silver spray
   Up from the path would spurt,
And every lady in dismay
   Would clutch a silken skirt.
Of course the royal joker was
   Profuse in his regret,
And all the dames would shriek because
   Their pants were wet.

Such is the legend that the guide
   Will tell to me and you,
If in Seville you chance to bide,
   A week or haply two.
But when the merry fountain sprayed,
   The joke I failed to see;
For as I gazed the dam guide played
   That trick on me.

34

TIME'S TYRRANY

The spires of the Escurial
    Leap lovely to the sky,
And in pride immemorial
    Time's tyrrany defy;
While down in darkness boreal
    The Kings and Consorts lie.

Their marble tombs are white as snow,
    And fine like sculptured lace;
And yet, each carven lid below,
    With grinning skull for face,
Are skeletons that stink, I know,
    Despite their royal race.

We tourists stopped to stand and stare,
    And while the guide extolled,
Within that human frigidaire
    The French dame, camisoled
Too flimsily, went green I swear,
    Goose-puckered with the cold.

I shivered too, but not with chill;
    I thought of all that line
Of Mighty Majesties so still,
    Of skeletons supine,
Whose skulls grin up—even as will
    In due course—yours and mine.

COLUMBUS

In this Cathedral of Seville,
    Beneath a dizzy dome,
I saw three washer-women kneel
    And scrub the flags to foam.
With mop and pail they laboured where
    A Tomb was towering high,
And shocked by their flipacious air
    To them said I:

"Fair dames, in a Genoa slum
    A weaver's boy was born,
Who from his father's loom would run,
    Dream-driven and forlorn.
To dockland gutter he would stray,
    And stare and stare to sea,
As if he knew beyond it lay
    His Destiny".

"This weaver's boy," I told the three,
    "Died in Valladolid.
Afar from his beloved sea
    A broken heart he hid.
And now in languorous Seville,
    In rich cathedral gloom,
We Western pilgrims come to kneel
    Before his Tomb."

36

The washer-women scrubbed away
    As if I were a bore.
"American!" I heard them say,
    And sloshed the marble floor.
While in that proud Tomb lay the bones
    Of one of mighty fame;
And yet I'll bet these lousy crones
    Knew not his name.

ESCAPIST

Among the tourists I alone
    Now stand in silence where
Upon this altar step of stone
    Columbus knelt in prayer.
Before this very shrine he bent,
    By this same virgin blest,
E'er yet he made a Continent
    His golden quest.

Now nigh five centuries have gone:
    New York and New Orleans,
Chicago, Pittsburgh, Washington
    Surpass his wildest dreams.
Detroit, Seattle, Hollywood,
    Milwaukee and St. Paul
Exceed his hopes, but oh how good
    To scram from all!

Columbus, Man of Destiny,
    Revealed a region vast.
A pilgrim of romance I be,
    Discovering the Past. . . .
Though of the New World long a part,
    Because I love you best,
Old World, to you with hungry heart
    I come for Rest.

GOYA

As in Bordeaux I took the air
    An ancient house I passed,
And someone told me it was there
    That Goya breathed his last.
Adrift from his beloved Spain,
    The splendour of his day,
In twilight penitence and pain
    He passed away.

In peasant hovel he was born,
    And to the bull-ring rose,
Killing with insolence and scorn
    His *toros,* I suppose.
With gutter drabs no stucco saint,
    By courtly dames adored,
His right-hand held a brush to paint,
    His left a sword.

See in the Prado in Madrid
    A picture on the wall;
Grotesques and satires Goya did,
    But this out-horrors all.
A naked girl a monster dread
    Is clutching in his claws,
And blindly chewing off her head
    With bloody jaws.

In all the world there is, I swear,
   No picture more obscene;
One wonders in what dark despair
   The painter's mind had been.
What brain diseased could thus conceive?—
   Yet I forgive him for
In hellish horror, I believe,
   It symbols WAR.

DON JUAN

Sweet Stranger, stand upon this stone
        And pray for me,
Who pitifully would atone
        My perfidy.
Who did such evil in his day
        To maid and man:
Kind pilgrim, on this tombstone pray
        For Don Juan.

Thus read I on an ancient slab
        By hospice door,
Whose walls with poverty were drab,
        Whose roof was hoar.
And in its halls so vast and bare,
        Each on a bed,
A hundred ancients, crushed with care,
        Were gnawing bread.

Their cheeks were hollow, dim their eyes;
        They coughed and coughed.
While some just stared with sad surmise,
        Some *berets* doffed.
Two priceless pictures starred the wall,
        By Masters done,
Proclaiming that Death comes to all,
        And spareth none.

Like animals these men await
    Death's final grace,
While others bide beyond the gate
    To take their place.
Such is the charity of one
    Who in his span
Much evil did beneath the sun—
    Poor Don Juan!

EL TORO

Green mountains reared against the sky,
And tranquil as a herd of cows,
With horsemen nonchalantly nigh
I saw a hundred bulls a-browse.
In supple strength and pride they grazed,
And life was simple, sweet and full;
With placid peace their eyes were glazed—
         How good to be a bull!

But one outstood beyond the rest,
With inky dewlaps, orange eyes;
High-horned and rampant for the test
Of red revolt and sacrifice.
So from the herd they cut him out,
And following a pilot ox
They harried him with goad and shout
         Into a dung-deep box.

Then in that dark and narrow pen
He stood a week of dreary days,
While taunted by down-peering men
He yearned for brother bulls a-graze:
Hoof-loose in God's green spaciousness,
The purity of hill and plain,
The dewy dawn, the breeze caress . . .
         Ah, liberty again!

A door swung wide—with horn up-fling
He hurtles to the happy light.
Rapture! Then in a sandy ring
He halts, bewildered at the sight:
Tier upon tier, from sand to sky,
Of gloating faces, glad and grim;
Full fifty thousand poised on high,
                    Their vision fixed on him.

Red rags before his eyes they flaunt,
Till mad with rage, but unafraid,
He hurls his passion to the taunt
And scars the crimson barricade.
With lance and dart his heart they break;
Blood-boltered there he stands alone;
Yet I for hopeless valour's sake
                    Would set him on a throne.

Would place him far above them all . . .
His blood now mingles with his breath;
Upon his knees I see him fall,
As dauntlessly he waits for death. . . .
Oh! Spain, to heaven high you stink!
And as I take the car to town,
A dame, American, I think,
                    Pukes on her satin gown.

MATADOR

Unless there is a lot of goring
I always find a bull-fight boring.

Lopez, the famous Mexican,
   Was starring in Madrid,
And mobs acclaimed that mighty man
   For daring deeds he did.
His tunic braid was primrose gold,
   His pants were lily white,
As round the sanded ring he strolled,
   A dazzle to the sight.

But haply in a thousand fights
   A matador may slip;
With women, wine and hectic nights
   His hand may lose its grip.
So as he dealt the lethal blow
   The bull lunged out once more,
And Lopez, pride of Mexico
   Was mingled with its gore.

A pretty maid from U.S.A.
   Was sitting by my side,
And as they bore the man away
   Right bitterly she cried.
She sobbed to see a Mexican
   Who round the ringside struts,
Be carried forth, a dying man,
   A horn-thrust in his guts.

'Twas sad to view—then suddenly
   She laughed and laughed aloud;
Aye, she betrayed a wanton glee
   Before that grieving crowd.
"I'm glad to see him killed!" she cried;
   "It's such a devil's game!" . . .
Somehow I'd like to think she lied,
   But I think just the same.
With skill and art their parts they play,
   Six bulls are duly slain;
With dreary logic they display
   The cruelty of Spain.
But still I go to bull-fights for
   I hope I may be thrilled
To see another Matador
         BE KILLED.

FAT LADY

Oh! Lady fat, from Tennessee,
With bifocals and fallen belly!
Your face is pale as pale can be,
You tremble like a shaken jelly.
Yet resolutely you are climbing
With horror from your front-row seat
While thirty thousand throats are chiming
The bloody joy of bull defeat.

You saw the beast bewildered, bleeding,
And bellowing in bitter pain,
A stupid brute, the horde unheeding,
Who howl and gloat to see it slain.
Amid the mockery and baiting
You saw it kneeling on the sand,
With blind futility awaiting
A fate it could not understand.

Alone, alone with thirty thousand
Conspiring to provoke its death,
Their sadic rage by blood-lust rousened,
Lady, you saw its bubbling breath.
And now your thought is to *vamoose,*
For of black bulls are other five;
And so you cry: "Excuse! Excuse!
Please let me go while they're alive."

"Excuse me and excuse me please.
Let me escape this crimson flood,
Before upon its crumpled knees
I see another bull belch blood."
And so you crush up through the crowd,
Your frantic thought to get away,
(Despite their protestations loud)
Before another bull they slay.

"Excuse you, Lady!" It is they
Who glare at you with looks of gall
And to you grudgingly give way
Who should pray you: "Excuse us all."
Fat Lady, from far Tennessee,
We set you from our lusts apart:
In our insensate cruelty
We reverence your human heart.

BACK STAGE

To celebrate Ascension Day
Six innocents are sacrificed.
In churches all the morn we pray,
Then in the afternoon we slay
Six bulls as advertised.

And as from the arena I
Slip to escape the crowd,
Five dead bulls on the flag-stones lie,
And as the sixth goes down to die
The cheers are overloud.

But by the bulls two horses wait,
And one is brown, one grey.
Yet for the bulls they have no hate;
Blood-laquered from their sorry fate
Two bags of bones are they.

Yet each ten times I saw heaved high
In that mob-frenzied hell,
And with each toss amazed was I
To see they did not drop and die
From that red rituel.

But no, they have survived the fray,
Its glory and its thrill.
Their harness has been put away;
Patient they wait next Sabbath day
Their sewn-up guts to spill.

I tender sugar in my hand:
They sniff—and then a boy
Gives each a blow . . . They understand
That callous language in a land
Where cruelty is joy.

But how next Sunday I should smile
As morning Mass I take,
To see them shamble up the aisle
And at the altar kneel awhile
                    For Jesu's sake!

SONGS OF MYSELF

OLD CODGER
(1951)

My years are seventy and seven,
But other ten I beg of Time,
That five may be devoutly given
To votive verse and loyal rhyme;
Each day to dream with pencil poise,
And make designs on paper white,
Recording all the simple joys
That minister to my delight.

Then leave me five to lay aside
My patient pen and weary-wise
In home of loving to abide
And wait my fate with quiet eyes;
To grow a silver beard, maybe,
And rarely from seclusion stir,
With pussy purring on my knee,
A frail fireside philosopher.

So Reader, should you chance to scan
This page in Nineteen *sixty-one,*
Oh! Will you say: his race he ran,
Or: still he has some laps to run?
I wonder. . . . Well, before I go,
Let me be purged of passion base,
And whether there be God or no',
Sweet Time, give me a breathing space
To groom me fitly for His grace.

DUST

My desk was thick with dust, and so
        My name upon it
I wrote; then with a heart aglow
        Composed a sonnet.

But soon my old housekeeper came
        With busy duster,
And wiping from the desk my name,
        Restored its lustre.

And then that grim Charwoman Time,
        Ere Fame I tasted,
Effaced my wistful snatch of rhyme,
        And it was wasted.

Ah me! The rapture, the delight,
        The hope of glory!
. . . Our silly names in dust we write—
        Dust ends the story.

MY VIRTUES

The fount of humour sparsely springs,
And it is granted unto few,
To see the funny side of things,
To get the comic point of view.
In hospital I chanced to eat
With one whose arms were sheared away,
Yet as I glumly cut his meat
He humbled me, he was so gay.

Serenity you'll often find
In simple folk designed to die;
The patient heart, the quiet mind
Give shame to gripers such as I.
I am not of the humble meek,
I know the fever and the fret;
Serenity is far to seek,
But by God's grace I'll gain it yet.

Let me not fight with any man,
Yet mostly with myself make peace.
Let me enjoy my mortal span,
And tranquilly accept release.
Let dawn discover me with glee,
And sunset be my smiling friend:
So Humour and Serenity
Shall glad my journey to the end.

MY VICES

When I am sad I cannot sin,
  But when my heart's aflame
It's then I see the devil grin
  And point to paths of shame.
When I am sick I have no urge
  To break Commandments Ten,
But when I am with life a-surge
  I mock the laws of men.

When in December cold I pine
  I follow folks to church;
But when Spring kindles in the vine
  I leave them in the lurch.
When ailing oh how good I am,
  But when I'm fighting fit,
For morals I don't care a damn,
  And that's the truth of it.

When as with lusty force I sing
  Of woman, wine and mirth
I wonder if my transgressing
  Is not just joy of earth?
And though I sail with even keel
  I think it's rather hell
To practice virtue when I feel
  So dangerously well.

MODERATION

What pious people label vice
    I reckon mainly pleasure;
I deem that women, wine and dice
    Are good in modest measure;
Though sanctity and truth receive
    My hearty approbation,
Of all the virtues, I believe
    The best is Moderation.

Be moderate in love and hate,
    Soft pedal on emotion;
And never let your passion get
    The better of your caution.
Should Right or Leftist seek to goad
    You from the course that's level,
Stick to the middle of the road
    And send them to the devil.

Though rich the feast be moderate
    In eating and in drinking;
An appetite insatiate
    Is evil to my thinking.
Though ladies languidly await
    Your kisses, on your way shun
Their wiles, but—well, be moderate
    Even in moderation.

56

Avoid extremes: be moderate
  In saving and in spending;
An equable and easy gait
  Will win an easy ending. . . .
So here's to him of open mind,
  Of sense and toleration,
That hope of headlong human-kind,
  The Man of Moderation.

IMPORTANCE

Respected brothers of the Pen
Who deem your writing will be read
By legions of the living when
Your name is numbered with the dead—
Could you foresee how soon forgot
You'll be in spite of printer's ink,
How you would realize you're not
So damned important as you think.

And you, oh mighty potentate!
Of what avail your lofty line
When to the bone-corral they crate
Your carrion as they do mine?
Could you but know how sadly soon
Into oblivion you'll sink,
Your pride will be a pricked balloon. . . .
Poor Prince! You're smaller than you think.

Besotted fools of pride and place,
Of pomp and power, of wealth and fame,
Disdainful death will fast efface
The pallid record of your name!
Take heed, ye Arrogant of Earth!
E'er to obscurity you shrink,
Time takes the measure of your worth,
And you are smaller than you think—
Aye, vastly smaller than you think.

AN ARCHITECT

Said I: "I'll build in airy rhyme."
Said he: "I'll build in stone and steel."
And so for fifty years of time
I watched the film of life unreel,
And put my findings into books
That had their day of shallow fame,
While he with approbative looks
        Payed tribute to my name.

But when I'm dead his stones will stand,
His steel for ages will endure;
His dreams are anchored in the land,
His immortality is sure.
For while his rhymes on rock are built,
His poems in grey granite soar,
My mansions have their feet in silt,
        My sculpings are no more.

Now near the pay-off of my days,
I envy you, my boyhood friend.
As your creations greet my gaze
I know you triumph in the end.
So let me build a stye of stone,
Aye, sweaty mason let me be;
And see my hope in it alone—
        Of immortality.

LOW-BROW

To show you how low-brow I am
    I sadly must admit
When reading Mary and her Lamb
    I wish I'd written it;
I'd rather, I can tell you flat,
    When for Parnassus bound,
Have authored *Casey at the Bat*
    Than odes of Ezra Pound.

And if a painter I might be
    I'd fain be like the Dutch,
And daub fat people full of glee
    Who eat and drink too much;
To souse and song I'd give my heart
    With brush meticulous,
Since for Picasso and his art
    I care no tinker's cuss.

If music chanced to be my line
    The gods I'd sooner thank
If Old Kentucky Home were mine
    Than fugues of Caesar Franck.
A march by Sousa and a waltz
    By Strauss are more to me
Than all the classics time exalts
    In solemn symphony.

You see, a common bloke am I
    And vulgar ways I go;
I sit in pubs and on the sly
    Enjoy a good leg show.
So if you be with culture crammed
    You'll scorn the likes o' me. . . .
Hell! What of it? If I be damned
    I've heaps of company.

MELANCHOLY MOTORIST

I think a car has something human
That serves one with a willing heart;
I coddled mine just like a woman
And kept it sedulously smart.
And as we roved the world together
And knew adventure near and far,
Braving the brunt of bitter weather
I learned to love my little car.

A year ago I came to sell it,
(Oh! Not because it was so old)
But people said—I grieve to tell it,
It was outstyled and should be sold.
"Get rid of it," my daughter said,
"While you can ask a price that's pretty."
Get rid of it—I scratched my head,
Thinking her words more wise than witty.

And so I sold my lovely dear,
And saw a stranger drive it gladly;
He wasn't an expert, I fear,
For he was steering rather madly.
I winced to hear the crash of gear,
And loathed his money as he paid it;
With heart of woe I watched it go,
And somehow felt I had betrayed it.

I saw it only yesterday,
And gazed at it with bitter grieving;
So warped and worn, so foul forlorn,
A rueful wreck beyond retrieving.
It seemed to look reproach at me;
And as by local tinker driven
It jarred away, I prayed that we
For our unkindness be forgiven.

For faithful service has no price
In man or beast or metal shining;
Ingratitude's the meanest vice
And takes a plenty of repining.

MY CHAUFFEUR

My chauffeur is a handy chap
And I admire him quite a lot;
In grim mechanical mishap
He's always Johnny-on-the-spot;
While I'm as stupid as a gopher—
Oh! How I wish I were my chauffeur!

My chauffeur has a hand of steel;
In practice he is rudely right;
You've no idea how I feel
A perfect duffer in his sight;
And though to copy him I try,
He's miles a better man than I.

My chauffeur smooths my daily path,
Contrives my ease to earn his pay;
But should the rabble rise in wrath
'Tis I would perish by the way.
I with my unearned increment,
Securities at six per cent.

The bloke who sweats in smeary toil
Makes wage that he may sweat some more;
Who wrests a living from the soil
Keeps barely wolf beyond the door.
And that is why, a useless loafer,
I take my hat off to my chauffeur.

For what we give in unearned gold
For duty done by wage or fee
Comes back to us a hundred-fold
In service rendered faithfully:
To those who grime for us we should
Give gold, ah yes, and—Gratitude.

MY BABY CAR

I have a silvery Rolls Royce
And in its beauty I rejoice;
But oh with what a cheery shout
I hail my little runabout.

My chauffeur has a uniform
And holds a baby car in scorn;
But let him sneer and jeer and flout,
Give me my dinky runabout.

It's sweet and neat and fighting fit;
I fuss and fiddle over it;
It's sleek and shiny as a trout,
My nippy, whippy runabout.

Although it's only six horse power
I do my sixty miles an hour;
On mountain steeps its heart is stout:
None daunt my dogged runabout.

Oh! It is good at eighty-five,
Even a baby car to drive,
And though I have a touch of gout
I won't give up my runabout.

They say that second childhood must
Have toys to treasure—mine, I trust,
Till life at last shall fizzle out,
Will be my faithful runabout.

BRIGHT ENCOUNTER

As wearily I went my way
   A-feeling more than blue,
I met a little girl today
   Whose face I never knew.
Then suddenly to my surprise,
   As she was passing by,
She looked at me with happy eyes
   And smiled so sunnily.

I am so sensitized to pain
   And in our human hive
I grieve the servitude and pain,
   The struggle to survive.
But as I walked weighed down with woe,
   To sorrow reconciled,
A tiny tot I did not know
   Looked up at me and smiled.

Sweet innocent, I blessed her as
   I went upon my way,
And that dark cloud my spirit has
   Was lit as by a ray.
So magically glad was I
   That I too smiled and smiled,
From midnight mood delivered by
   The sunshine of a child.

CONSOLATION

With Beauty I have been in touch
   And lived with such delight,
I would not worry overmuch
   Were I to lose my sight.
For in the few moons left to me
   Sweet comfort I would find
And richer beauty I would see
   In vision of the mind.

Such melodies of ravishment
   Have lingered in my ear,
I would not grievously lament
   Could I no longer hear;
For in this inner ear of mine
   Is music loved so long,
Its echo would be so divine
   That silence would be song.

Such plenitude I've known of love,
   Of children, wife and friend,
I would not curse the gods above
   If loveless in the end;
And though blind, deaf and lone I be,
   How I would count it bliss
Could I but write real poetry,
   Not silly rhymes like this!

CONTRAST

Of all the people whom you meet
        In city mile
How few there are who gaily greet
        You with a smile!
For radiance you look in vain
        In human mask;
You only see the fret and strain
        Of daily task.

Only the very young are gay
        With empty cheer;
Yet soon on them life's hand will lay
        Its load of fear;
They too will join the drudge and drive
        In dust and din,
The weary struggle to survive
        So few will win.

Then let us seek a soaring trail,
        A singing stream;
A sunset fading primrose pale,
        A moon a-dream;
And where rich pines embalm the air
        And rumours cease,
In hush as holy as a prayer
        Commune with Peace.

CRUISE DE LUXE

Though bliss it be to grandly roam
        In foreign land or sea,
The joy of joys is coming home
        To domesticity;
And with content to settle down
        From travel wear and tear,
With slippers, pipe and dressing-gown
        In snug arm-chair.

When you have climbed the Pyramid,
        Admired the Taj Mahal,
Beheld a bull-fight in Madrid,
        Gondoled the Grand Canal,
How gleeful seems the garden patch
        With blooms of bonny hue!
How *Towser,* when you lift the latch,
        Leaps up on you!

You've drank gin-slings in Singapore,
        Loafed in the *souks* of Fez,
Sun-bathed on Capri's silver shore,
        And scaled the heights of Eze.
For travel education is,
        And how you see and learn . . .
But oh! The climax of your bliss
        Is your return!

Aye, you may comb the blessed earth
  And roam the seven seas,
But when beside the quiet hearth
  You cull your memories,
Then with the books and friends you love,
  You'll find in peace and rest,
The end of travel is to prove
  THAT HOME IS BEST.

GRANNY

My Granny smoked a cutty pipe
And lit it at a fire of peat;
Her face was like a pippin ripe,
Framed by her mutch and sagely sweet.
She sat upon a three-legged stool,
With by her side a cat apurr,
And talked of when she went to school,
And Grandfather came courting her.

They married in their teens, I guess,
And of braw bairnies she had seven;
'Twas counted shame to mother less,
Though four preceded her to Heaven;
She never had a kitchen help,
She did her housework all alone:
With seven little daups to skelp,
She worked her fingers to the bone.

And now I sit before a fire
In sculped Carrara marble set;
I've luxury to heart's desire,
And I am old as Granny—yet
I have not in my eyes the joy
Of hers beneath that cottage thatch,
As when she hailed a tiny boy
Who had to reach to lift the latch.

No urchin by the olive glow
Waits wistfully beside my knee;
Her youth, a hundred years ago
How happily she told to me!
Her "but and ben" had scarce a clout,
But Oh! How she was gay and glad!
Alas, my fire is dying out . . .
And I—I have no little lad!

LYRICS OF THE LOST

GLADIATOR

Irresolute in rigid rain
He shudders in his shoddy clothes,
Seeks for a handkerchief in vain,
With icy fingers wipes his nose.
A lean and livid lad he stares,
Gripping his canvas suit-case tight,
At those beneath the neon glares,
Now crowding in to see him fight.

A welter weight, six rounds to go,
Then take a knock-out—that's the "fix".
Yet if he makes a sporty show
And don't pull off no monkey tricks,
Another match they've promised him.
Could be, they'll let him win that bout,
And if he is in smashing trim
With luck he'd knock the next guy out.

Why not tonight? The double cross
Is common in this game of guile . . .
But no, one socks to please the boss,
Or else is left to sleep awhile.
Aye, one must be a butcher block
And take a bashing with a grin,
Survive the pounding and the shock
To be, at last, *allowed* to win.

He sees the crowd go milling in,
The sordid, sleek, sadistic mob;
And soon with hoarse, derisive din,
They'll spur his mauler to the job;
They'll goad the bruiser to his task,
With gritting teeth and spittle-gulp,
To see his face a crimson mask,
His body battered to a pulp.

So in the puddled, oily light,
Besprayed by every passing car
He wonders if the sky of night
Will ever glimmer with *his* star . . .
And now with cotton dressing-gown
And tawdry trunks he turns to where
The public wait to turn thumbs down,
And mock him, blood-bright in the glare.

THE BRUISER

So iron-grim and icy cool
I bored in on him like a bull.
As if one with the solid ground
I took his blows round after round:
Glutton for punishment am I,
Rather than quit prepared to die.

Like dancing master was the boy,
Graceful and light, a boxer's joy.
He flapped a left and tapped a right—
I laughed because his blows were light;
The gong was like a golden chime,
As darkly I abode my time.

It's hard to stand ten grilling rounds.
I saw despite his leaps and bounds
That he was tired and failing fast;
But little longer could he last,
While I as solid as a rock
Grinned and withstood shock after shock.

Round eight: I launched to the attack.
I gave him all, held nothing back,
Disdained defence, with hammer blows:
The blood was spouting from his nose;
One eye, cut open, glistened wild . . .
Sudden he seemed a helpless child.

Round nine: They'd washed the blood away,
But bang! It spouted bright and gay.
His face was all a gory mask,
And yet no mercy would he ask.
Ah yes, the boy was gallant game,
Yet I must down him all the same.

Round ten: His eye like oyster gleamed.
I could have blinded him, it seemed.
Then as he weaved, faint and forlorn,
Strange pity in my heart was born.
I dropped my hands unto my side:
"For God's sake, strike me, lad!" I cried.

He struck me twice, two loving taps,
As if he understood, perhaps.
Then as the gong went like a knell,
Fainting into my arms he fell.
We kissed each other, he and I . . .
"A draw!" I heard the umpire cry.

MUSICIAN

Damn you, Beethoven! See, I've crashed
Your plaster bust upon the floor.
Into a dozen fragments smashed,
You will reproach me nevermore.
Only a single eye I see,
Staring so dismally at me.

I was so proud the day I brought
Your bust, that head magnificent,
Into my garret, bravely bought,
For on it my last coin I spent.
It seemed to symbolize my fate,
To song divinely dedicate.

Well, song has failed me, music too;
My poor piano I have sold.
My shelf is bare, my rent is due,
My attic bitterly is cold.
Oh! Saturnine and stormy head!
I might have bartered you for bread.

Yet better you be shattered there,
As all my hopes are shattered now.
You are the proof of my despair,
With jagged lips and broken brow,
Who lured me half a lifetime through
To dream that I might live in you.

Ah well, I'll never play again,
Nor grubby children will I teach.
As salesman, maybe not in vain
A simple living I'll beseech. . . .
Poor fools! who strive uncomforted,
By music's dole to win your bread.

GUITARIST

His aged hands were grained with grime
      Warped was his old guitar,
And as I paused a little time,
      So near and yet so far,
He looked at me with sightless stare,
      Yet *knew* that I was there.

He must have done. He played an air
      I sang in days gone bye.
'Twas *Jeannie of the Nut-brown Hair;*
      As softly as a sigh
He played, yet oh! So sad the strain
      It woke an ancient pain.

For though she left me all alone,
      Bleak years and years away,
I think my minstrel must have known—
      His jazz he ceased to play,
And strummed so gently just for me
      That heart-break melody.

Blind folk, I think, are often *fey,*
      And second sight have got,
For every time I pass that way,
      Although he knows me not,
He looks at me with empty stare
      And plays that old-time air.

. . . There by the tragic plane we stand:
  No kisses, only sighs.
Her hand is groping for my hand,
    Her eyes drown in my eyes . . .
Dark Tunesmith, echo my despair!
    Soft, soft her nut-brown hair.

ACCORDIANIST

His old accordian he played
    With virtuosity.
Such trills and triolets he made,
    And though he could not see,
Oh! How delightful to his ear,
    How gladly he would grin,
As in his darkness he could hear
    The pennies fill his tin.

Poor devil! He'd been blind from birth,
    And never had he known
The radiant excellence of earth,
    In night he lived alone.
Despite the music in his soul
    With life so sour and grim,
The chink of pennies in his bowl
    God's music was to him.

I thought: Could he but give to me
    A trifle of his skill,
How heaven-happy I would be
    To harmonize and trill.
Nay, it is not an idle whim,
    Though foolish-like it sounds,
I swear if I could play like him
    I'd pay a hundred pounds.

And so I listen in the rain
    To his appeggios;
His raw-red hands he chafes in vain,
    A blob hangs from his nose.
And as his misery I grieve,
    Yet deem his notes divine,
With envy in his tin I leave
    A five-pound note of mine.

FIDDLER

Oh! I have built a house at last,
To fill with music night and day;
For I have laboured in the past
And had so small a time to play.
My house is of a whin-grey stone;
Its walls are bare for poor I be,
But with my fiddle all alone,
   I'll have rare company.

My fiddle's old and so am I.
For it I've often longed in vain.
Bleak years and years I've layed it bye,
But now I'll take it up again.
For in four frail gut strings I know
All music sleeps for me to wake,
And here before the peat-fire glow
   Fine melody I'll make.

I'll leave my fiddle by the bed,
And take it in the morning bright,
So all the dreaming in my head
Will weave into a web of light.
Or lone lament—I'm fearing so,
For I have waited far too long,
And all a life of want and woe
   May well into my song.

But no! I'll make these wintry walls
Like Spring, with dancing day and night;
And when the Great Conductor calls,
My fiddle I'll be holding tight.
My last love! Worth its weight in gold . . .
Yet—on its strings my fingers lie
So warped and worn, so stiff and cold. . . .
      Too late!—*I want to cry.*

MY DOUBLE

In hail and rain and sleet and snow,
In gale and fog and freezing cold,
I see him to his labour go,
Yet he is old as I am old.
I shrink and think: Life is not fair.
He looks like me, yet Fate has ground
Him in the bloody mire, and where
He makes a bob I make a pound.

Aye, how he seems the spit of me,
And had I not the knack of rhyme,
I, too, might muck in misery,
Or grovel in the gutter grime.
I grieve that there be rich and poor,
And from my study snug and warm,
I watch from luxury secure
My broken brother breast the storm.

And sad of soul again I say
Alas that there be poor and rich;
God speed the day when life will pay
An equal wage to desk and ditch.
Aye, even more—with just decree,
Pay *him* a pound and *me* a bob . . .
Yet though I mucked in misery,
By God! I'd stick my rhyming job.

And so I see with heart of rue
His trudge to toil in daylight dim . . .
But what the devil can I do?
So many millions are like him.

CAGED LARK

She tried and tried to make me sing,
That sick girl in the wicker chair,
As with my bleeding breast and wing
I beat the bars in my despair:
Said she, "If you belonged to me
This moment I would set you free.

"I've half a mind to reach your cage
And open wide its door of wire.
The Matron would be red with rage:
'Who slipped the latch?' she would inquire.
And if I said it was not I,
Would God forgive me for the lie?"

The lone girl in the wicker chair
Is very low and soon must die;
Like sun-flower golden is her hair,
Like dark anemone her eye.
So beautiful, so soon to go . . .
Fain would I sing to ease her woe.

She whistles with her scanty breath;
To make me sing she tries and tries.
Her face is like a mask of death . . .
If I could cheer her as she dies
I'd break my heart remembering
The melodies of ghostly Spring.

I'll cease to beat my bars in vain,
With panting beak and wings outspread,
Because I see it gives her pain . . .
Look! How the sunset kindles red!
As once on wings I used to soar
I'll sing as ne'er I sang before.

What joy lights up her wasted face!
Her gladness is beyond belief.
Her blessing is above all grace,
My rapture has alloyed her grief. . . .
I'll sing and sing, *caged souls are we,*
Beseeching God to set us free.

ALPHONZE

Some people are like postage stamps,
        Made to be licked;
Or like lost dogs and lousy tramps,
        Born to be kicked.
I think that I am one of these,
        Unfit for strife,
Destined to menially please
        Through-out my life.

For here am I at sixty-two,
        A waiter still;
And bow as I present to you
        Your little bill.
Solicitously hovering,
        Your crumbs I flip,
Hoping servility will bring
        An extra tip.

No notion of my entity
        Your mind intrigues;
You don't know my identity
        From my colleagues'.
I'm lacking personality,
        An automat,
Less human than the pretty "she"
        Who brings your hat.

And if I recommend a dish
        Or choice tit-bit,
How wistfully I have a wish
        To taste of it.
But of your menials the least,
        To service born,
Give me the leavings of the feast,
        The scraps you scorn.

And yet my human pride I've got
        And hard I try,
So that my little kids may not
        Be such as I.
They say a waiter needs no brains;
        No bulge you'll see
Behind my ears—and that explains
        Why I am me.

But Sir, give me a kindly thought
        Next time you dine,
And with obsequence I've brought
        Your quail and wine.
And though I play my humble part
        And get my due,
'Neath skin we're kin, and I've a heart
        The same as you.

DECADENCE

The Prince, they say, has had his day
  And it was proud and high;
And now you meet him in the street
  On foot as you and I.
And though you note his shabby coat,
  A monocle he sports,
And has the flair so *débonnaire*
  Of protocols and courts.

The Prince is lean, his lips are green,
  His face is putty grey;
A meal of meat he cannot eat
  Because he cannot pay.
From Savile Row of long ago
  A threadbare suit he wears,
Yet as I pass he cocks his glass
  And stonily he stares.

But yesterday upon my way
  His haughtiness I met,
And such his glance of arrogance
  I dropped my cigarette,
For very shy and meek am I,
  Yet as I turned around
I saw him quick bend down and pick
  My fag from off the ground.

And so this morn I braved his scorn
    As in the sun we strolled;
A mild gold-flake I begged him take
    From out my case of gold.
Sour as a quince I saw him wince,
    His eye-glass he produced.
"No thanks," said he; "Hum! pardon me—
    Have we been introduced?"

INSURANCE TOUT

Each day's a battle for a guy like me,
Its end dim victory or dark defeat;
I'm lean and livid, care-carked as you see,
My only aim to make enough to eat:
To buy the wife and little children bread,
To keep our sordid roof above their head.

I brace my prospects with a dental grin;
I put it up to them as man to man . . .
"To carry no insurance is a sin—
Let me explain our new endowment plan.
For those you love it's up to you to sign . . ."
(I wish I could afford to think of mine!)

"You'll mull it over—well, that means a lot.
I'll call again—say, in a week or so.
You're short of ready cash, but who is not?
Insurance is so vital, as you know.
The premium is small, the boon immense:
It must appeal to one of your good sense."

And so I go *blah, blah,* from each to each,
Spouting the line of talk I know by heart,
Handing to all the same old hackneyed speech
They taught me at the office at the start:
Until my prospect I wear down to sign,
With vague reluctance on the dotted line.

96

My wife and kids are what most worries me,
For even though the premium I could borrow
The Doctor would advise the Company
My heart was weak and I might die tomorrow.
So for my dear ones I must fight and fend,
Going *blah, blah,* unto the bitter end.

PROUD DESTINY

"Young man, a noble part you play
   To mould the mind of youth,
To guide it on the starry way
   Of Wisdom and of Truth . . ."
So spoke that old, fat-headed fool,
   The Chairman of our School.

I wish he had my class to teach
   Just for a single day;
I don't think he would want to preach,
   But rather want to pray.
And count of avocations curst
   A teacher's is the worst.

I put my dreary books away,
   My head is like to split;
Tomorrow is another day,
   I must prepare for it:
A pile of essays to correct,
   Till bedtime, I expect.

My boys are little beasts, I know;
   They hate me more or less;
I wield the cane with vigour, so
   They've reason I confess.
Their grubby minds I grimly cram
   To pass a fool exam.

Oh! Could I quit this life tonight
  And live a lusty spell;
To be a man, to wench and fight
  And raise a ruddy hell!
Alas! I haven't even spunk
  To go and get me drunk.

"Young man," said he, "your part is proud
  To shape the dreams of Youth."
. . . Oh! How I wish one of my crowd
  Had proved his saying sooth,
And with a sling-shot pinged his rear—
  I would have laughed, I fear.

JOB GARDENER

When other people are so poor
It's jolly nice to be secure.

The man who does odd jobs for me
    Stopped me the other day.
"Please sir, you've no old coat," said he
    "You'd care to give away?
We pinch and scrape, the wife and I,
    And scant have we to eat,
Yet howsoever hard we try
    We just can't make ends meet."

So I gave him my oldest coat,
    Moth-eaten, worn and grey;
But oh you should have seen him gloat
    And carry it away.
"It's far too good for me," said he;
    "So much above my class."
And yet next Sunday I could see
    Him wearing it to Mass.

Mine is annuitable ease,
    Immune from gain or loss;
I work the when and how I please,
    And no man is my boss.
And so it doesn't seem just right,
    (Though normal, I suppose)
That one who toils from morn to night
    Should beg my cast-off clothes.

Yet that's exactly how it was:
    Four other coats I own,
But I'm discomforted because
    His fingers to the bone
He wears, yet cannot purchase one,
    And to my sad surprise
In thanking me for what I'd done
    The tears were in his eyes.

FAITH

The tragedy innate in life
    Is with me as I write,
And in my heart the naked knife
    Is twisting noon and night;
And yet today upon my way
    I saw a soothing sight.

Old Marthe was coming from the Mass
    And fingering her beads;
With sympathy I sought to pass,
    For grievous are her needs,
And comforting's a precious thing
    When pious pity pleads.

Yet though her eyes were all ashine
    Her tears were those of joy:
Said she, "Dear Doctor, you divine
    I'm praying for my boy . . .
He's poorly, and you understand
    How wounds of war destroy.

"He coughed and coughed the weary night,
    His face was wan to see,
So I went with the dawning light
    In church to bend the knee . . .
Then as I prayed for Heaven's aid
    The Saints smiled down on me.

"Aye, as I rose each Holy One
    Was gazing down on me;
Each Saint was lighted by the sun
    And beautiful to see:
So sweet they smiled I knew my child
    The Lord would spare to me."

No woman's faith would I destroy
    Though dark was my demur;
With wasting woe her boy I know
    From bed will never stir. . . .
Yet as I grieve I too believe
    The Saints smiled down on her.

AIR MOTHER

She talked of flying and of men
    Who perfected the aeroplane;
Her only child would listen—then
    His eyes would kindle to her flame.
"If I were half my age," said she,
    "I too would dare the crystal skies."
Then tense he told her: "You will be
    The mother of a man who flies."

"The future of the world," said she,
    "Is in the hands of those who dare
To pierce the heaven's purity,
    The cleansing sweetness of the air;
Above all human spite and sweat
    Uplifted to the starry span. . . ."
Said he: "Old Lady, don't you fret;
    Your son shall be a flying man."

Then came the war. With heart aglow,
    Although with love her eyes were dim,
A lad with wings she saw him go,
    And that's the last she saw of him.
The desert mocked her dark despair;
    No hope, no sign, no stark surmise
Of gallant airman sprawling there,
    A vulture feasting on his eyes.

And now she curses aeroplanes
   And thinks how happy we all were
Before men broke the golden chains
   Of earth and soared into the air.
And looking at the bane and blight,
   And bloody havoc wings have wrought,
One wonders, though by grief distraught. . . .
   May that poor mother not be right?

THE WILD ONE

"Son, there's nothing I can say,
  Nothing I can do.
You will go your foolish way,
  'Tis the last of you:
Why for strangeness and the storm
  Leave a hearth so warm?"

"Mother, what you say is true:
  Sweet's the heather heath,
And the roads of wrath and rue
  Lead to lonesome death.
But for all your bitter blame
  I'll go all the same."

"Son, three cows are in the byre,
  Praties in the sod;
There's the peat to feed the fire—
  Why be tempting God?
Leave the shielding for the wild . . .
  I'm a-feared, my child."

"Mother, never you will hear
  Word from me of woe;
I will send you lines of cheer
  From the where I go;
For a mutch with ribbons blue
  Send you siller too."

"But if letters never come,
   I'll have quit to be;
And in hushness of the home
   Wail and weep for me . . .
Boy who dared the fairy foam,
   Crossed the moon-mad sea."

SYLVAN SONGS

POEMS

A poem should be like a brook,
   As dulcet to the ear;
And it should need no second look
   To make its meaning clear:
As chrystal as a rill it should
   With music meet your mood.

A poem should be like a bird
   And to green joy belong,
That should inspire each jewelled word
   With pregnancy of song,
And be of brooding thought no part,
   Appealing forthright to the heart.

A poem should be like a flower
   That gems a sullen space,
To live ineffably its hour
   Of ecstasy and grace:
A lily, violet or rose,
   That in sheer beauty glows.

A crystal brook, a flower, a bird
   Are poems perfect planned;
We have no need of graven word
   Their grace to understand:
So wrapt in them is my delight,
   A poem I've no need to write.

THE INNOCENTS

Last night a little fire I lit
   Deep in a ferny dell;
With piny cones I kindled it
   And sat a silent spell.
So peaceful was the solitude,
   When sudden with surprise
I saw around me in the wood
   A ring of lambent eyes.

Oh! I had thought myself alone,
   Afar from earthy ires,
So by my fire as still as stone
   I watched those other fires;
The eyes that flickered here and there
   With daring, doubt and fear;
But when they paused to stare and stare,
   I knew that they were Deer.

Alas! I made a little sound
   For I to sleep was fain,
And they were gone with single bound
   And all was dark again.
Yet when I roused me in the night
   And raised my head to see,
My little fire was still alight
   And they were watching me.

Somehow love in my heart awoke
    For buck and doe and fawn,
Yet when the light of morning broke
    My dappled friends were gone.
But I will ne'er forget my night
    Of sylvan solitude,
My fire of piny cones alight,
    The tender eyes that shone so bright
Deep in the briery wood.

NATURE MAN

The happiest man I ever knew
　　Was scarcely clad at all;
He had no bath like me and you,
　　But owned a waterfall.
And every sunrise he would wade
　　The streamlet silver bright,
To stand beneath the clear cascade
　　　　　　With sheer delight.

The happiest man I ever knew
　　Lived in a forest glade;
His hut of palm-leaf and bamboo
　　With his own hands he made.
And for his breakfast he would pick
　　A bread-fruit from the tree,
Or lobster he would gaily flick
　　　　　　From out the sea.

The happiest man I ever knew
　　Could barely read or write,
But beer from honey he could brew
　　To get drunk every night.
He had no wife as I'm aware,
　　Nor any bastard brat,
But lived a life without a care,
　　　　　　With laughter fat.

The happiest man I ever knew
    Was innocent of rent;
Low labour he would scorn to do
    And never owned a cent.
But he would strum an old guitar
    And sing a sultry song,
Insoucient as children are
                Of right and wrong.

The happiest man I ever knew
    Recked not of government;
His wants were simple and so few
    His life was pure content.
And as I thole this rancid mart,
    In which I plot and plan,
How glad I'd be, with all my heart,
                That happy man.

SYLVAN DESTINY

My olive trees are very old,
A hundred years, or two or three;
Their trunks fantastically boled
Look mediaevally at me.
My mild-eyed goats are gravely glad
To shade them from the hungry heat,
And as I tend them, scantly clad,
It happies me to see them eat.

Poor toiler! Don't you envy me
With no man to dispute my state;
My life superlatively free,
My solitude inviolate.
With never cloud of care to fret
My dreaming in a silver glade,
While piping on a flageolet
I read Catullus in the shade.

Oh! Am I wise or am I not
Who choose to live apart from men?
My home a tiny, red-tiled cot,
My hope to ply a humble pen.
My olive trees are twenty-five,
My dainty-stepping goats are seven;
I praise the gods that I'm alive
To demonstrate my daily heaven.

What luck I bought this spot of earth,
Although it cost me all I had;
And every dawn with sober mirth
I'll everlastingly be glad.
A silver bell shall grace each goat,
Each olive tree shall be my friend,
So luminously and remote
Let me go gentling to the end.

CRYSTAL PAUSE

My mind is full of emptiness;
  I do not even dream.
I watch the little waves caress
  The sand with sunny gleam.
Like silver bells their music sweet
      Is all about my feet.

My mind with nothingness is filled,
  I'm tranquil as a tree;
To perfect peace my heart is stilled,
  In all I hear and see.
My being is absorbed and I
      Am part of sea and sky.

My mind is void . . . and yet I must
  Recall my name and place,
Shake off this oneness with the dust,
  This lineage with space:
Let thought seep back into my brain,
      And find myself again.

Life has so much to tell and teach,
  And memory to recall . . .
Yet oh to brood upon the beach,
  To scarcely think at all:
And tuned to earth and sky and sea
      Forget that I am me.

MIRZA

A year ago my goats were three;
    Now I have only one;
But I am eighty as you see:
    My days will soon be done.
My son-in-law has said he'd give
Me only six years more to live.

While goats are grave and strangely wise,
    Sheep have no sense at all.
Mirza has knowing in her eyes
    And cometh to my call.
When faggot-bowed for home I jog
She follows faithful like a dog.

Her hair is soft and silky white,
    Her eyes like amber are;
She has been mine from kiddy height,
    My comfort and my care.
I have not left her for a day:
She will not eat if I'm away.

Aye, goats are wise beyond belief.
    She loves me I am sure;
When I am gone she'll pine with grief,
    And though we are so poor,
We've been so happy, she and I,
It seems a pity I must die.

Come, Mirza come, we must go home
   And you'll give me sweet milk,
And I with tenderness will comb
   Your fleece to sheen of silk,
And polish up your silver bell. . . .
"No, Son-in-law, she's not to sell!"

CHERRY ORCHARD

A lad and lass fared forth at dawn
  To pluck the cheerful cherry;
Their foot-prints pearled the dewy lawn,
  Their laugh was bird-like merry.
When youth and June compose the tune,
  What meaner one can matter?
As high he climbed their voices chimed,
  And silver was their chatter.

He clipped the fruit she gleaned below,
  And ringing was their laughter.
Their cheeks were cherry-like aglow,
  Beneath the leafy rafter.
And then there was a crystal pause
  As soundless as the grave is:
But soon I heard a bell-like bird—
  I think it was a mavis.

A lad and lass returned at eve,
  Hushed by some secret gladness;
Idyllic air they seemed to breathe,
  Their eyes lit with sweet madness.
While from the grove I heard a dove,
  To love its note beholden,
No silver speech made each to each,
  Just silence—Oh! How golden!

FIRST PARTING

Where is everybody gone?
Is there no one in the house?
Windows are wide-eyed and wan,
Not the twinkle of a mouse.
Desolate I wander round,
Ever since the hint of dawn;
Not a movement, not a sound—
Where is everybody gone?

Would you tear a rose apart,
Scatter wide its velvet leaves,
Brittle-break its lovely heart,
Careless of the how it grieves?
And a home is like a rose,
Exquisite in artless art,
Love and beauty to enclose—
Could you break a home apart?

So I wander all about,
Looking here and seeking there,
Harking for a sudden shout,
Fleeting feet upon the stair.
Emptiness is everywhere,
And my mind is on a rack—
Darkness, terror and despair . . .
Should she never more come back.

What a foolish man am I
Of such foolishness to dream!
Fast her holidays will fly
Till the days less lonely seem.
But—dear God! the piercing pain
As I open wide a drawer
Where her summer frocks have lain . . .
Oh! The rose-sweet scent of her!

PANTHEIST

When purblind people are with wars
      And passions overspent,
Ocean and sky and sun and stars
      Make no comment.
The moon looks down with ageless scorn,
      The planets do not grieve,
The dawning is no whit forlorn,
      Uncaring is the eve.

So let us be a one with these
      In crystal innocence,
The unconcerning of the trees,
      The brooks' indifference.
And let no lust and greed outrage
      The peace of our sweet earth,
For holy is our heritage,
      And blessed is our birth.

Aye, let us be like brook and tree
      Unstirred by human strife;
Like sun and moon and sky and sea
      Aloof from human life.
Yea, let us be like Nature blind
      To hate and havoc high;
Ignore the madness of mankind,
      And bid the world go by.

FREE

The joys we ought to value most
Are those that have no lucre cost;
A sunrise or a sunset are
Of gratis sights the finest far;
The constellations of the night
Gratuitously charm our sight;
And all the beauty of the earth
Cannot be weighed in money worth.

I love the cloistering of trees,
The scent of clover on the breeze;
Plump apples gemmed with morning dew,
Lone lamb clouds lost up in the blue;
The mating rapture of the thrush,
The eventide of holy hush;
The soar of mountains to the sky—
Such sights no Midas gold can buy.

Dame Nature is no niggard, she
Displays her best for all to see;
So learn to love such lowly things
As violets and linnet wings;
Life's richest gifts to you and me,
My friends, are fabulously free:
And finally, no miser's wealth
Can buy the ecstasy of health.

THE WEE PEOPLE

Though I am but a lisper
   In realms of Poetry,
The Fairy Folk they whisper
   Their fancies unto me.
I cannot write a poem,
   As anyone may guess,
Yet Fairy Folk bestow 'em
   On me with eagerness.

I'm just an old reporter;
   I can't compose a lay.
I do not try—it's shorter
   To let the Pixies say.
For when in bed I'm lying
   Without a single thought,
The little folk come flying,
   And murmur—oh a lot!

For this rhyme—if you've read it,
   (Nay, do not think I joke)
Don't give me any credit,
   But thank the Fairy Folk.
For I'm the saddest duffer
   Of all earth's singing sons . . .
So Reader, should you suffer,
   Confound the Impish Ones.

THE SEER

. . . Then in the street quite suddenly
  The folks began to cry;
A crazy crowd they seemed to me,
  And only sane was I:
Yea, standing in the market place
Insanity in every face
  I saw and wondered why.

Aye, all at once the mob went mad,
  They wept, they wailed, they laughed.
And there I stood stock-still and sad,
  For everyone was daft.
For something strange was in the air,
A crazy germ from God knows where,
  A hell-erupting draught.

So I was chill because I knew,
  Being so clear of mind,
That now the end of all was due,
  And God would blast mankind.
To me alone was knowledge given
Of secrets whispered in High Heaven . . .
  I saw where all were blind.

. . . Then like a flash the moment passed,
    And oh I was so glad.
Deferred was that destructive blast,
    Dear God compassion had.
Yet as I laughed aloud with glee,
A thousand eyes regarded me,
    And deemed that I was mad.

ROVER'S REST

I would seek a still house,
Blessèd by tranquility;
Far from wind and wave carouse,
And the sea's urgency.
After wandering the earth,
After wastreling and war,
I would win a hushed hearth,
From the tempest far, far.

From the vehemence of blood,
Where beyond meadow bars
Cows in night-time chew the cud,
And their eyes reflect stars.
Where the owl goes *woosh woosh*,
Weavingly with ghost wings,
And above the hearth hush
One wee cricket sings, sings.

I would own a still house,
Sit beside a wood flame,
Hear the rustle of a mouse,
Beady-eyed, half tame.
From the hives of men apart,
With a robin on the sill,
I would home with husht heart,
Waiting one more mute still.

THE RETURN

To my old home I came,
Where I was born and bred;
I lit the hearth-fire flame,
I made my boyhood bed.
The walls were bleak with blame,
The nooks were dark with dread.

To my old home I came
From world-wide wandering;
With nought to show but shame
For sin and squandering.
Sickly and old and lame,
Death dourly pondering.

In my old home will I,
With doom-deep weariness
Remain until I die,
While wraiths of wistfulness
Around me peer and pry,
And pity my distress.

With ghosts will I remain
Of those who held me dear;
And I will bed with pain,
And I will bide with fear . . .
Sweet shades! grieve not in vain:
I come to you again
I left for fifty year.

AT THE BEND OF THE ROAD

With on my back a bitter load
      I climbed the hill,
And at the bending of the road
      I sat me still;
Thought I, to rest awhile is good,
      Though not too long:
Then birdlike from the sunny wood
      I heard a song.

It was not loud, but oh so sweet,
      With joyous trill!
I listened, then with heavy feet
      Went up the hill;
With heavy heart the ridge I topped,
      When turning there,
I saw where I had chanced to stop,
      A maid most fair.

I felt an urging to go back,
      Though sadly spent;
But level now I found the track,
      So on I went.
Aye, on I went to seek romance
      In joy and pain . . .
Then yesterday I took by chance
      That trail again.

There at the bending of the road
          A withered crone
With faggots in a heavy load
          Sat all alone;
Said she: "I've waited for you long,
          With love apart."
And then she crooned that olden song,
          Still in my heart.

Silent we sat a little while,
          Both bowed with years,
And there was heaven in her smile,
          Despite her tears;
And so I took her faggot load,
          For none had I,
And hand in hand we climbed the road,
          Climbed to the sky.

CAGES

I built a cage of ivory
    To hold my little bird,
For she was precious unto me
    And lovely more than word.
With frame of snowy filigree
    I sought to make her glad;
But oh it grieved my heart to see
                My bird was sad.

I built my dear a crystal cage
    That snared the silver stars,
And thought to hear her lyric rage
    Tremor the gleamy bars;
But though I knew her trill more sweet
    Than any living bird,
A faint and piteous *tweet, tweet*
                Was all I heard.

I built my love a cage of gold
    To joy her into song,
And wistfully, with woe untold,
    I waited long and long;
But from that home so exquisite
    No tiny tune would come,
And though my heart with hope was lit,
                My bird was dumb.

132

And so the door I opened wide
  And let my pet go free,
And now my cottage door beside,
  She sings a song for me.
Oh! Such a radiant melody
  She sings from morn to night,
The blossoms of my almond tree
        Thrill with delight.

And so my gorgeous cages three
  Are dusty on the shelf;
For in my passion to be free
  How could I cage myself?
But though she flit on bough above,
  Beyond all thought and word
Her joy is mine, for how I love
        My bonny bird!

LARK ECSTASY

I am no ornithologist;
I ain't wised up on birds;
A heap o' schoolin' I have missed,
I got no fancy words.
Yet that there lark above the hill
That sings wi' might and main
Of pleasure gives me such a thrill
It's almost like a pain.

Most birds sing steadfast on a bough,
His stance is in the air;
The ether is his perch and how
He tells us he is there.
That's why his song's so pure and clear,
Like beads of crystal spun,
Delirious with atmosphere
And drunk with sky and sun.

The thrush sings from the hawthorn hedge,
The blackbird from the may;
The robin from the chimney ledge,
The wren from cherry spray.
The nightingale when day is done
Wakes woodland with his air—
But oh! The lark's the blessed one
Who seeks the splendour of the sun,
And sings from Heaven's stair.

ROBIN RAPTURE

My robin ruled the apple tree,
  His glee was piercing sweet.
So taken with his song was he,
  He scarce had time to eat.
And as he wet his bill with dew
  And saw his brood take wing,
The joyous Spring and Summer through,
  He never ceased to sing.

My robin perched upon the wall
  And trilled with Autumn zest,
No ruby leaflet of the Fall
  Was brighter than his breast.
He greeted me with morning dew,
  The eve echoed his glee:
As nearer to my door he drew
  I *knew* he sang for me.

My robin stood upon the sill
  And pecked the window pane.
Alas! the house was dark and still,
  And all his cheer was vain.
Then when the snow was wavering
  From cold and cruel skies,
My little robin ceased to sing
  And closed his eyes.

Sweet spirit of embodied joy,
    You piped the season through,
And now the gods your note destroy,
    I sing a song for you.
Aye, though the sentiment's absurd,
    Fantastical maybe,
If there's no heaven for a bird
    Let there be none for me.

STRANGE THIRST

Perched high upon an office stool
    I plied a plaintive pen,
Thinking a chap's a bloody fool
    To hive in homes of men;
When there's the wilderness to span,
    The desert to explore,
And he may camp where never man
    Has pitched a tent before.

And so it grimly came to pass,
    Because I willed it so,
I proved myself a precious ass
    And went where wastrels go.
I fashioned my fantastic fate,
    Insanely resolute,
Seeking some spot inviolate,
    Unfound by human foot.

The puny pines were whimpering
    Their plaint of winter woe;
The lythe brook held the bitter sting
    Of immemorial snow;
Yet oh! Joy-crazy as a child,
    I flared the hemlock high,
To think that in this haggard wild
    The first to burst was I.

To think that bird and beast and tree
    In this so secret place,
Had never seen the likes of me,
    Nor reckoned of my race.
To think this hank of rag and bone
    Saw now what none had seen,
And I was all alone, alone
    Where man had never been.

And so despite defeat and scathe,
    As fated from my birth,
Exultantly I kept the faith
    With elemental earth.
My brothers sober ways did plod,
    I chose the path of pain. . . .
And if I could re-live—by God!
    I'd do the same again.

THE TRAIL OF TROUBLE

Because my life was drab and stale
    In stifled city air
With careless heart I took the trail
    That led to anywhere.
The sky was fell, the wind a knell,
    The road was rough with rubble,
And yet because my fate it was
    I took the Trail of Trouble.

In safety and in smugness lay
    The boulevards of my birth,
Yet fecklessly I went my way
    Of darkness and of dearth;
And though to meet my foolish feet
    Came danger at the double,
Because I thought it was my lot,
    I took the Trail of Trouble.

For some of us are born like that
    And never can we change.
We flout the fairness of the flat
    And rove the rocky range.
That goes for me—though blurred I see,
    And grey is my chin stubble,
A reckless old son of a gun,
    With saddle-pack at rise of sun,
Here's fare-you-well to everyone . . .
    Hooray! the Trail of Trouble.

MONGREL

A puppy dog without a collar
   Annexed me on my evening walk;
His coat suggested fleas and squalor,
   His tail had never known a dock.
So humble, trusting, wistful was he,
   I gave his head a cautious pat,
Then I regretted it because he
   Accompanied me to my door-mat.

And there with morning milk I found him,
   Where he had slumbered all the night;
I could not with displeasure hound him,
   So wonderful was his delight.
And so with him I shared my porridge—
   Oh! How voraciously he ate!
And then I had the woeful courage
   To thrust him through the garden gate.

But there all morning long he waited;
   I had to sneak out by the back.
To hurt his feelings how I hated,
   Yet somehow he got on my track.
For down the road he sudden saw me
   And though in trees I tried to hide,
How pantingly he sought to paw me,
   And yelped with rapture by my side.

Poor dirty dog! I should have coshed him,
    But after all 'twas not his fault;
And so I took him home and washed him,
    —I'm that soft-hearted kind of dolt.
But then he looked so sadly thinner,
    Though speckless clean and airy bright,
I had to buck him up with dinner
    And keep him for another night.

And now he is a household fixture
    And never wants to leave my side;
A doggy dog, a mongrel mixture,
    I couldn't lose him if I tried.
His tail undocked is one wild wiggle,
    His heaven is my happy nod;
His life is one ecstatic wriggle,
    And I'm his God.

PIES

A poet is a goofy guy
With dandruff in his hair.
I'm glad a poet am not I,
Indeed I little care
For bards who sing
Of Love and Spring—
I'd rather sing of Pie.

I'd rather rhyme of pastry and
The trove of orchard fare,
That mother moulded with her hand
To fabrications fair,
Of loganberry,
Plum and cherry,
Apple, peach and pear.

Or hap, those deep, delicious pies
It was her joy to bake,
Of chicken breast and turkey thighs,
And kidney and beef-steak:
I can't forget when gravy wet
Their rich and crispy flake.

With pumpkin, lemon, raisin, mince
She sure had proud success;
I've never ate their equal since,
And never will, I guess:
If Ma bakes pie up in the sky
She'll merit holiness.

142

Of gooseberry and custard what
Fond memories arise!
Of cinnamon the very thought
Brings moisture to my eyes . . .
Let poets tune to rose and moon,
I'll pipe of mother's pies.

EELS

Let poets sing the joy of Spring
  As I have in my time,
But now I seek the lyre to tweak
  Of less exalted rhyme.
A simple lay of every day
  More to my mood appeals:
Let me revive the memory I've
  OF EELS.

Oh! Have you ever, daft with joy,
  On holiday from school,
Sloshed up a burn, a bare-foot boy,
  From gold to silver pool?
Green weed streams in the glassy flood,
  Then suddenly you feel
Between your toes, inch deep in mud,
  The wiggle of an eel.

You stomp down hard and grab it tight,
  Your hands like bands of steel;
It wriggles like a streak of light,
  Then nowhere is your eel.
Yet what a whopping one it was,
  And how you darn your luck;
And stealthily you tread because
  It's still there in the muck.

Then once again you tread on it,
    Embedded in the slime,
And though it squiggles quite a bit,
    You've got it cinched this time.
You take it home with heart aglow,
    For Ma to fry or pot,
Then sigh a little, for it's so
    Much smaller than you thought.

I've fished the world of sea or shore
    For salmon, trout and pike;
For bass, bluegill and albacore,
    For tuna and the like.
Yet never have I known the joy
    In thrill of singing reel
As when a bare-foot, eight year boy
    I grabbed an eight inch eel.

PIGS

My mother sow with babies ten
   Is proud as any queen;
Each morning I wheat-straw the pen
   For pigs are truly clean.
My piglets are so cute and sweet
   I grieve to see them grow,
Each nuzzling a tiny teat,
   A plump and rosy row.

And grow they do; with every day
   They seem to gain in girth,
And as I watch them squeal and play
   I rock with ruddy mirth.
Yet as I note their merry jigs
   I shudder some, because
I hate to think of roasted pigs
   With apples in their jaws.

And then one morn old Mother Sow
   Looks up and seems to say:
"It's you must feed my babies now
   With barley meal and whey.
For though they poke with coral snout,
   My fount of plenty dries . . .
The orchard waits—say, what about
   Our bit of paradise!"

So then the pen I open wide
   And let them all go free.
Oh! How they hustle eager-eyed
   From pear to apple tree!
The orchard grass is juicy green,
   The windfalls star the sod,
And while Ma Sow is like a queen
   I feel akin to God.

Poor innocents! When all too soon
   Will gleam the butcher's knife,
Let each beneath the harvest moon
   Enjoy enchanted life.
And so the merriest of men,
   Beneath benignant skies
I give my little piggies ten
   Their bit of paradise.

WHIMSICALITIES

EATERIES

I went into a Hashery:
"Poached eggs on toast," said I;
"Please let the hen-fruit new-laid be,
And let the toast be dry."
The waitress was a saucy doll
Who looked at me and laughed,
As to the cook I heard her bawl:
                    "Two on a raft."

I went into a Steakery:
"A sirloin grilled," I said;
"Please let the outside browny be,
And let the in be red.
Let it be thick, with fat a streak,
And with fried onions covered." . . .
And then I heard that beldame shriek:
                    "A teebone smothered."

I went into a Beanery,
For I was low of means,
And of the wench who waited me
I ordered: "Pork and beans."
Yet through me still a horrid thrill
Of disapproval runs,
Remembering that maiden's shrill:
                    "Pig and the noisy ones."

CHASTITY

Do they envy her as she flashes by
    In her shiny limousine,
In her satin gown with her head held high
    And her look of a movie queen?
Do they see the lines in her painted face,
    And the boredom glooming through?
Do they envy her in her haughty place?
        THEY DO.

Do they know she is just a painted doll,
    A girl in a gilded cage?
Well, not exactly a gangster's moll
    But the toy of a man of age.
Do they deem her a whited sepulchre
    And a blot to womanhood?
Do you think they would swop their lots with her?
        THEY WOULD.

And bending over the kitchen sink
    Where the supper dishes soak,
Do they thank the Lord as they gladly think
    They are just plain honest folk?
With her sheeny pearls in a triple cord
    And her face of a fallen saint,
Are they glad that virtue's its own reward?
        THEY DAM WELL AIN'T.

PEEPS

In callow youth my crusty college,
    Although it fed me facts in heaps,
Omitted to instil the knowledge
    That P-E-P-Y-S spells Peeps.
And as I pride myself my step is
    Precise where diction is concerned,
When someone said: "Pray, who is Peppies?"
    You may imagine how I squirmed.

Despite the old boy's fornication,
    And dashing rakes and demireps,
I liked his diurnal relation,
    And oftentimes I called him "Peps".
Yet I am grieved beyond the telling,
    And disillusion o'er me sweeps,
To think, with all that swanky spelling,
    Old Sam was simply Mister Peeps.

Well, what care I; for what the hell is
    Pronounciation when all's said;
It's my belief the way we spell is
    The way a surname should be read.
And so pedantic scorn unheeding,
    It's "Peppies" he will be for keeps. . . .
Ah no, old Sam, when you I'm reading
    By gosh! I'll never call you PEEPS.

MY SPECS

Alas! I fear that every day
  My family I vex,
As crustily they hear me say:
  "Where have I put my specs?"
I hunt them here, I hunt them there,
  I search each likely spot;
I ought to have an extra pair,
  But somehow I have not.

I probe the arm-chair, turn the bed,
  I grovel on the floor;
I mumble, grumble, scratch my head,
  And search my pockets o'er.
I revisit the toilet seat,
  And oh the time that passes,
As I this litany repeat:
  "Where are them goddam glasses?"

Says Ma: "Where did you leave them last?"
  Such dumbness floors me flat.
Says I: "I'd find them mighty fast
  If I could tell you that."
Yet though I'm Deacon of the Church
  I cuss—you may suppose,
When Ma says: "Pa, why don't you search
                   Your nose?"

THE KISS

When Will came home his wife was knitting;
With back towards him she was sitting,
And did not see him as he went
With stealth, and over her he bent,
Planting, instead of husband peck,
A lover kiss behind the neck.

Then—then her ear he gave a clout,
And when with fear she turned about,
And shrieked: "Why are you cuffing me?"
Said Will: " 'Tis very plain to see:
I bussed ye, lass, then smacked because
Ye didn't turn to see who 'twas."

THE HAGGIS

Said Jock to Jean: "Whit did ye do
    Wi' yon wee haggis, plump an' grey,
I carried home for me and you
    To cheer our hearts on Hogmanay?"

Said Jean to Jock: "I didna' ken
    It wis a haggis—In ma doot
I gazed an' gazed at it, and then
    I took the tongs an' threw it oot.

"Ye shoulda' telt me. When you brought
    It in the cat came at the run,
An' sniffed at it—I think she thought
    'Twas something naughty *she* had done.

"Poor Puss! Wi' shame she looked at me,
    An' did the best that she was able
To cover it . . . Jist look how she
    Scratched a' the varnish aff the table!"

CUCKOLDS

Said Charles: "I trowed my wife was true,
    But now I doubt it;
Our eyes are brown, our babe's are blue—
    Pa, what about it?"

"Don't worry, Charlie," said his Dad.
    "Iron out your frown.
Your Ma and I blue optics had,
    And yours are brown.

"I've often wondered if you were
    My lawful son;
As any wife is apt to err,
    She might have done.

"And then I thought: my eyes are blue,
    Yet Grandpapa's
Are of the same hot hazel hue
    As Grandmama's.

"So don't let us our spouses shame
    By mean suspicion,
But keep an open mind and blame
    Remote transmission."

156

AUNT JENNIE

Old Aunt Jennie used to lay
A hand as gentle as a dove,
Upon my brow, stroke down and say:
"My laddie, that's the way of love."
Then suddenly with upward scruff
That made me laugh, it seemed so funny,
She'd give my mouth and nose a ruff,
And snap: "My boy, that's Matrimony."

There must be truth in what she said,
For though the marriage bond has blisses,
Most lovers learn when they are wed
There's more to bread and cheese than kisses.
Aunt Jennie did not know romance,
So there was reason for her stricture,
And yet in youth she had her chance,
Since she was pretty as a picture.

Today I heard a lover's plea,
(And I am sure he truly meant it)
"Be mine for life!" I hope that he
Had not a lifetime to repent it.
Aunt Jennie, soothing soft as fluff
My face, says: "This is love, my sonny."
Then with a rasping upward ruff:
"And that, sweet brat, is Mat-rimony."

OLD SOURPUSS

Today I met a man who laughed
   At everyone with mocking glee;
I thought the fellow must be daft,
   For nothing funny could I see.
         He even laughed at ME.

For I am rarely moved to mirth,
   And less disposed to smile than sigh;
Yet as I groaned with gloom of earth
   I wondered: Was this sunny guy
         A loony—or was I?

Well, now I get a heap of fun,
   For I have changed my point of view;
Like him I laugh at everyone—
   Oh! More discreetly, it is true. . . .
         I even laugh at YOU.

THE TEST

Sometimes a bit of rhyme I see
　　In magazine or book
That makes such fond appeal to me
　　Its flaws I overlook;
It may be just a simple lay,
　　Yet humanly so pat,
That when I've scanned it twice I say:
　　"I wish I'd written that."

But when I read some classic ode
　　Of gods and mighty men,
To finish it I have to goad
　　My patience now and then.
Although to thrill to it I try,
　　Its organ note goes flat,
And honestly I cannot sigh:
　　"I wish I'd written that."

Some poems lift aloft the mind,
　　Some whisper to the heart;
Unto the last I'm more inclined,
　　Though innocent of art.
Some verses get beneath my skin—
　　Like *Casey at the Bat,*
Or *Jim Bloodso* or *Gunga Din*—
　　Why didn't I write that?

These bards have got the edge on me,
    I've missed the lyric bus;
My rhymes and metres, I agree,
    Are sadly obvious.
My balladeering lays I rue,
    I'm just a copy-cat. . . .
Goldarn that devil, Dan McGrew—
    Oh why did I write that?

DEATH OF A CROAKER

You've heard of Montreal Maree,
   That rose of scented sin;
But are you hep to Doc' McGee
   Whose lubricant was gin?
The poor old Doc' has gone, I fear,
   To dry and dusty doom;
Yet why does Maree shed a tear
   So frequent on his tomb?

I'll tell you. It was in the whirl
   Around our Christmas tree,
Outshining every glamour girl
   Was Montreal Maree;
And of the rowdy bunch of us
   Who round her feet did flock,
None was half so assiduous
   And ardent as the Doc'.

Then Maree mounted on the stage
   To do her special show,
Her Floradora dance, the rage
   In circles of Sourdough.
And as the boys stood up and cheered
   Them shapely limbs to see,
The gayest of the gang who peered
   Was gallant Doc' McGee.

Then suddenly she paused to show
    A needle and some thread:
"Can any of you smarties sew?
    I've split my tights," she said.
A hundred answered to her call:
    "We surely can," cried we;
But most vociferous of all
    Was grey-haired Doc' McGee.

I heard the warning of Maree;
    I saw the frenzied rush.
Alas! Too late—poor Doc' McGee
    Was trampled in the crush.
Aye, when we dragged him to the light
    That gay old guy was dead;
Yet lo! His dauntless hand held tight
    A needle and some thread.

BIDE-A-WEE

You've heard, may be, of Maw McGee
    Who from Old Reekie came;
A lorn and lonely widder she,
    And sorry for the same;
Who put her scanty savings in
    A tiny shop for tea,
In Lucky Strike, that bed of sin,
    And called it Bide-a-Wee.

The which is Scotch for Rest-A-While,
    But somehow no one did,
And poor Maw with a sickly smile
    Her woe and worry hid.
Her hand-made scones and cookies were
    Forever growing stale,
For sourdoughs vinously aver
    Tea's splendid—for the trail.

Then one day Montreal Maree,
    In gaily passing bye
Saw silver-haired old Maw McGee
    Partaking of a cry.
So bold she breezed into the shop:
    "I like your joint," says she;
"And every afternoon I'll stop
    To have a cup of tea."

Right there she tuckered in with toast
    And orange-pekoe brew;
Of shortbread that was Scotland's boast
    She bought a pound or two.
Then to the dance-hall dolls she spoke:
    "I sink zere ees no doubt
Zat poor ol' leddy she go broke:
    We gotta help her out."

And so next day 'twas joy to see
    Them babies bargin' in,
And Maw was busy as a bee
    Amid a merry din.
And then the hooch-hounds lent their aid;
    Said they: "It's jest like home."
Why, even spoonin' marmalade
    Was Black Moran from Nome.

The Nugget Bar was lonesome-like
    From four to five each day,
And wondering was One-eyed Mike
    What kept the boys away.
Says he: "Where are them sons o' guns?
    I'll stroll the street to see."
When lo! he found them buying buns
    In jam-packed Bide-a-Wee.

The boys looked sheepish, I'll allow,
    As One-eyed Mike strolled in,
To see him kiss Maw on the brow
    And greet her with a grin.
"Why, bless you, dear, give me a pot,
    And make it strong," says he;
"Since Mother died I've quite forgot
    The taste of home made tea."

So in the Camp of Lucky Strike
    Maw sure has made the grade,
And patronized by One-eyed Mike
    She plies a pretty trade.
To all the girls a mother's part
    She plays but oh how she
Is grateful for the golden heart
    Of Montreal Maree!

THE CHECK-UP

My health had never been in question;
I felt as good as other men,
Until my wife made the suggestion
I have a check-up now and then.
The Doctor fellow fussed and fiddled
Until I fair got in a fright,
And then his stethoscope he twiddled;
Said he: "Do you get up at night?"

"Sometimes," I told him, little thinking,
"I like a bedtime beer or two,
And no one can deny when drinking,
That what you swallow must go through."
He looked at me with sudden bleakness:
"Ah now," says he, "I understand;
What troubles you is prostate weakness,
And I must take your case in hand."

He orders me expensive potions,
Despite I be of little wealth;
And fills me full of fearful notions
Pertaining to my state of health.
He gives me mensuel inspections,
And seems new trouble to provoke,
For now he's talking of injections,
And hell! He says I'm not to smoke. . . .

So lads who hold a hefty neck up,
To sluice a throttle dry as bone,
Don't go to doctors for a check-up,
But just let "well enough" alone.

MY NOT-SO-LITTLE MARY

I've written stanzas in my time,
   And some were rummy;
So now I want to make a rhyme
   About my tummy;
This organ I am viewing now
   With some perplexity,
Disliking with a furrowed brow
   Its smug convexity.

But though its bold exterior
   My vanity belittles,
I sing of its interior
   Wherein I launch my vittles;
That cavity mysterious
   That handles all my eatings,
Benign or deleterious
   With gastronomic greetings.

I love my grub; I hate to sit
   And feel my innards hollow;
Yet wonder what becomes of it
   With every bite I swallow.
It's true I might read up its fate,
   But science I find boring,
And so I let it go its gait,
   Its functioning ignoring.

I love my heart; its faithful beat
   Obtains my approbation;
But when delicious food I eat
   I feel a veneration
For that proud part of me that makes
   My waist a hummock. . . .
Yea, spite of gas and belly aches
   God bless my stomach!

DIRT

Dirt is just matter out of place,
  So scientists aver;
But when I see a miner's face
  I wonder if they err.
For grit and grime and grease may be
  In God's constructive plan,
A symbol of nobility,
  The measure of a man.

There's nought so clean as honest dirt,
  So of its worth I sing;
I value more an oily shirt
  Than garment of a king.
There's nought so proud as honest sweat,
  And though its stink we cuss,
We kid-glove chaps are in the debt
  Of those who sweat for us.

It's dirt and sweat that makes us folks
  Proud as we are today;
We owe our wealth to weary blokes
  Befouled by soot and clay.
And where you see a belly fat
  A dozen more are lean. . . .
By God! I'd sooner doff my hat
  To washer-wife than queen.

So here's a song to dirt and sweat,
        A grace to grit and grime;
A hail to workers who beget
        The wonders of our time.
And as they gaze, though gutter-girt,
        To palaces enskied,
Let them believe, by sweat and dirt,
        They, too, are glorified.

HEAT

I am just an ancient cove
  With a little room,
And in it a little stove
  Fights December gloom;
For my blessings great and small,
  Such as bread and meat,
I thank God, but most of all
  I praise Him for Heat.

When my tiny stove is lit
  Loud may be the storm,
I can huddle over it
  Snug and safe and warm.
One needs roof and couch and clothes,
  One must drink and eat,
But I reckon each of those
  Just a form of heat.

Warmth is life and cold is death;
  Snow is my despair;
I must go before my breath
  Freezes in the air.
So my little stove I hug,
  Blankets round my feet,
Poor in purse but safe and snug,
  Blessing God for Heat.

THE MUSIC MAKERS

We have a dago painter in
Who carols all day long;
Above the traffic's muted din
I hear his sunny song.
So if I had to work by hand
Instead of with my nob,
I'd like to be a painter and
To warble on the job.

Our plumber, though lethargic, has
A lyric gift, perhaps;
For arias he whistles as
He tinkers at my taps.
The trills he has at his command
No frozen pipe can irk:
I'd love to be a plumber and
Make music as I work.

It helps a lot, with throat or lip
In life's contentious coil
To make a pretty partnership
Of melody and toil.
The times are grim, so here's to him
Who does not gripe or shirk,
But gaily tries to harmonize
The joy he has in work.

A WOMAN'S WAY

When I was three and she was four,
    The rowdiest of girls,
She soiled my pretty pinafore
    And pulled my curls.
When I was five and she was six,
    In kindergarten school,
She bullied me and with her tricks
    Made me a fool.

When bobby-socked and flapperish,
    With hockey sticks for toys,
She spoke of me as "that poor fish"
    To other boys.
When with her chewing gum in cheek
    She got work as a sten—
Ographer at twelve bucks a week,
    I just made ten.

Though always next door neighbours we,
    Her scorn I did incur,
And while she cocked her snoot at me
    I hated her.
Yet now, complacently elate
    Her triumph you should see:
Her life disdain to culminate
    She's married me.

KNOCKING IS OUT

Said old Grandpa, that silver sage
  Who mellows in the sun:
"I guess I've reached the goofy age
  When I like everyone.
I'm too old now to nurse a thought
  Of cussedness or spleen;
I don't do things I didn't ought,
  And keep my shirt-tail clean."

Then as his bowl of soup he stirred
  He let this dictum fall:
"When I can't speak a kindly word
  I'll speak no word at all.
You fellers may your hammers ply,
  But when you knock and knock,
Include me always out, for I
  Am sold on sunny talk.

"I aim to say no spiteful thing;
  With folded hands I sit,
And if a thought inbeds a sting
  I jest don't utter it.
I know you young 'uns think I'm dumb
  When with a shoulder shrug,
(A candidate for Kingdom Come)
  I zipper up my mug.

"Yep! Now my hammer's on the shelf
     And I won't take it down,
For I've decided in myself
     A smile outbids a frown.
So with a mild and mellow gaze
     I purge my soul of gall. . . .
Please Lordy, let me live with praise
     Or not at all."

A VERSATILE MAN

I've painted nearly all my life
   Yet never sold a daub;
Despite reproaches from my wife
   I still keep at the job.
I just completed one today,
   As happy as a boy,
And though I can't *give* them away
   My pictures bring me joy.

I've written verses from my youth
   Yet haven't published one;
I've never tried, to tell the truth,
   But oh it's heaps of fun
To make a poem of a thought,
   And though it's waste of time,
Because it pleases me a lot
   I keep on making rhyme.

I strum upon an old guitar
   And tiny tunes compose;
Oh! Very sweet they often are
   But no one ever knows;
For no song-plugger ever has
   Conspired to make them known,
And yet I'm very happy as
   I sing them all alone.

Had these three talents I possess
    Been fused into a whole,
I might have tasted a success
    And scored a modest goal.
Well there's no reason to be sad
    When all is said and done:
I'm just a dud, but how I've had
    A wagonful of fun!

PROFANE POET

In olden days if you were rash
   Enough to print a swear,
You used a letter and a dash
   To indicate your "dare";
Then Grandmama would shake her head,
   And Cousin May would blush,
And if the cuss-word Father said
   Mama would murmur: "Hush."

But nowadays in printer's ink
   If I say dash and hang,
And asterisk, the ladies think
   My verse is lacking tang.
The naughty words I must express —
   Ah! things get wuss and wuss:
A poem's not complete unless
   It coruscates a cuss.

Well, to the fair sex I comply,
   Though sadly am I loth;
To no sweet dame could I deny
   A good old-fashioned oath.
A bard of bald profanity
   Reluctantly I am. . . .
Reproachful Reader, pity me—-
   Oh blast and dash and d—n!

POETS

A poet is a human joke;
The humouristic people poke
Their fun at him and laugh a lot:
I'm glad a poet I am not.
He writes a volume none will buy;
From it the customer doth shy:
Though fine as Keats and wise as Plato
He drops it like a hot potato.

A poet's life is cruel hard,
And if I were a blooming bard
I'd go around in patchy pants
And live on dole of maiden aunts.
A poet has a sorry time:
Thank God I'm just a man of rhyme
And in plain verse my thoughts compose,
Or even condescend to prose.

So you who wrestle with the Muse
And to abandon it refuse,
Regard with due humility
Your lyrical futility;
And think of poets ranked sublime
Who grace the Pantheon of Time,
Of Milton, Shakespeare, Pope and Donne,
Of Browning, Burns and Tennyson.

So friends, with these let's be content,
Nor seek to join the poor per cent
Of goofy guys who homage pay
To piddling poets of today.

RHYME-MONGER

Most everyday like egg I lay
          A lyric smooth,
Of even time and ready rhyme,
          My skill to prove;
I ponder it as snug I sit
          In book-lined den,
And when it's done to lunch I run
          Like clucking hen.

When I immerse myself in verse,
          Pursuing rhyme,
Life's fuss and fret I fain forget,
          So speeds the time.
The Muse incites the man who writes
          Sweet words to clink,
And to him sings delightful things
          He failed to think.

A verse a day keeps care away
          And happy I'm
To count with lip and finger tip
          Syllabic chime;
And having laid my egg and made
          My lyric drive,
I park my pen, so happy when
          A poem I've.

POEMS OF PEOPLE

REQUIEM

Though we were sleek and rotten rich,
   No greasy florins would we spend;
We dumped him in a dirty ditch
   And doomed him to a pauper's end.
One devil's day of storm and sleet,
   With none to mourn and none to pray,
From poverty, pain and defeat
                 He passed away.

A great and saintly soul revealed
   In harmonies now deemed divine,
We left him in the Potter's Field,
   With never on the grave a sign.
His sick wife from her bed arose,
   To seek in vain the resting place
Of one whom all the world now knows
                 For tuneful grace.

His years were only thirty-five,
   Yet music's miracle was he;
None other twice as long alive
   Has matched his magic minstrelsy.
No gentler being, pure as snow,
   Was ever dumped from charnel cart
To grave unmarked . . . His name you know—
           MOZART.

ALBERT

My husband is a worthy man,
   He occupies much space.
He runs the house to fit his plan
   And everything's in place.
He has a kind, forbearing smile,
   He knows just how to treat me;
And yet I wish once in a while
   He would get drunk and beat me.

My husband is a noble guy,
   His sentiments are proper;
He never would forgive if I
   Should ever come a cropper.
He is of such a moral mood,
   'Twould give me joy, believe me,
If every now and then he would
   With some bright bitch deceive me.

Should I attain to widowhood,
   (His heart is weak, I fear)
I'll tell the world he was so good,
   And shed a tepid tear.
Aye, Albert is a model mate,
   He guides and counsels me. . . .
Yet in my heart oh how I hate
   His damned nobility.

EDWIN

When my dear husband died in grace
    I vowed I'd never take another;
Yet here, prepared to take his place
    And share my home comes his twin brother.
How strange that God should take away
    The saintly one and leave the sinner:
For Edgar—Edwin used to pray,
    And now the wicked one's the winner.

'Tis true the two were like as peas
    When first they left their mother's nipples;
Yet Edwin shone at tennis teas
    While Edgar at the Anchor tipples.
In sooth the black sheep and the white. . . .
    (Poor Edwin might have been a Vicar)
Yet Edgar is so nice despite
    His wenching and his love of liquor.

They say a woman loves a rake—
    It may be so, I never knew it.
I should be lone, for Edwin's sake;
    If I re-marry I may rue it.
Yet Edgar's such a handsome brute
    I fear he may my double-bed win—
The pious and the dissolute. . . .
    What shall I do? Alas, poor Edwin!

WILLIAM

How merciless can children be!
    Dark truth within them lies.
My little daughter said to me,
    With candour in her eyes:
"Oh! Mother dear, you seem more gay
    Since Daddie went away."

Said I: "Oh! No, I just pretend;
    You know I cried and cried,
And thought my heart would never mend
    When your poor father died.
For your sake, child, with laughter light,
    I make the gloom seem bright."

Yet children have so strange a ken
    I wonder if it's so;
If I'm not happier since when
    My William had to go.
He was a kind and loving spouse,
    And Master of the house.

Then as we gravely sipped our tea,
    Said my sweet daughter Ann:
"Oh! Mumsie dear, I would not be
    The wife of any man. . . .
Can I not be a widow too,
    And laugh and sing like you?"

MY PREDECESSOR

"Dear David died a year ago",
  Said my sweet wife to me;
"I'd like to shed a tear or so
  For him, if you agree."
"A very worthy thought," said I;
  "In fact I'll go with you. . . .
Poor David! it is tough to die
  When one is forty-two."

So to the cemetery we
  With sober faces went,
And I looked glumly on as she
  Above his tombstone bent.
At first with her I sympathized,
  For I knew David well,
Then suddenly I realized
  I hated him like hell.

Why did he have to go and die
  And leave his spouse to me?
A happy bachelor was I,
  Exuberantly free.
Elaine is fond beyond belief,
  Yet as we homeward hied,
I was the one who sobbed with grief
  Because poor David died.

HERBERT

He loved the country, she the town,
   And so he stuck it with the Store,
In stale apartment battened down,
   Amid the city's reek and roar.
And when Babe went to women's clubs
   And played a gainful game of cards,
He drank his beer in local pubs
         And prowled the boulevards.

Then when from business he retired,
   And smoked his pipe with time to waste,
He thought: "By Nature-love inspired
   Now I can gratify my taste.
A cottage and a strip of ground,
   A garden—that's my cup of tea. . . ."
At last the very thing he found,
         And took Babe down to see.

With eyes aglow and heart abrim
   He showed her round the garden gay;
Some wistful roses raptured him,
   But she had nothing much to say.
And when he spoke of growing food,
   With bleak regard she damped him down. . . .
Alas! he saw it was no good,
         And drove her back to town.

And now he roams the greasy streets,
    A little rabbit man who dreams
Of growing carrots, spuds and beets,
    And cabbages and lima beans.
Yet when fat wife to bridge has gone,
    And into dopey dream he slips. . . .
Lo! gossamer is on the lawn,
                A rose is at his lips.

EDWARD

Of children we had only one;
Alas! A little crippled son
        Was all I bore;
And after seven years of care
And gloom and grief we did not dare
        To pray for more.
Now Edward's hair is almost white
And mine is gentling in the light
        With silver touch;
We're growing old . . . it's long ago,
Yet still I clasp with heart of woe
        A tiny crutch.

I keep it up the garret stair,
Well hid, for Edward cannot bear
        To look on it;
He thought that I had best destroy
This sad momento of a boy
        For life unfit.
I wonder if he did not blame
Me darkly that the lad was lame––
        I've heard him say
There was not in his family
A taint of ill and sound was he
        In every way.

He freezes up, his face is set,
He fondly thinks he can forget
             Yet evermore
I know, like me, with inner ear
A ghostly *tap tap* he will hear
             Upon the floor.
For mouselike as I climbed the stair
I came on him all unaware
             And saw him clutch
Close in his arms with weary woe,
And sob and sob with grief, although
It's oh so long and long ago—
             A tiny crutch.

ASCENT TO HADES

The day I died Will said to me:
"Don't grieve—a few short years
And reunited we will be
Beyond this vale of tears.
My own dispatch is overdue
To paradise above:
Full soon I will be linked with you
In everlasting love."

But Heaven is a lonely place
When one's love is not there;
And so I begged a moment's space,
Ghostwise on earth to fare,
That I might see my Will again,
And still my fond alarms . . .
When lo! I saw him to my pain
Clasped in another's arms.

Alas! he looked so young and bright,
His joy was sad to see,
For in his passion and delight
He had forgotten me.
Knowing that angels may not cry
I smile and all is well . . .
May he be happy—yet how nigh
Can Heaven be to Hell!

SHE TOOK THE VEIL

She took the Veil: I wondered why,
    And could not understand;
For oh I loved her like to die
    And sought to win her hand.
But no, she chose the Living Grave,
    Though paths of light we trod,
And in a convent grim she gave
                Herself to God.

Her cheeks were like the rambler rose,
    Her eyes a lupin blue;
No sweeter blossom could unclose
    To greet the morning dew.
And yet she chose the cloister gloom
    Rather than be my wife,
In grisly garb to dreary doom
                Condemned for life.

Is it some madness of the mood
    That makes a maid to pray,
When her dream might be motherhood,
    A wife's her worthy way?
My heart for her with worship throbbed
    Beyond all saintly pride,
And now I curse the God who robbed
                Me of my bride.

TIME'S CRUELTY

Though we were half a world apart
　　Her image haunted me,
And so I sought my old sweetheart
　　Across estranging sea;
Although since I bade her goodbye
　　Were thirty years and three.

So to her cosy cottage door
　　With quickened pulse I came . . .
Lo! Everything was as before,
　　The garden was the same;
With on the gate an ancient plate
　　Enamelled with her name.

"Miss Susan Grey, Mus. Bac." it read:
　　So she still carried on
At teaching scales to make her bread,
　　Though half a life had gone . . .
Then the door opened to my knock—
　　God! How I had a shock!

Who was this frailing crone who peered
　　From lavender and lace,
With wonder at my salty beard,
　　With blankness at my face?
Yet on her finger was the ring
　　I gave one fairy Spring.

So to my great surprise I said:
  "Does Missis Brown live here?"
She gravely shook her silvered head:
  " 'Tis not this street, I fear;"
Then having nothing more to say
  I bowed and went my way.

That's all . . . For women in life's wear
  Grow old before their time;
And she was bent and crushed with care,
  And I in lusty prime.
It hurt—my name I could not tell . . .
  Yet oh it spared her hell.

JONES IN CAPRI

By sunny seas I puff at ease
    My pipe of briar,
And pity those who warm their toes
    Beside a fire;
While others seek the London reek
    In daily doses,
How it is sweet at dawn to greet
    December roses.

Yet I was just a drudge who must
    Slave in the City;
From morn to dark rheumatic clerk
    In warehouse gritty.
No hope had I of brighter sky,
    In Brixton greying,
And so I quit to do a bit
    Of foreign straying.

And here I've found a tenting ground
    Of peace and plenty,
A beauty land of *dolche* and
    Of *far niente*.
I do not know a fret although
    My funds are scanty;
Spaghetti takes the place of steaks,
    Of beer—*chianti*.

So here beside this happy tide
   My heart has fixed on,
My pipe I'll smoke and never poke
   A fire in Brixton;
Aye, here I'll stay while solar ray
   Cures my lumbago,
And with my sum of thrift become
   Almost a Dago.

PLAYWRIGHT

I had a friend of eighty-five
Who might today be still alive,
But that he let the doctors sound
And poke him till a flaw they found:
"Your liver's in a parlous state,"
Said they: "We ought to operate."

"I am too old for that," said he.
"It may be bad, but let it be.
It's lasted me throughout my life,
And don't deserve the surgeon's knife.
Just let it go a year or two;
The Lean Man waits, I'm nearly due."

But as he was a man of fame
They operated just the same.
Alas! he never left his bed,
And in a fortnight he was dead.
And so I think—conclusion grim,
The goddam doctors butchered him.

His name? Maybe you know it too,
So don't let "croakers" fool with you.

NOVELIST

When I was young and free from guile
   I knew a writer of renown,
Who told me with a charming smile:
   "I never let a woman down.

"When some sweet creature I desire,
   I pray she will be kind to me;
And when of her I truly tire
   I buy her an annuity."

Then thought I, with an inward frown:
   "All right for you, you've heaps of pelf;
You never let a woman down,
   But what, old chap, about yourself?

"The price to you is just a dole
   To pay for dainty flesh and bone;
You buy a precious human soul,
   But how dirt cheap you sell your own!

"Though each new year a conquest crown
   You in your sybaritic hell,
Yourself you let down, down and down. . . .
        You dog, you smell!"

JOURNALIST

Ere patriotic passion died
He made a song of love and pride.
With blood and tears he wrote, I think,
Yet when it paled to printer's ink,
A million echoed his refrain:
                    England again!

There was such faith, such noble rage,
Such glow and glory in his page,
Such bugle call to high emprise,
Honour and hope and sacrifice,
Unto the stars rang out his strain:
                    England again!

England again! One winter day
I heard a Fleet Street fellow say:
"Poor So-and-so is destitute.
Too bad a bard of his repute
Should starve . . . A patriot so stout·
                    Let's help him out."

England again! Today I heard
In pauper's grave he was interred,
And wonder in his misery
Did he lament "When one can see
The land he worships run to rot,
A man's a bloody fool to be
                    A PATRIOT."

POET

Had he been Scotch, like you or me,
He might have saved a braw bawbee
           For rainy day;
But being Irish he would lend
His bottom dollar to a friend
           Who'd never pay.
He had his whack of dizzy fame,
And though the dough in lashins came,
           It went like smoke.
He'd blow it in on sport and spree,
And so perennially he
           Was stoney broke.

Then in due course his vogue was past;
He saw his star eclipsed at last,
           His books unsold.
The editors sent back his stuff,
His publishers were peeved and gruff,
           His friends grew cold.
If those he helped had paid him back,
He might have rustled quite a stack,
           But few came through;
And so to poverty he sank,
While to console himself he drank—
           Fool thing to do.

And then I heard some fellow say
That he was paralysed and lay
                    In Belvedere.
And so with heavy heart I took
Along with me his favourite book,
                    And saw him there.
He hailed me from a pauper's bed:
"You've brought my master-piece," he said,
                    With twisted laugh.
"You cast a pearl before a swine.
Behold! I cannot even sign
                    My autograph."

Alas he's gone into the Night,
Like many a man who burned too bright
                    The festive flame.
And so my story being true,
I leave it, Reader, up to you
                    To guess his name.

PATRIOT

Sweet God! What a heavenly morning!
　　Was ever a sunrise so fair!
How golden the gorse is adorning
　　The hill; hark the lark in the air!
And yet no delight I exhibit,
　　But wistfully look at the sky. . . .
For here I am under a gibbet
　　　　Preparing to die.

To die when the year's in its glory,
　　When earth is exultant with glee;
To come to the end of my story
　　When gladness is all that I see.
When praise of God's handiwork hallows
　　With rapture one's every breath,
To pause on the brink of the gallows,
　　　　Awaiting my death.

A traitor my enemies call me,
　　A hero am I to my friends.
No matter: Whatever befall me
　　In heaven or hell, here it ends.
My patriot heart is unbaffled,
　　Though doomed to defeat is my hope,
As proudly I stand on the scaffold
　　　　My neck in the rope.

I'm hearing the bells in the steeple;
　　My murderers foul I forgive.
I go with the prayers of my people,
　　I die that my country may live.
My eyes on the sweet sun are steady,
　　My heart is alift to the sky. . . .
"Right O, Mister Hangman, I'm ready."
　　　　"*Sir Roger*, good-bye."

IN THE UNDERGROUND

That they were made for one another
        How could they know?
'Twas in the Underground's foul smother,
        Its ebb and flow;
At six o'clock—rush hour, they met,
Both cold and tired and sopping wet.

How could they know with nerves so frayed
        In sad, vile weather,
That in a million they were made
        To come together?
Jammed soggily in that grey mob
He checked an oath and she a sob.

How could they know they were twin souls,
        Sheer bliss their crowning?
They faced each other, blind as moles,
        Half bored, half frowning:
With joy they should have cried aloud,
And kissed and clung despite the crowd.

But no, they went their weary way
        Without a thought,
And in the tide of traffic they
        Were swift upcaught:
No doubt he cursed her damp umbrella;
She thought him: "just another fellow."

And yet oh how they might have been,
      With dancing heart,
Of cityful joy's king and queen,
      Never to part!
How could they know each was for each
      The perfect mate!
They met, they passed, no word of speech,
      Two lives frustrate.

CHILDLESS

They say love makes the world go round,
But though my husband is a dear,
No family I dare to found,
For I am overcome by fear;
And even one black sheep in seven
Would make a hell out of my heaven.

How many tote a load of care,
And are with ill-starred offspring curst?
Of all the crosses hard to bear
An erring daughter is the worst.
How many are with anguish torn,
And wish a son had ne'er been born!

My sister has a girl that's lame,
With bones that never will be well;
My brother has a son of shame
Who ornaments a prison cell;
My neighbour has an idiot boy,
Who poisons at its source her joy.

These are but three of many more,
Who make me glad I have no brood;
For I am coward to the core
And shrink the chance of motherhood. . . .

Weak woman, voicing direful doom;
A President may wait your womb.

208

LITTLE SISTER

She always had a crave to write,
  And when we walked from school,
Her bits of verse she would recite
  Until I felt a fool.
She filled a ten-cent copy-book
  With lines and lines of rhyme,
Until she had to wash and cook,
                And had no time.

She ran the home—that's quite a chore;
  Her hours were hard and long.
Right heavy was the load she bore,
  And her not over-strong:
To milk the cows, to clean the byre,
  To wash and darn and mend;
To chop the faggots for the fire,
                Toil, toil no end.

"To paint the prairie," said she,
  "How words are weak and vain!
The earth as level as the sea,
  The sky God's window-pane.
How I would give my sum of days
  For beauty's sake if I
Could sing one starry hymn of praise
                Before I die!"

Now she is dead and I'm alone,
    And still I sow and reap,
And work my fingers to the bone,
    While she is soft asleep.
So selfless was the way she took,
    For these be bitter times. . . .
Poor Sis! Well, there's her copy-book
            Of childish rhymes.

BROTHERS

When care and sorrow fret the brow
    And weary is the head,
It's mighty soothing, you'll allow,
    To just flop down in bed.
When you have little sweet to say,
    And long to be alone,
It helps a lot to drift away
    Into oblivion.

And when from life at last you creep,
    So fed up with it all,
What comfort it must be to sleep
    With face turned to the wall!
To know your woe and care are past,
    And with a heart at peace,
To throw life's burden off at last
    In merciful release.

Oh! Sleep and death are brothers twain
    Who differ in degree;
From Sleep you wake to woe again,
    And no escape may be.
For Sleep is just a gentle pause
    That may brief solace bring—
But Death—how blessed is! Because
    There's no awakening.

FINALITY

I know a word so sweet of tone
   It echoes like a silver shell,
Yet is as weary as a moan,
    As desolating as a knell—
           "Farewell!"

Another tuneful word I know,
   In whose soft cadence I can never
Feel other than a sense of woe,
    Of hearts forlorn and hands that sever—
        "Forever!"

And if perchance you link the two
   In sequence of a bitter breath,
And come to learn—unhappy you!
    How loveliness is locked with death,
God help you! May you never know
    That dirge of hope and high endeavour,
That melody weighed down with woe—
        "Farewell forever!"

L'ENVOI

I wish my verses I could give,
   Instead of sell.
Unfortunately I must live,
   Though none too well.
But if you borrow, beg or steal
   This tome to get,
I hope that you will never feel
   The least regret.

I hope that in it you may find
   A word of cheer,
An image kindly to your mind,
   A smile, a tear;
A single line you want to quote,
   A small refrain:
Then I will never think I wrote
   My verse in vain.

And so I knock upon your door
   And beg your time,
A pedler with a humble store
   Of homespun rhyme.
Yet do not think that I will blame
   If you be coy;
No, Friend, I thank you all the same,
   And wish you joy.

SONGS FOR MY SUPPER

CONTENTS

DOMESTIC DITTIES

RHYMES FOR IRONY

LYRICS FOR LEVITY

RHYMES FOR A RECLUSE

LYRICS OF THE LOST

RHYMES FOR REVERENCE

FRONT PIECE

The lot of bard is bitter hard
  In this metallic day,
For rhymes unread bring little bread
  To keep the wolf at bay.
My dole is spent to pay the rent,
  Yet though my hearth be cold,
With raucous voice I still rejoice
    At eighty old.

All up and down the callous town
  Vainly my wares I cry;
Oh it is hell when you've to sell
  And nobody will buy.
Though bare my shelf I tell myself
  With pallid nose a-drip:
"Buck up, old chap; whate'er the hap
    You must not slip."

Don't pity me, for brash I be;
  And brawly carolling
I'd rather fare in rags than wear
  The raiment of a king.
So calm I wait the common fate
  That comes to foe and friend,
Praying that I my pen will ply
    Unto the end.

RHYMES FOR RESENTMENT

RAW RECRUIT

They said to me: "Thou shalt not kill,"
   And well I understood.
"Thy brother's blood thou shalt not spill,"
   They spake, and it was good.
And then I could not understand,
   Yet had to do their will;
Cold steel they put into my hand,
   Saying: "Go forth and kill.

"Go forth with rage of race and slay;
   Pile up the corpses for
What's murder called in Peace—alway
   Is hallowèd in War.
The Church has blest your bloody blade,
   The which in peace it cursed;
So go forth, son, all unafraid,
   And do your bloody worst."

What's wrong in Peace in War is right,
   So I will do their will,
And bear me bravely in the fight,
   And kill and kill and kill.
Yet as I brave the battle test
   With dripping sword in hand,
Proving me equal with the best . . .
   Christ, help me understand!

THE MIGHTY ATOM

In World War One with glee I read:
    "Last night we raided Germany.
It was," (the morning paper said),
    "A devastating sight to see:
On Mannheim roofs we dropped a ton
    Of bombs,—great damage has been done."

In World War Two my journal said:
    "Our raiders made a splendid run;
A thousand bombs were put to bed,
    Block-busters, each at least a ton.
Observers state: There is no doubt
    Mannheim is almost blotted out."

Today I read: "A suitcase small
    Can hold a bomb that will destroy
A mighty city, shambling all."—
    The knowledge does not make for joy:
London, New York and Moscow might
    Be cinders in a single night.

Time marches on. The atom hurled
    From heaven may with blasting breath
Annihilate this crazy world,
    Decreeing universal death . . .
God grant sheer fear of doom may fend
    Humanity from hellish end!

BITTER SHADE

I am bewildered: I would know
The why I rot this sod below,
Who lived so full of hope and joy,
So little more than laughing boy?

I dreamed of destiny divine,
Fore-runner of a lustrous line
Of loved ones, in old age to die,
And with fore-fathers fitly lie.

I was too young blood-strife to know;
I held no hate, I had no foe.
Was it for this that I was made,
This hollow glory-accolade?

O cursed birth to sacrifice
On war's red altar hero-wise,
Rough-reft from home and sunny sky,
On field of fear and flame to die!

I pass, but may the ages breed
A race that's free from clan and creed,
From flag and feud and phoney lies
Of patriotic paradise!

14

RETURN TO NORMANDY

He runs as if to leap with wings
    The ramparts of romance;
In blythesome blue the lavrock sings
    Above the fields of France,
Now billowing with golden grain,
    That once were stiff with slain.

From cottages where roses glow
    Sun-happy maidens smile;
Gay taverns that he used to know
    Bid him to rest awhile;
But ruddy topers starkly stare
    As if he were not there.

He enters in the old *église*;
    What joy to see once more
Those ivied walls now wreathed in peace
    That once were rocked with war! . . .
Then in a graveyard lush and lone
    His name leaps from a stone.

Gone is his innocent delight,
    Gone, gone his laughing glee;
For now he knows in maiden sight
    A wraith unseen is he:
One of a mighty martyred host,——
    Poor lonesome lad! Poor ghost!

WAR WIDOW

'Twas with a heart of leaden woe
    Poor Alphonze went to war;
And though it's true he did not know
    What he was fighting for,
He grieved because unto Marie
    He'd been but three weeks wed:
Tough luck! Another three and he
    Was listed with the dead.

Marie was free if she were fain,
    Another spouse to choose;
But if she dared to wed again
    Her pension she would lose.
And so to mourn did she prefer,
    And widow to remain,
Like many dames whose husbands were
    Accounted with the slain.

Yet she was made for motherhood,
    With hips and belly broad,
And should have borne a bonny brood
    To render thanks to God.
Ah! If with valour Alphonze had
    Not fallen in the fray,
Proud Marie would have been a glad
    Grey grandmother today.

Yet maybe it is just as well
    She has not bred her kind;
The ranks of unemployment swell,
    And flats are hard to find.
For every year the human race
    Richly we see increase,
And wonder how they'll find a place . . .
    Well, that's the curse of Peace.

So let us hail the gods of war
    With joy and jubilation,
Who favour foolish mankind for
    They prune the population;
Aye, let us thank the hungry guns
    Forever belching doom,
That slaughter bloodily our sons
    To give us elbow room.

UNEMPLOYED

That work is grim I know full well,
    And weary is the strain;
But to be out of work is hell,
    To beg for it in vain.
See! I am young and willing too,
    No drudgery I shirk;
And yet I humbly plead to you:
    "Please give me work."

Oh there is something sadly wrong
    When for sheer toil I ask;
And though I'm tall and swift and strong
    No one will give me task.
Aye, though my brain be none too bright,
    To sweat I have no dread;
In justice then grant me the right
    To earn my bread.

So here I am prepared to give
    My best of brawn and thew,
That I may be allowed to live
    As we poor devils do.
To beg for pence is held a crime,
    And laws are for the rich . . .
But oh to beg in this our time—
    To dig a ditch.

SCULLERY MAID

A Cinderella of the sink.
No Prince Charming will ever think
    To stoop to me;
No children will I ever bear—
Pale, puny, snot-nosed brats to share
    My misery.

I rub and scrub, I wash and sweep,
Where warily cockroaches creep,
    And mice are bold;
And I'll go on and on like this,
A maid sweet destiny will miss—
    Until I'm old.

Until a worn and toothless hag
Rheumatically I will lag
    Before I croak;
Far too unsavoury for sin,
I'll take my comfort out o' gin,
    A bleary soak.

Oh could I only make the grade
To be a lady's chambermaid
    How glad I'd be!
But as a dreary kitchen drudge
It seems as if God had a grudge
    'Gainst gels like me.

A pallid orphan of the slum,
No chance to me has ever come
    In life to rise:
And so with wistful heart I go—
A Sunday shilling picture-show
    My Paradise.

TROPICAL TRAMP

I have no brief for Work, I think
    It's just a bloody curse,
Enough to drive a man to drink,
        Or even worse.
Of all inventions of mankind,
    A simple soul to irk,
The most pernicious to my mind
        Is Work.

Hard work don't get you anywhere,
    It pays wi' aches and pains;
So praises be, I'm breathin' air
        Where savage reigns!
Hand it to him for common-sense;
    Dame Nature serves his need,
And he chalks up to her expense
        His feed.

Toil is a game for mugs, it wears
    Your guts out till you die;
It breaks you down wi' woes and cares,
        But wise am I.
And so to foolish sweat farewell;
    So long to city murk:
In language impolite, —to hell
        With Work!

PROUD BOAST

To hell, say I, with party strife!
Why cannot honest folk agree?
I've never voted in my life,
And there are lots of guys like me,
Who hold that any man's a fool
To fight his fellows when he could
With them harmoniously pull
        In Brotherhood.

It's just as simple as all that.
Among my pet dislikes I list
Republican and Democrat,
Conservative and Socialist.
And so I go my lonesome way,
And never in dissension mix
With silly mugs who are the prey
        Of Politics.

Because I have no axe to grind,
Nor any faction faith to prove,
I hold the hope that human-kind
Will weld at last in common love.
So when I hear election strife
I'll go afishing in my boat,
Content that never in my life
        I've cast a vote.

REBEL

In flighty youth I sought to flee
      Man-made control,
And in the name of liberty
      To save my soul;
From niggard Wild with gun and rod
      I reft my food,
And I was grateful unto God,
      And all was good.

Since then I've loathed the word "obey"
      And bowed to none;
With guts and grit I've fought my way,
      And welfare won;
And so I hate their servile State,
      Their Labour Lords,
Who herd the mob to helot fate
      With windy words.

Aye, to their democratic spout
      Unreconciled,
With gipsy heart will I go out
      Into the Wild;
Seek sanctuary where I can,
      Be proudly free,
And to the bidding of no man
      I'll bend the knee.

Let bosses plan and regiment
    And legislate,
I'm damned if I will be content
    To serve their State.
In life I've given none the right
    To master me,
So to the end I'll fight and fight
    For Liberty.

TWO WOMEN

I knew a woman powerful bad
    In parson's view;
For frequently affairs she had,
    And love-nights knew.
But ailing mothers she would tend,
    Their bairnies feed,
And her last penny she would spend
    For friend in need.

Another dame I know who walked
    In pious ways
And would have been profoundly shocked
    At these my lays;
A spinster and a virgin, sure
    In grace to dwell,
Who deemed that every evil-doer
    Should suffer hell.

Though these two women sisters were,
    They did not speak;
One steeled her heart to those who err,
    One braced the weak . . .
Yet if a Judgement Day befall,
    I wonder which
The Head of Heaven's Court will call
    A BITCH?

THE POLITICIANS

In olden days our rulers roared
    With wrath and went to war;
They girdled on their battle sword,
    For that's what it was for.
They buckled on their battle shield,
    And when their men they led,
Quite often on the gory field
    They bled and bled.

But now our rulers talk and talk,
    And wordy windbags are;
Immune from bloody battle shock
    They never know a scar.
In conference with "ifs" and "buts"
    They rib each other raw;
And while we poor mugs spill our guts
    They jaw and jaw.

If those who rule us had to lead
    Us blokes into the fray,
And on the field of battle bleed,
    I guess some other way
They'd mutually find to right
    Life's game of greed and grab:
But while we suckers fight and fight,
    They gab and gab and gab.

26

RENEGADE

That grimy chap who mends my pipes
Of social injustice gripes
      With brandished fist;
But though to humour him I try,
He blasts the rotten rich and I
      Am on his list.

But yesterday, —'twas April first—
Two Reds into his workshop burst,
      Great news to tell.
Cried they: "You've won the Football Pool!"
Said Bill: "I baint no April fool:
      You go to 'ell!"

But when they proved the news was true,
Adown his monkey-wrench he threw:
      "No mucky mess,"
Cried he, "of drains and taps for me;
The bloody nation now will be
      One plumber less!"

"A hundred thousand quid!" said they;
"The Party will rejoice today
      Your dower to list."
Said Bill: "Get out you mugs; I guess
Today the Party will be less
      One Communist!"

THE BUILDER

In scabrous streets I roamed alone
    A city battle-scarred,
And spied a statue hewn from stone,
    Set in a mason's yard:
A naked man of brutish brain
    Who gripped a granite block,
And heaved it high with savage strain,
    Flesh rawed by rock.

And as I stared, from shadow crept
    A lean and livid Jew,
Who told me: "Weary I have wept
    And waited long for you.
Twin souls in art are you and I;
    This shape for you I carved;
The Builder it is called, —please buy,
    For I am starved."

"It is too sad," I answered him,
    And gravely shook my head.
"Too gaunt and grey and crudely grim,——"
    "Life too is grim," he said.
But I just gazed, then turned away . . .
    'Tis fifty years ago,
Yet I remember as today
    His look of woe.

I wish I had that statue now,
    Of wild and weary stare,
Of straining limb and brutish brow,—
    Stark symbol of despair;
That naked man, uncouth, unskilled,
    Toil-racked and hollow-eyed,
With jagged boulder braced to build
    A Dome enskied.

WHITE COLLAR MAN

I passed a tipsy gipsy who
    Was sprawling in a ditch;
He blasted me for all he knew,
    And called me: "Bloody Rich!"
Although I am not rich at all,
    And count my pennies twice,
The views of me that he let fall
    Were anything but nice.

And then he hollered: "I am free;
    No bosses I obey;
No master lords it over me,
    My life's a holiday.
I tinker when and where I choose,
    To make a bob or two,
Enough to buy my bread and booze,
    And scoff at toffs like you."

Then as I went my worthy way
    I wondered—was he right?
Because of what the folks might say
    I dare not get me tight.
I dare not slumber in a ditch,
    Rheumatic joints to swell,
Or make love to a gypsy bitch,
    Deep in a downy dell.

But worst of all, I am not free
    To do whate'er I will;
To pay my taxes and my tea
    I toil to meet the bill.
And as I plod from Sunday Church,
    Believe it if you can,
I wish I could with liquor lurch
    Like that brash gypsy man.

SOLITARY

Of punishments unto my mind
       Exceeding hell,
The damnedest is to be confined
       In prison cell;
In barren cell of bitter stone
       And gruesome gloom,
Six feet by ten, alone, alone,
       —A living tomb.

To count the endless nights and days,
       The years and years,
Till death in pity shall erase
       That term of tears.
Oh better far in quarry sweat
       To labour sore!—
Oh lucky those who pay their debt
       On gallows floor!

Fate makes a man a felon low,
       Or hero high;
The callous gods on men bestow
       The death they die.
And so I curse the Judges who
       Their gibbets spare,
And damn poor souls their wrong to rue
       In life despair.

MY HIGHLAND HOME

My mother spun the household wool,
  And all our kiddy clothes would make;
I used to go barefoot to school,
  While bannock took the place of cake.
One shirt a week was all I had,
  Our home was just a but-and-ben;
But oh I was the proudful lad,
  And life was rich with promise then.

Although I supped on milk and brose,
  And went to bed by candle-light,
I pored on books of noble prose,
  And longed like Bobbie Burns to write.
Now in this age of the machine
  I look back three-score years and ten:
With life so simple, sane and clean,
  Oh were we not more happy then?

We deemed not of electric light,
  Nor ever thought that we would fly;
Our sons were not called up to fight,
  And in a foreign field to die.
So now when threats of war appal,
  And millions cower to monster men,
Friends, don't you think that after all,
  We were a heap more happy then?

33

UNDERDOG

A prisoner of toil I be,
    And though I've done no wrong,
In life's grey penitentiary
    Oh how the time is long!
And with what weariness I wait
    Sweet death to spring the gate!

Sometimes I look from out my ditch
    To blossomed bungalow,
And see the children of the rich
    With happiness aglow,
While mine must muck in mine and pit,
    —Ah! That's the hell of it.

For brawn is all we have to give
    From brutish poverty;
We live to sweat and sweat to live,
    And millions are like me,
Dull serfs of darkness, care and dearth,
    Cursing our day of birth.

Oh you who sit in silken ease,
    Clean collared every morn,
Give thought to those who in disease
    And misery are born,
The underdogs in evil coil
    Of that grim tyrant Toil!

34

Yet ere I pass into the night
  How happy I would be
Could but my kiddies read and write,
  And not be oafs like me . . .
Then would I know from pit of pain
  I have not slaved in vain!

CURBSTONE PIPER

A penny-whistle minstrel I
 Play in the street,
Hoping I'll make enough to buy
 A bite to eat.
My tinny notes are sour and shrill,
 My tunes are old;
For how it's hard to lilt and trill
 With fingers cold!

And so inside a chapel near
 I seek a seat;
For there the organ I may hear,
 Divinely sweet.
O heaven-joy of warmth and rest!
 O tears that smart!
And there's my penny-whistle pressed
 Against my heart.

So in the gutter I repeat
 Some organ strain,
Some air melodiously sweet,—
 Alas! In vain.
For pity folks their pennies give,
 Yet still I try
Sweet sound to make,—for I must live . . .
 God help me,—why?

INDIVIDUALIST

I only like my fellow men
    Round twenty-five per cent;
I meet somebody now and then
    Who clicks to my content.
Society I tend to shun;
    Alone I'd rather be;
Of boon companions I have none,
    And scorn Fraternity.

I've fought my way alone in life
    And won to modest wealth;
But I am racked and scarred with strife,
    And slipping in my health.
Though feckless folk have less than I,
    That is as it should be;
I've earned my all, and that is why
    I loathe Equality.

I've known the naked Communist
    In rancid lands afar;
And with the foggy socialist
    I've jawed in pub and bar.
Their shopworn slogans seem a bore,
    And to the core of me,
The more I know of laws, the more
    I'm daft for Liberty.

BILL SMITH

My name's Bill Smith: I'm no man's dope;
   I work my fingers to the bone,
And save my screw, for it's my hope
   To have a workshop of my own.
I'm Labour,—independent brand:
   Let lousy socialists be damned!

"Would you exploit your fellow men?"
   They ask me.—"Sure, with all me heart,"
I say; "And if I would, what then?
   For so would you if you were smart.
I have some brains beneath me 'at,
   So blast the proletariat!

You spend your pay on beer and fun;
   You always want to bum a bob;
But when my daily work is done,
   I'm looking for an extra job.
I'm saving everything I can,
   So I won't be a working man.

It's individules 'oo 'ave made
   This country rich beyond its dreams.
The source of wealth is private trade,
   To hell with socialistic schemes!
Oh Reds of every rank and hue,
   It's Bill Smith thumbs his nose at you!"

SOVIET STRAINS

RAILWAY GANG

I watched ten women from the train,
  Who heavy rails were packing;
Their backs were bent to stress and strain,
  Their dress was mostly sacking:
"You see," the Comrade said to me,
  "We practise Sex Equality.

"These splendid creatures play their part
  In our new Five Year Plan.
Each has its proud success at heart,
  And works like any man.
Even with child they toil, you see,"
  The Comrade said to me.

Bare-footed in the dreary rain
  They heaved with hands that bled.
I watched them from the shabby train . . .
  "No toilers they for bread,
But heroines, you must agree,"
  The Comrade said to me.

I would not know,—maybe they were;
  Maybe their hearts were gay,
Despite their worn and weary air . . .
  "They're dreaming of the day
  When masters of the world we'll be,"
  The Comrade said to me.

40

OLGA

As we were voyaging the Volga
We had a sweet girl guide called Olga;
But when, as haply may occur,
My young friend Wilbur fell for her,
And asked if she with him would wed,
Fair **Olga** shook her sunny head.

Said she: "I have been married twice,
And though a change of spouse is nice,
I pray you, clearly understand
My heart is in my Soviet Land,
While reading *Pravda* I can see
Your States are stark with misery."

Then when he said a sad goodbye,
And offered her a silken tie
Of fine design and rosy hue
He bought upon Fifth Avenue,
She said: "Though very lovely it's,
We cannot accept perquisites."

So Wilbur went back to his State
Of Maine, and no doubt found a mate.
Yet in his dad's glue factory,
In business deals transactory,
I wonder, does he think of Olga
Who chose to stick it on the Volga?

MOSCOW METRO

Although I'm not devoid of malice
    And have for Bolshevics no brief,
I must admit that like a palace,
    And beautiful beyond belief,
The Moscow Underground can claim
    The Subways of the world to shame.

Gum-booted girls, asweat like swine,
    In squalor helped to tunnel it;
Each one a Soviet heroine
    Climbed chalk-faced from the clayey pit,
Hoping to win a Crimson Star,
    Or right to kiss a Commissar.

Now glamorous beyond all dream,
    With fresco, bas-relief and frieze,
Its marble and mosaic gleam;
    And one with eyes of wonder sees,
In alcoves ringed with ruby lights,
    Proud statues of Stakhanovites.

Then there arrives a jam-packed train,
    And is assailed with fury for
With curses one must strive and strain
    Even to gain the corridor;
And no man in this turmoil human
    Would yield a seat to pregnant woman.

Aye, it's a sight to marvel at,
    Of amber, jade and ivory;
And though the proletariat
    It lures from hovels,—all I see
Are soldiers grim who guard the doors,
    And hags in rags who scour the floors.

THE CONTRAST

At the Soviet station hags
Greeted us with filthy flags;
Yet their bleak and bitter smiles
Haunted me for miles and miles.

But at Polish stations we
Plunged into a climate free;
Sentinels made proud salute,
Spick and span from head to foot.

'Twas before the War,—today
Poland cowers to Soviet sway,
And their women, wrapt in rags,
Hail the trains with filthy flags.

PROLETARIAT PARADISE

Yea, you may count me Communist,
    Yet not your Kremlin brand;
In Moscow I believe they list
    My name among the banned.
They mutter that for chaps like me
    They save a lethal cell,
Who preach a paradise to be,
    While they conceive a hell.

My Communism is the kind
    The Prince of Peace proclaimed:
A gentling pity of the mind,
    A meekness unashamed.
Aye, though their devils of unruth
    The veils of virtue rend,
I know that justice, love and truth
    Will triumph in the end.

Oh sure I am a Communist
    If you will only count
As light that lesson you have missed,
    The Sermon on the Mount.
So damn that Kremlin Commissar
    For whom a sneer sufficed
To tell me—Marx is greater far
                Than Jesus Christ!

44

AT LENIN'S TOMB

I chewed my quid, yet quailed a bit
   As sentinel with savage glare
Told me I must not dare to spit
   Within the sacrosanct Red Square.
But when behind the Tomb safe hid,
   I spat—and *something more* I did.

And then I thought: with patience grim,
   A waxen culture under glass,
Poor Lenin lies. I pitied him;
   How wearily he watches pass
The pallid proletariat!
   What did he do to suffer that?

His mongrel mob are serfs today,
   And there's no freedom in the land;
No comrade dares to disobey
   The dictates of a dastard band.
Czarist and Soviet servitude
   Are equally of hell-hatched brood.

Twin stars above the Kremlin glow;
   The raving radio rends the night.
The monster flag lit from below
   Ripples in waves of ruby light;
Bright symbol of that crimson flood
   One day to drench this world with blood.

RED DIPLOMAT

Of course he could not be compelled
   To cower to tyranny;
Yet hostages they grimly held
   His wife and children three.
So at the order of recall
   He stared with vision blurred;
Though death was dark behind it all,
   "Suspended" was their word.

The men of steel he must obey;
   They gripped him in a vice.
He knew that if he dared to stay
   His dears would pay the price.
And so he sailed to cynic doom,
   Beyond all human hope:
The torture and the trial room,
   Confession and—the Rope.

On board we reckoned he was queer;
   He seemed to shun our sight.
And in his stateroom we could hear
   Him sobbing in the night.
Or else the gibber of a prayer,
   And then—no sound we heard . . .
He must have kicked aside a chair:
   "Suspended" was the word.

DICTATORS DIE

The tame sea mumbles at the shore
   With grey and toothless gums;
Tomorrow it may rear and roar
   With rage of battle drums . . .
So thought I as I opened wide
   My morning rag and read
A headline hugely magnified:
       Stalin is dead!

Now I'm an old rheumatic boy
   Whose hair is scant and hoar,
Yet flooded with a sudden joy
   I danced upon the shore;
Though why I should exult at death
   I cannot understand;
Yet there, despite asthmatic breath,
   I jigged upon the sand.

When tyrranous dictators die
   A million million laugh,
And you can read in every eye
   Of joy—their epitaph.
And so beside the senile sea,
   In sunset gory red,
I cried to God with wanton glee:
      "STALIN IS DEAD!"

MERCY

I dreamed . . . Before the Judgement Seat
     I saw two felons stand,
Stark naked, fettered by the feet,
     Yet holding hand in hand.
And then from Heaven's Holyhead
     The Judge of all looked down:
"And who may be," he mildly said,
     "This craven and this clown?"

Yet when they told him he was sad,
     Though merciful his mien,
Saying: "Great qualities they had,
     And Saints they might have been.
So to a braver, sweeter morn,
     In future aeons far,
Let them to righteousness be born
     Beneath a holy star.

"Scapegoats of immemorial sin,
     Through long oblivion,
Let them to Christlike virtue win,
     In some celestial dawn . . ."
And so into the womb of Time,
     For ages to repent
And expiate their every crime—
     Hitler and Stalin went.

DOMESTIC DITTIES

FISHERMAN

When I'm feelin' sick o' soul
  From worldly wishin',
I jest grab my willow pole
  And go off fishin'.
Though folks of inflation gripe,
  And nations totter,
I jest dream an' light my pipe,
  And watch the water.

People think I'm none too bright:
  To them it's funny,
I go fishin' when I might
  Be makin' money.
Some day I might have a try,
  (I kindo' doubt it);
Money's fine, but mostly I
  Kin do without it.

Sunshine's more than gold to me,
  And I am happy
Underneath a maple tree
  When trout are snappy.
Even when they do not bite,
  If skies are blue,
And larks chortle with delight
  I'm happy too.

Philosophers are fisherfolk;
    A monument
Of patience I my corncob smoke,
    With calm content.
For as I watch a tranquil stream
    My troubles cease:
My hook is baited with a dream,—
    I fish for Peace.

SILENT GRANDPA

When I was one and twenty
    I was a lively lad;
'Tis true my brain was empty,
    But what a tongue I had!
Yet now I'm nighing eighty
    I falter by the way,
And though my thought is weighty
I haven't much to say.

They claim that empty bottles
    Are those that make most sound;
It's strange how silence throttles
    What wisdom I have found!
What memories are welling!
    What faces I recall!
When so much bids for telling,
    Best not to speak at all.

It's funny how big talkers
    Have little things to say.
In time's memorial lockers
    I stow my thoughts away.
My grandson is loquacious,
    My son's a gabby chap—
But Grandpa is sagacious,
    And shuts his trap.

JIM

"Jim's got a job at last," said she,
  "And I'm just crazy glad.
It nearly broke my heart to see
  Him coming home so sad.
I tried to cheer him up at night,
  My laughter nigh a sob;
But now all's going to be right,—
        Jim's got a job.

"I pray to Heaven it will last:
  (We've just been wed a year).
Our penny-pinching will be past,
  Our worry and our fear.
In black despair I've heard him swear:
  'For you a church I'd rob.'
But now I'll bid goodbye to care,—
        Jim's got a job.

"My boy will battle with the best
  And bring me back his pay;
A sweetness strange is in my breast,
  A baby's on the way.
How heaven-glad a girl can be
  To feel life in her throb,
To think that two may soon be three . . .
Oh God, you are too good to me!
        Jim's got a job."

THE BEAUTY PRIZE

Since Myrtle won a Beauty Prize
    Our home is not the same;
Her head has swelled to twice its size,
    She dreams of movie fame.
She spends her time before the glass
    To pose and prink and preen;
I'm scared since Myrt became—alas!
        A Beauty Queen.

For I am just a common jerk,
    A carpenter by trade;
But oh how hard I used to work
    Until the house was paid!
Now Myrt is in the magazines,
    A toast of all the town:
I guess that in the end it means
        She'll throw me down.

Well, everywhere it's just the same;
    Successful dames no doubt,
When once they grab a chunk of fame
    Will kick the old man out.
I'm wondering when I'll be dropped,
    Like all them other guys . . .
Oh cursed day when Myrtle copped
        A Beauty Prize!

IN THE WAY

I'm jest a fossilized old scout,
    A-livin' in the past;
I see folks try to figger out
    How long I'm like to last.
I've had my share of weal and woe,
    I'm ninety old today,
And somehow I begin to know
    I'm kindo' in the way.

They leave me cuddlin' up the cat
    Deep in my old arm chair,
And loudly talk o' this and that
    As if I wasn't there.
I reckon it is time they took
    My carcase to the clay,
For I can see the way folks look
    I'm only in the way.

I've lived too long, I feel I should
    Make up my mind to go;
My sense o' hearin' ain't too good,
    My sight is gittin' low.
There's no one kindo' wantin' me,
    And I can only pray
The Lord won't think—if Heaven be—
    Old Grandpop's in the way.

MY BARBER'S CHAIR

In business of my own to set
      Me up in modest way,
I'm saving all the tips I get,
      And scrimping night and day.
I would not sit upon a throne,
      Nor be a millionaire:
My one ambition is to own
            A barber's chair.

Then I will labour for myself
      In little shop a-shine;
'Tis I will pouch the daily pelf,
      And not this boss of mine.
So as my razor blade I hone
      And clip and comb your hair,
I dream of days when I will own
            A barber's chair.

A little shop, a little wife,
      With young 'uns two or three,
Gee! We will lead a rosy life,
      And they will worship me!
And as to school my kiddies hie,
      How they will halt and stare
To see their poppa standing by
            His barber's chair.

56

But oh it takes a weary time
   And needs a cheery heart,
To rope in dollars dime by dime
   Enough to make a start.
The wife and weans I fear are far,
   But how the dream is fair!
More beautiful than any star,—
    My Barber's Chair.

GRANDMA

Granny washes up the dishes
   In the water warm and soapy,
And her hands she sadly wishes
   Were not so rheumatic ropey;
But tonight her heart is glowing,
   For instead of climbing bedward,
To the movies she is going
   With her grandson Thomas Edward.

For each Saturday he takes her,
   Kids her she's his little girl friend.
Oh how jubilant it makes her,
   Thinking of her giddy week-end!
How she dolls with frills and laces!
   And her ancient heart rejoices
At the *thought* of picture faces
   At the *thrill* of movie voices!

Grandma thinks: "He must not know it,
   Little of the talk I'm hearing;
Though half blind I must not show it,
   Just pretend . . . But oh how cheering
For two hours so swiftly flitting
   To forget my joints rheumatic,
Get away from baby-sitting,
   Reading Scripture in the attic!

58

JANE

I like my little housemaid Jane,
    But oh about her health she's fussy;
She tells me every ache and pain
    Until I'd like to spank the hussy.
I give her gargle for her throat,
    For rheumatics an embrocation;
And liver pills of famous note
              To combat constipation.

One day a-listening to her woes
    I could not master my vexation.
Says I: "My lass, don't you suppose
    Your ills are of your own creation?
Just think a little less of 'you',
    And more of those who hold you kindly:
Forget yourself and you will view
              Your ailments blindly."

Quite willingly my words she weighed,
    And now no longer introspective,
She's such a happy little maid,
    With mind unselfishly objective.
No more *malade imaginaire,*
Her friends with fondliness she smothers:
Proving that joy is just to care
              And comfort others.

BREATHIN'

I asked a centenarian
   The why he was not dead;
He spat his quid, that ancient man,
   And this is what he said:
"If you be lovin' life a lot
   Wi' all its bright bequeathin'
Don't give the calendar a thought,
      —Jest keep on breathin'.

"Don't let the dam' world worry you,
   Refuse to be upset;
An' if folks seek to hurry you
   Be sparin' o' your sweat.
Let each day like a Sabbath be
   Wi' peaceful sap a-seethin':
Jest pattern on to cow an' tree,
      —An' keep a-breathin'.

"Jest cultivate a walkin' crawl,
   An' travel on the flat;
Jest take to talkin' wi' a drawl,
   An' none too much at that . . .
Well, that's the why I'm loth to lie
   In coffin sheathin':
My hobby's Respiration, I
      Jest can't quit Breathin'."

HOUSEWIFE

As I'm an old and cranky cove
    I hate the female sex;
I'd like to herd them in a drove
    Until they break their necks;
Except the ones who do not shirk
    The duties of the home,
Whose hands are calloused to hard work
        And laundry foam.

When I meet any woman I
    No more her favours beg;
Though being only human I
    Still love a shapely leg.
But while to ladies disinclined
    My dudgeon I disgard,
If when I shake their hands I find
        The palms are hard.

Let poets sing of mitts that cling
    With soft and silken touch;
My heart goes out to those that bring
    A sense of kitchen clutch . . .
So here's to heroines galore,
    From boudoir ease disbarred,
Who don't disdain to scrub the floor,—
        Whose hands are hard.

THE GIRLS OF LONG AGO

I rate the girls of long ago
    Ahead of those today;
They used to sit and knit and sew
    Where now they want to play.
I may be stuffy in my ways,
    Old-fashioned and uncouth,
Yet let an aged codger praise
    The lassies of his youth.

At home how gladly they would wait
    To entertain their beaus;
Where now what they appreciate
    Are cars and picture shows.
With crochet, lace and fancy work
    They made the parlour gay:
The household chores they did not shirk,
    The maids of yesterday.

My mother was that kind of girl,
    She had no wish to roam:
Despiteful of the social whirl
    Her heart was in her home.
It used to be her happy boast
    To keep the hearth aglow,—
So now let this old codger toast
    The girls of long ago.

MA'S GOD

Ma used to tell me—in some dim age
The Lord made mankind in his image:
Good job! What worship more fit than
                Almighty Man!

Then Pa would sound off: "God is spirit."
Which somehow modified His merit;
For spirit I imagine as
                A form of gas.

Then Sonny-boy, professor-taught,
Proclaimed: "God's outside human thought.
He is the Wholeness of the Whole,
                The Cosmic Soul."

Well, though I'm dumb and self-deceivin',
Like Ma I'll jest keep on believin'
That I'm a part o' God an' he
                Is part o' me.

FAMILY MAN

Said Pa: "Too long you've played the clown
        And monkeyed with your life."
Said Ma: "Why don't you settle down
        And take yourself a wife?"
They're dead . . . I wish that they could see
        The answer to their prayer,
—A meek-eyed man of family,
        With dandruff in his hair.

My life was light and loose and free,
        And all I made I spent;
But now, what went in fun for me
        Scarce serves to pay the rent.
And I could curse these two old folk
        For counselling they gave,
That doomed me to domestic yoke,
        A home-providing slave.

Yet all my neighbours are the same,
        Resigned, phlegmatic fools,
Suburbanites who play the game
        According to the rules;
Subscribing to the common fate,
        Respectably inclined
To take unto themselves a mate
        And propagate their kind.

If I again were young and free
        My ways I'd never mend,
But merry bachelor I'd be,
        And playboy to the end . . .
So lads, beware the nuptial snare;
        Laugh loud while yet you can,
For soon or late you'll meet your fate,—
        A rabbit family man.

LOYALTY

"And so you want to leave," said I,
    "Because you're offered better pay?
Quite right! I've often wondered why
    You did not go before today.
I cannot give you any more;
    I tell you this as man to man,
And with your years of life in store,
    Please John, you do the best you can."

Said John: "I hate to go like this,
    But I'm so glad you understand;
It seems a chance too good to miss,
    It means advancement and command.
And yet—no place I'll ever find
    That holds so much in trust and cheer:
Excuse me, Sir, if you don't mind
    I'll keep on working here."

So John is with me to this day,
    More like a son than anything;
My daughter's in the family way,—
    'Twas John supplied the wedding ring.
So now I'm ready to retire
    And let the young folks run the show,
And I will sit beside the fire . . .
    Youth must be served, the old must go,—
        Heigh ho! Heigh ho!

MOTHER'S BUTTON BOX

The pictures never fail to please,
    When memory I tap,
Of Mother sweetly shelling peas
    With sunshine in her lap;
Or sitting by a fire that glows,
    And darning Father's socks;
Or rummaging with specks on nose
    In her old button box.

Five hundred buttons were her store,—
    I know, I counted them;
Some matched those on the pants I wore,
    Some sparkled like a gem.
Such colours as I never dreamed,
    Of every shape and size:
Ah! Though a lad to me it seemed
    A playbox paradise.

When I was down with chicken-pox
    And could not go with boys,
I asked for Mother's button box,
    And scorned my books and toys.
I ranged the buttons battlewise
    On blanket hills and dales,
With childish rapture in my eyes,
    Forgetting all my ails.

But came Big Brother with a laugh;
    He mocked my war array,
And scattered all my troops like chaff,
    Jibing: "What baby play!"
Aye, with a hoisting of the sheet
    The platoons on my bed
He heaped in pitiless defeat . . .
    I wept,—I wished him dead.

Now Mother's gone and Father's gone
    And Brother's in his tomb,
While weak and wan I linger on,
    Indifferent to doom.
Amid a world I never made,
    That rack and ruin rocks,
I doze and dream of days I played
    With Mother's button box.

TIMOTHY

Each day I take my uphill walk
    To sit upon a stile,
And to a terrier I talk,
    Who wags his tail the while;
Who licks my fingers even as
    His dad did years ago:
Tim is his like, and also has
    His look of loving so.

Ten years from now I'll climb this hill
    And on this same stile sit;
Oh I'll be spry and supple still,
    Though grizzled quite a bit.
And I will rest with pipe and book
    Above the singing sea,
While Timothy the Third will look
    With eager eyes at me.

Look at me long, as if to say:
    "Old chap, you're getting slow;
Let's keep a-walking on our way,
    For I am young, you know."
Then I will pouch my briar pipe,
    And grip my staff anew:
"Aye, Tim," I'll say, "I'm over-ripe,
    Not full of pep like you."

Same hill, same stile, same daily plan
    As on my way I jog;
Yet one year of a life for man
    Counts ten for any dog.
And though a sprightly son of Tim
    May leap upon my knee,
For this old cove I know—with *him*
    Will end dog dynasty.

DRUNKARD'S DOG

Each time a brandy keg I broach,
After a semi-sober spell,
My dog looks at me with reproach,
And I feel meaner than all hell.
He slinks away behind the barn,
And will not answer to his name,
As if he did not care a darn,
     Or maybe shared my shame.

But if I wake in gutter grim
He's there to ward and lick my face;
The village curs won't speak to him,
He seems to be in dog disgrace.
A mongrel that no one would own,—
Aye, even beggars would despise:
And yet he lives for me alone,
     With sheer love in his eyes.

Oh I will sober up some day,
And we will take a woodland walk.
How he will be like puppy gay!
Aye, he'll do everything but talk.
And when he tells me I'm his god,
I'll be as solemn as a priest.
He'll die upon my grave-yard sod,—
     Which of us is the beast?

SNOOKY

Snooky was a cocker bitch,
(Of course I had her spayed),
Devoted to me to a pitch
I never met in maid.
And every evening, prompt at six,
She'd stare up at the clock,
And fetch her leash for me to fix,
          To take a walk.

Then after strolling round a bit
I'd sit down in the park,
And when my pipe was snugly lit,
Smoke on till after dark.
Always the same worn bench I'd choose,
And had for months of days,
For I'm a cove who loves to muse,
          Routine my ways.

And then one eve in sunset glow
I sought my usual bench,
But Snooky would not sit, although
I gave her leash a wrench.
She backed, and howled and pulled away,
Such sudden strength she had:
I must admit, in some queer way
          I thought her mad.

Ah well! I let it go at that,
And how that pup was pleased!
When on another bench I sat,
She jumped upon my knees,
And licked my face and yelped with glee . . .
Then—then a blinding flash!
I heard, as hot earth spattered me,
                    A rending crash.

I should have said—'twas in the War,
When bombs fell every night;
And so I stared with horror for
I saw a sorry sight.
With Snooky licking at my face,
My usual bench, I found
Had gone, and gaping in its place
                    Was charnal ground.

I've written dog yarns in my time,
(Most doggerel, I guess);
But this I've made into a rhyme,
With feeling, I confess.
My word may not be worth a cuss,
Yet this my tale is *true;*
Dogs have a sense unknown to us,
                    And Snooky knew.

EXPECTANT

Because I was so big with child
       I walked head high,
And maiden eyes were soft and mild,
       And proud was I;
Even a harlot gently smiled
       As I went by.

When other women in my case
       I chanced to meet,
We looked each other in the face
       With knowledge sweet;
And lilies seemed to light the space
       Of sordid street.

But some were pale and poorly clad
       And pinched with care;
Not all were glad as I was glad
       A child to bear;
And so for pregnant women sad
       I spoke a prayer.

Like lost leaves in a wailing sky
       In vision wild,
Faces of women drifted by,
       Denied a child.
And as their tears I heard down fall
       This was my prayer:
"O Mary, pity women all—
       Who cannot bear!"

74

MY PATCHWORK QUILT

This vivid patchwork quilt you see,
    Now lying on my bed,
With jauntiness will cover me,
    When I am dead.
Although my mourners gape and grin,
    When in my tomb you tilt
My last remains, please shroud them in
    My patchwork quilt.

Being despite my business cares
    A man of sentiment,
I love its eight and forty squares,
    Each different.
My Mother picked the stuff for me,
    And patiently she built.
A pattern that's a joy to see,
    My patchwork quilt.

Each time I go into my room
    It greets me like a cheer;
I think of poor Ma in her tomb,
    And wish her near.
I love its rainbow colours, much
    As clansman loves a kilt.
How I caress with tender touch
    My patchwork quilt!

I could have silk and eider-down
 To grace my cosy couch;
But on all fancy frills I frown
 With homely grouch.
So gay and gaudy let me lie,
 Yet happy to the hilt,
With comforting me till I die,—
 My patchwork quilt.

RHYMES FOR IRONY

THE OLD WOMAN

A-near the last of life
    Death tax to save,
To my son and his wife
    My cot I gave.
I deeded dish and clout;
    Now all is theirs,
And they can turn me out
    Who were my heirs.

They grudge me in their greed
    Peat for my fire;
The bite of food I need,
    My church attire.
They haste for me to die,
    And sore I see
The pig that's in the stye
    Means more than me.

Because I'm near to blind
    I cannot knit;
The cow they make me mind,
    And so I sit
And hear it crop the grass
    Beside the way,
And as the neighbours pass
    They shout good-day!

78

But oh I'm sure and sure
   They pity me,
To be so old and poor
   And scarce to see.
I think I hear them say:
   "The daft old wife,
To give her all away
   Within her life!"

AT THE FUNERAL

I weep with those who shed their tears;
      While many wonder why,
Though worn and wasted by the years
      Her mother does not cry.
Is it because her ending nears,
      And soon she too must die?

Or has she seen so many go,
      And wept of tears a flood,
She has no bitter drop to flow
      For her own flesh and blood?
Though she has buried children nine,
      Her grief should match with mine.

For oh her lass was my beloved
      And would with me have wed,
Had not the old folks disapproved,—
      And now my dove is dead.
Forever more my heart will bleed . . .
      Curse them! Why did I heed?

She was so sweet, so fair to see;
      We loved beyond control.
Aye, she was gone with child to me:
      She died to save her soul.
Only her mother knows,—that's why
      She does not cry.

80

JUBILATION

It was the last day of the War;
The enemy were in retreat,
And we were cheering in a bar
      Their desperate defeat;
Said he: "I'll seek my cabbage patch
And write a song of Victory."
Said I: "Another down the hatch
      I'll put, or two or three."

He was a poet,—which I'm not.
I've heard them call his work divine;
While I'm a fisherman, a sot,
      Some say—a drunken swine.
And so I saw him climb the hill,
To write beneath his ilex tree
(The while the foe were fighting still),
      His song of Victory.

And that's the last I saw of him.
A gunner with his final shot
Was looking for a target trim,
      And spied his garden spot.
And so the poet posed on high,
Was shattered by a random shell,
The last man in the war to die,
      While I—got drunk as hell.

So here's my moral, sadly true:
Don't celebrate in poet's ink,
But do as we poor *bougres* do,
      Just drink and drink.

AT THE RITZ

The daughter sidled like a crab,
    Against her mother pressed.
The sight gave me a cruel stab,
    Though richly were they dressed.
The girl was so forlornly fair,
    The mother masked despair.

I minded when she too was fair,
    And fashionably wed.
"A child I never want to bear,"
    She petulantly said;
And tried to balk it, yet it came,
    Her Cross, grotesquely lame.

A babe had better not be born,
    Than crippled be for life.
A mother's heart with woe is torn
    To spite a selfish wife.
When it came forth with shape awry,
    She hoped that it would die.

Ye women who would fain prevent
    The fruiting of your womb,
Beware of Nature's punishment,
    A child of woeful doom,
As anguished you must go your way
    Unto your dying day.

A SOUR NOTE

Giants of genius three I know,
Their names in sky of fame star-woven:
Shakespeare and Michelangelo,
    Then (to my mind) Beethoven,
Whose lustre Time will never wan,
Outwitting bleak oblivion.

Yet earthly gods have feet of clay,
And I would fain blot out a picture
Portrayed by critic of his day,—
    (Oh not by way of stricture),
To show how he was music's thrall,
And had no thought of *self* at all.

"A sloven man with towselled hair,
A stuffy room with dust a-smother;
Some dirty linen on a chair,
    Foul dishes on another;
A baby grand, and stark in sight
A you-know-what,—to be polite."

Aye, there's the image cruel clear,
And though I'm something of a stoic
It makes me wince each time I hear
    The Symphony Heroic . . .
As he would have detested jazz,
So loathe I that—Etruscan Vase.

TYCOON

My picture in the *Morning Star*
    I look at with distaste;
For I from comeliness am far,
    Chub-chinned and wide of waist.
To think that I should come to that,—
    Falstaffianly fat.

To think that Nature strove to shape,
    Experiment and plan,
Through jelly, polyp, reptile, ape
    This climax of a man!
In smug frock coat and bowler hat,
    This greasy plutocrat!

Though I have gear and gold galore
    What does it mean to me?
I'll hie me down unto the shore
    And stand beside the sea,
As naked as I was at birth,
    A child of Mother Earth.

Yea, I will stand with belly tense
    Beside the roaring sea's
Monotonous magnificence,
    Content in bitter breeze
To be a man where menfolk are,
    And—blast the *Morning Star!*

SCHOOL MA'AM

Oh Sicily's a bonny isle
 For boon vacationing;
And in its blue and golden smile
 I lived a lyric Spring.
And that is why I was so glad
 To laud its lure again
To that poor, pale Italian lad
 Who faced me in the train.

Monotonously streaming past,
 The Kansas prairie
Was bludgeoned by the Winter blast
 And drearyful to see.
But when of soft Sicilian skies
 I spoke, how he was stirred!
And harked to me with starry eyes,
 Yet never uttered word.

Of one wee village by the sea
 I babbled to the boy;
Of sardine net and almond tree,
 And gentleness and joy.
And then the man who sat by him,
 As paradise I praised,
Broke in on us with visage grim:
 "That's where the kid was raised."

So when they rose I saw his hands,—
    Ah! Sorely was I shocked,
For they were bound with iron bands,
    His wrists were steely locked.
And as they gravely walked away
    It gave me quite a turn
To hear the train conductor say:
    "That Dago punk will burn."

THE CRASH

I tipped the taxi man a pound
To speed me to the flying ground;
And then I cursed with might and main
To find the places on the plane
Were taken,—there was none for me,
       Boss of the Company.

Before my irritation vain
They told me: "There's a smaller plane
Will follow the four-motor one
That's tuning up upon the run."
And so amid the gay goodbyes
       I watched the big ship rise.

Reluctantly it seemed to me
It took the air, and I could see
Something was wrong.—It circled round,
And swung back to the starting ground,
Then sudden made an earthward dive . . .
       No one was left alive.

Although my heart is none too stout
I helped to bring the bodies out,
Till from that cursed spot I fled
When in my hearing someone said:
"Among the dead five children are,
       All crisped unto a char."

I thanked the Lord for sparing me,
Fat Chairman of the Company,
Although He let those kiddies five
In brazier be burned alive . . .
Said they: "What of the smaller plane?"
            Said I: "I'll take the train."

AT THE LION D'OR

I went into a restaurant
   Renowned for fancy fare,
Whose gilded door I used to haunt
   In days when dimes were rare.
But now my purse was dollar tight,
   And as I'd fasted long,
Said I: "This is the gorgeous night
   Of woman, wine and song."

For I a serial had sold
   The *Sunday Evening Post,*
And now I walked with heels of gold,
   Exulting: "Darn the cost!
I'll call for terrapin and wine,
   And caviare and squab:
Like a millionaire I'll dare to dine
   Where once I begged a job."

Where once I washed the dishes and
   The *maître* used to frown,
He waits with pencil in his hand
   To take my order down . . .
When through the rosy window pane
   I see in gloom and grime,
The ghost of "me", who begs in vain
   The diners for a dime.

Says Jules: "Sare, we have roasted quail."
    Says I: "Ye gods of grief!
Why don't you put yon bum in gaol,
    He's just a lousy thief.
The devil take your fancy fare!
    I'll get me drunk tonight:
That wretch! He's robbed me of a rare
    Ten dollar appetite."

LONGEVITY

"I'll make the ninety mark," he said,
   "For I am eighty years today;
A sane and sober life I've led,
   And I am fit in every way.
A lusty, gusty chap I be,
   Aware of no infirmity.

"Few folks have loved life more than I;
   I've never known a doctor's care.
Of sheer old age I mean to die,—
   Why, I might be a *centenaire*.
If years a hundred I could claim,
   Say, that might be my bid for fame!

'It is for that that I must plan,—
   Each day to live to longer live.
Yes, I will be a grand old man,
   And papers will my picture give:
A patriarch to marvel at,—
   A hundred old! . . . My God! What's that?"

    *   *   *   *   *

We buried him a week ago.
   The local doctor's diagnosis
Of ill that hit him like a blow
   Was something ending in "thrombosis."
So friends, don't be of death a scorner:
   The Old Guy's cowering round the corner.

NEUROTIC

I sat upon an upturned boat
   Beside the weary waves,
And listened to their sullen note
   In saturnine sea caves:
When to my horror and amaze
   A corpse oozed in my gaze.

A hideous host of tiny crabs
   Crawled on its hands of clay;
The little fish we know as dabs
   Had gnawed its cheeks away.
Oh was it woman? Was it man?
   I know not,—scared I ran.

I sped and told the coastal guard,
   Their hurry to beseech,
But no *cadavre* evil starred
   They found upon the beach.
Such search, they said, could hardly **fail:**
   They seemed to doubt my tale.

I sometimes wonder too; yet I
   Now shun the senile sea.
From off a stile I watch crop by
   The sheep upon the lea;
Yet how I vision on the beach
   That crab-crawled hand beseech!

FASHIONABLE WEDDING

I see her passing up the aisle
    Upon her father's arm;
Her bridal robe is white, her smile
    Has lost none of its charm.
Ah! If the bridegroom only knew
    Who watches from a pew.

And now she proudly passes me:
    I look straight in her eyes,
And as they meet my gaze I see
    Them widen with surprise.
Aye, with dismay I see them stare
    To see me sitting there.

For I am seedy and half drunk
    And pallid as a ghost.
To what dark hells have I not sunk
    Since once I led a host
Of radiant riders of the air
    On missions of despair.

Then secret week-ends by the sea,
    Rapt nights no one will know,
When utterly she gave to me
    Her body white as snow.
So close we clung, with plighted word,
    —And now she weds a lord.

And he is old and very rich,
  And thinks she is a maid;
I know he's bedding with a bitch,
  But need not be afraid;
For though I suffer pangs of hell
  No power could make me tell.

The knot is tied, the crowd bestir,
  Like thief I sneak away.
Ah well! I've had the flower of her,
  This "ace" had had his day:
So in a pub deep drinks I'll quaff
  And laugh—and laugh.

SEX

I used to care for cats but now
   I fondle them no more;
They raise such an infernal row
   When I am fain to snore.
They make so hideous the night
   I'd like to break their necks,
As in the alley-ways they fight,
   Obsessed by sex.

By day they arch their backs and purr
   And leap upon my knee;
And as I gently stroke their fur
   Their calm reposes me.
By night foul fiends of tooth and claw
   Their sinews fierce they flex,
Lashed on to lust by Nature's law
   Of ruthless sex.

But why revile the feline race?
   Are humans not like that?
And cursed with passions just as base
   And brutish as the cat?
Man-mind may be a jungle dread
   That evil visions vex:
Beware, Sweet Souls, the scaly head
   Of Serpent Sex!

SANDY

Because she stole my Archibald
I'll rob her of her Alexander,
(Or Sandy, as he's mostly called),
Poor fool! He doesn't understand her.
Of my divorce she was the cause,—
Designing bitch if ever was!

But yesterday in Ciro's bar
To Sandy I was introduced,
And with a cocktail he looked far
From male who could not be seduced.
Lucille, I saw, looked at me queerly:
I'm pretty sure she loves him dearly.

So now sweet vengeance will be mine,
For I am set to ply my charms,
And in an *amour* clandestine,
Luscious I'll lapse in Sandy's arms:
Then she'll divorce him in her turn,
And Sandy I will duly spurn.

A little loving on the sly
Is fun. —Poor Sandy! Oh of course he
Will want with me to mate, but I
Prefer to be a gay *divorcée*,
Until I'm getting *passée*, then I'll
Rope in some fat guy, rich and senile.

A precious bitch! Well, yes I am:
What's more, I do not care a damn!

MAX

When Max is sick his doctor's pills
    With sympathy I buy;
When he is drunk his liquor bills
    I settle with a sigh.
I take care of his notes of hand,
    And satisfy each dun,
For I have heaps of money and
    My fancy man has none.

And even when he goes away
    And leaves me for a while,
Knowing he will come back some day
    I greet him with a smile.
For him a sporting car I pay,
    And meet each gambling debt;
And now I thrill to hear him say:
    "My beautiful brunette!"

His deviltries I can forgive,
    His follies I forget;
In lazy luxury to live
    I keep my pampered pet.
Almost a mother I can be,
    But though I'm foolish fond,—
I'll blast his bloody brains if he
    Betrays me with a blond!

HECTOR

My husband is an upright man;
He does the very best he can
      To mould my life;
With dominant domestic love
He seeks in plastic me to prove
      The perfect wife.

For everything I say and do
Is always as he wants me to,
      So meek am I;
He would have me like ivy cling,
Or snuggle warm beneath his wing,—
      "Cluck! Cluck!" I cry.

Claims he: "Two hearts that beat as one;
Twin streams that to one river run,
      Serene from strife . . ."
Yet let me whisper: "Truth to tell,
Oft-times I want to cry: Oh hell!
I'd rather be in a *bordel,*
      Than Hector's wife."

AGUSTUS

"I am a virgin, Sir," she said,
 Though I be thirty-four.
With lad I've never been to bed,
 Nor played the pretty whore."

Said he: "Your frankness I admire,
 Your virtue I respect:
Your household services I hire,—
 No others I expect."

And as he looks at her, demure
 And timid as a mouse,
He does not dream her primal lure
 Was in a bawdy house.

So while he lauds her purity
 In lonely bed he lies:
Yet oh if he could only see
 The wanton in her eyes!

JIM

Rosemary's eyes are cornflower blue,
    Of lucent loveliness;
And fortunately mine are too,
    So Jim can never guess:
For though he likes her brown-eyed brothers,
    He loves her more than all the others.

Poor Jim! I often laugh inside,
    Though I should blush with shame
To see with what admiring pride
    He deems her of his name:
The blossom of a night of love,
    Domestic dalliance far above.

I've nothing to be sorry for:
    Her father soared to fame,
A flying hero of the War,
    He fell in combat flame;—
But none on earth will ever know,
    And I have Rosemary to show.

Ah yes, 'tis luck blue are my eyes,
    Since Jim's are black as jet.
It might be awkward otherwise . . .
    And yet I've no regret
I gave my lover of the skies
    My life's one night of paradise.

UNCLE JOHN

Said I to Uncle John: "I know
    A canny life you've led;
Yet if you had not ruled it so,
    Today you might be dead:
While now you'll dodder on and on."
    "Could be," said Uncle John.

Said I: "My job is in the air,
    And hazard are my ways;
Yet I have lived with rapture rare
    Indomitable days,
While yours are relatively wan."
    "That's right," said Uncle John.

Said I: "Although I am your heir,
    I have not any doubt
With all your care and frugal fare
    That you will see me out.
Despite your prostate, carry on."
    "Okay," said Uncle John.

Said I: "Give me a life that's gay,
    Although it be not long;
With high adventure all the way,
    And women, wine and song:
Tonight for love my watch I'll pawn . . ."
    "You're daft," said Uncle John.

UNCLE WILLIAM

There was once a double-you
    Midway in my natal name;
Lest its loss should trouble you,
    Let me herewith solve the same:
It alludes to Uncle Bill,
    Who ignored me in his Will.

Though I won his disapproval
    As a vagabond fantastic,
I admit his name's removal
    From my own was rather drastic:
To retain it I was willing,
    Had he left me just a shilling.

Yes, I was a lad unruly;
    Yet was he not my godfather?
And did he not oh most unduly
    Deem me fool and vow he'd rather
See me plunge to total wreck
    Than throw the life-line of a cheque?

That's why I, to tell you truly,
    Jettisoned that mid initial;
Though I flourish "double—youly"
    In my signature official:
Uncle's stingy shade to vex,
    With his name I sign my cheques.

LYRICS FOR LEVITY

WHAT WOULD *YOU* DO?

I asked a festive friend:
   "If certainly you knew
That soon the world would end,
   What would you do?"
Said he: "Unto the poor
   I'd give all I possess,
And beg on altar floor
   Forgivingness."

I asked a man austere
   Who had no wrong to rue:
"If end of earth was near
   What would you do?"
Said he: "I'd quit wise ways
   I've followed overlong,
And pass my closing days
   With Wine and Song."

I asked a Scientist
   With mop of silver hair.
He looked as through a mist,
   In cosmic stare.
"Vot do if in a year
   Ve should be chaos-hurled?
Vy, schmoke and trink my beer,—
   'Tis such a leetle Vorld!"

MEN ARE MUGS

For arid years she dreamed the day
        Of his return,
Her trader son so far away,
        Where jungles burn;
Where sullen rivers writhe and gleam,
        And hides are black . . .
And now her boy, to crown her dream,
        Was coming back.

She bent above the steamy tub
        Of soapy foam;
How grimly she must scour and scrub,
        To spruce the home!
Said she: "I'll don my robe of state,
        Of gems my sum;
Oh I must be immaculate
        When John will come!"

And then she turned: lo! John was there,
        A handsome chap.
Unkempt and tangled was her hair,
        A rag her wrap.
"How I look like a hag!" she thought;
        "Alas! my charms . . ."
When with a roar of joy he caught
        Her in his arms.

Said he: "Why weep you, Mammy dear,
              At my return?
I'm home again, your heart to cheer,
              With dough to burn."
Said she, as sudsy hands she shook,
              And wiped her eyes:
"I'm crying—*just because you took*
              Me by surprise!"

ATAVISM

'Twas in the days of Auld Lang Syne
　　When every Scot was crummy,
The mighty Master of Loch Fyne
　　Would scratch his noble tummy,
A-wondering what he could do
　　To help his henchmen true.

Then slabs of granite he would shape,
　　And rear them every mile,
That ragged chiels their backs could scrape
　　Of cootie domicile;
And every man of every clan
　　Might bless the great Argyle.

So haply when in Highland glen
　　A pillar stark I see,
I think of kilted, crummy men
　　Who rubbed their rumps with glee,
Or chafed their shoulder blades the while,
　　To praise the proud Argyle.

Then as I roam the heaths of home
　　And spy some hoary pile,
My dorsal bone upon the stone
　　I rasp in ancient style:
Though crummyless like them I bless
　　The great Duke of Argyle.

INSPIRATION

A carping critic queried me:
  "What's quickest to compose,
A verse of lyric poetry,
  Or page of lucid prose?"
Said I: "Of that there is no doubt,
  Though you'll not be agreeing,—
Good prose has to be sweated out,
  While lyrics lilt to being.

"Pure prose takes brains; you have to think;
  It claims consideration.
In pen, long pausing, dries the ink,
  Implying cerebration.
But poetry is like an elf:
  You lend your ear a minute,
And then your lyric writes itself,—
  Why, Pal, there's nothing in it."

'Tis true: though I'm a business fool
  Each day I make a sonnet.
The rhyming ripples as a rule,
  I never linger on it.
Fast functions my poetic gland
  As city streets I'm roaming . . .
There now! Another lyric's canned,—
  Hurrah for happy homing!

DOUBLE EVENT

And as he paced the corridor
  With face so wan and wild,
He told me he was waiting for
  The birth of his first child.
His wife was wishing for a boy,
  He hoping for a girl;
A son was to be christened Roy,
  A daughter would be Pearl.

Said I: "I wish good luck to you:
  I'm waiting for my second."
And then a nurse hove into view,
  And to him blythely beckoned.
He disappeared; I waited on,
  But looking in the glass,
Oh how my face was wild and wan!
  What hell we husbands pass!

Then he came out; his mug was red,
  He gave me a cigar.
"Thank God it's quite all right," he said;
  "How wonderful things are!
I'm all up in the air with joy;
  My head is in a whirl;
My wife will have her little Roy,
  And I will have my Pearl."

So I sat jittery as he,
   And chewed on his cigar:
In childbirth how pathetic we
   Expectant fathers are!
My heart, as moments slipped away,
   Ticked like a taxi-metre . . .
Twins are a blessing, yet I pray
   Jane won't be a repeater.

GYPSIES OF TOURAINE

The gypsies camping in our glade
Are not true gypsies, I'm afraid;
They do not beg, they do not steal,
They have an air of wealth and weal.
Their caravans are motor driven,
They look like people who have thriven;
And so I wondered what might be
The source of their prosperity.

I shyly asked a gypsy man,
The head, I think, of all the clan:
"Your wicker-work you cease to weave,
You hands are hornless, I believe.
No more you make your chairs and mats,
Your baskets and your harvest hats.
My curiosity forgive,—
But tell me, brother, how you live?"

Then with an air of roguish glee
Out spoke that swarthy Romany:
"We have a better racket now,—
You know the Government allow
A subsidy for every brat
We breed,—well, we can live on that:
And while you blokes are on the skids,
We plumply prosper making kids."

Thought I: to gain enough subsistence,
And have a fairly snug existence,
What system could be slicker than
The method of that gypsy man!
To earn a living from the Nation,
What nicer way than Procreation!
So let me, too, have children ten,
And mock the toil of honest men.

OUR BONE-YARD BUS

With wine, said I to Max, the Maire:
  "Your benefactor I would be;
Tell me the answer to your prayer?"
  "A charnel chariot," quoth he;
"A holy hearse with columns four,
  And sculpturings of cherubim."
"You'll have the very best," I swore,
  And filled his beaker to the brim.

The hearse arrived in solemn state,
  So fine and mortuary fit;
And our delight to celebrate,
  The village band preceded it.
The Maire was in the driver's seat,
  With scarlet sash and stove-pipe hat;
While gaffers grey I heard repeat:
  " 'Tis proud we'll be to go in that!"

The Maire himself was first to lie
  Beneath its silken canopy;
We guessed he hurried up to die,
  Its primal occupant to be.
And as we followed up the dead,
  With priest and prayer and holy vow:
"Max beat us to it," someone said;
  "He's laughing in his coffin now!"

DYSPEPTIC DAD

So puny is my appetite
    I little eat;
Yet my old lady doth delight
    In rosy meat.
Yes, she can make a sirloin steak
    Look sadly small,
While I on grated carrot take
    No joy at all.

At lunch with guile I try to smile
    But sad am I,
To savour sago pudding while
    She packs in pie;
As to tisane my inner man
    I must resign,
My aged spouse will make carouse
    On nuts and wine.

With cottage cheese I seek to please
    Digestive sloth,
And while a chick my dame will pick
    I sip the broth;
And yet as I with spinach toy
    I bear no spite:
Vicariously I enjoy
    Ma's appetite.

GRETA

His wife was a slattern, his son was a punk,
  His daughter was loverly kind;
So when he came home from the tavern high drunk,
  He gave them a piece of his mind.

Said he: "I've another son, bastardly born,
  A beautiful boy with a brain;
And he would regard all you loafers with scorn,
  For he's engineer on a train."

His son was astounded, his wife was ashamed,
  Then virtuous wrath they revealed;
That hen-pecked bread-winner they bitterly blamed,
  For youthful excesses concealed.

But glamorous Greta laughed loud in her glee:
  "Poor Pop, you don't need to explain.
My lovely new brother I'm longing to see,—
  Just think! *Engineer on a train!*"

POT BOILER

Prose is a cabbage,
    Rhyme is a rose;
Ours is a drab age,
    Patterned for prose;
Cabbage for food I raise,
    Roses are heaven's praise.

Seize on a sunny thought,
    Wrap it in rhyme;
Maybe its gleam will not
    Tarnish with time;
Weave it in prose and you
    Wave it adieu.

On no rich fare I feed,
    Lacking the price;
Cabbage my belly need
    Fain must suffice:
No one supposes
    One can eat roses.

No room have I to sow
    Blooms in my lot;
Close are my cabbages,
    Ripe for the pot . . . ,
God, in my garden's prose
    Grant just one rhyme of rose!

POET'S WIFE

I sold the *Sunday Evening Post*
   A rhyme I joyed in making;
I thought it just as good as most
   Of lyrics they were taking.
So slick and to the point it was,
   In metre easy flowing:
I cashed the cheque with glee because
   The milkman we were owing.

How neat and sweet it looked in print,
   And yet I dare not show it
To Dick, nor even drop a hint,
   Because he is a Poet.
But while his epics proud and high
   Ought to be bound in vellum,
I make wee stanzas on the sly,
   And what is more,—I sell 'em.

Dick cannot get his odes in type:
   The public would not prize them.
My tropes he would consider tripe,
   And haughtily despise them.
Alas! My rhyming to confess
   No power on earth will force me;
For if he knew of my success
   I fear he would divorce me.

So in the *Sunday Evening Post*
    My lyric wings I flutter;
And while I do not dare to boast,
    I buy the bread and butter.
For poesy may feed the soul,
    And though I dote on Shelley,
When in an economic hole
    It's verse that fills the belly.

A CALF NEEDS ROPE

I think that letter writing is
    A most infernal bore;
I make a postcard do the biz.,
    And even that's a chore.
But my young Cousin Percy tends
    To epistolic capers,
And every other day he sends
    A letter to the papers.

Of cuttings he has albums full
    On great and little matters;
And while I keep a temper cool
    A spate of ink he spatters.
He's simply nuts on human rights,
    And thinks the world's a mess;
So to let off his steam he writes
    A letter to the Press.

His lucubrations unto me
    He brings, my eyes to dazzle,
And as an author deems that he
    Can beat me to a frazzle.
Maybe he can;—and yet despite
    Assiduous pen-scrapers,
May I be damned the day I write
    A letter to the papers!

PROPOSAL

"I do not like your voice," I said,
    "It's low and husky;
Your hair unpleasingly is red,
    Your skin is dusky.
With painted nails I am at war,
    And yet—why is it
That I am always longing for
    Your visit?

"I do not like your sloppy dress,
    Your slouchy walk;
I think too high-brow, I confess,
    Your line of talk.
Yet though you are a painted doll,
    More dear to me
I calculate you are, than all
    Divinity.

"I like your teeth, I love your eyes,
    Your hands are nice;
If other traits I cannot prize
    Let these suffice.
So when it comes to wedding rings,
    Just name the day.
I guess, considering all things,
    Kid, you're okay."

CONSOLATION

I said to God: "Though ageful I
    Am still a man of sin,
And when to mend my ways I try,
    I see the devil grin.
I still enjoy a yarn that's blue,
    And like a bawdy book;
I have an eye for trollops too,
    Plus a disrobing look.

"When in the church pew I should squat,
    In billiard rooms I err;
I go to prize fights when I ought
    Prayer meetings to prefer.
With my grey whiskers I should be
    An up-and-coming saint;
But by a rhyme like this you see
    I absolutely ain't."

Said God to me: "You're okay, son;
    Virility is wealth;
And lust, when all is said and done,
    May be a sign of health.
So do not mourn your sinful state,
    Nor seek your ways to mend:
Be thankful you're a reprobate,
    And will be to the end."

THE BOTTLE

When first into this life I burst,
    My infant wails to throttle,
My mother gratified my thirst
    By giving me a bottle.
'Twas milk, of course, but how I made
    It gush to my subsistence;
And ever since, the bottle's played
    A part in my existence.

It's never done me any ill,—
    Least none that I'm aware of;
But if it does, I have the will
    Immediately to swear off.
So in my cellar cool and dark
    Are wines my heart to kindle,
And ere I lose this living spark
    I hope to make them dwindle.

If Ma had fed me at the breast
    I might have been teetotal.
Poor dear! She knew what was the best,
    And raised me on the bottle.
Let water from my board be banned,
    And though my nose it mottle,
Here's to wine's jolly sunshine and
    The boon that's in the bottle!

SIR GODWIN

Sir Godwin a Crusader was,
And went to war in Palestine;
He fought the fearsome Turk because
Belligerence was in his line.
And then it direfully befell,
That though with valour he did lance some,
The foe prevailed, and in a cell
A year they held him for a ransom.

Said Hassim Bey, his conqueror:
"Your wife piastres must be hoarding;
We cannot keep you longer for
You're costing us too much for boarding."
And then a messenger arrived,
A gallant knight, so young and handsome,
Saying: "Your Lady has contrived
At last to pay the Bey your ransom."

"How much?" Sir Godwin asked with doubt.
"A thousand guineas," said the other.
"For that the Bey will let you out,
So you can join your wife and mother."
Sir Godwin cried: " 'Tis not enough!
Though to the Bey it sounds a grand sum.
As a crusader tried and tough
I'm worthy of a higher ransom."

The Bey was cross, but he agreed
To wait until the gage was higher.
Said he: "Sir G. is hard to feed,
And lousy rags are his attire."
. . . A year passed. Came the messenger;
Two thousand guineas did he proffer.
"Your wife begs you return to her,"—
With scorn Sir Godwin spurned the offer.

The Bey was wild. "I'll shut you in
A smaller cell without a transome."
Sir Godwin answered with a grin:
"I can't accept so mean a ransom.
For pure of heart and proud am I,
And" (sotto voice) "You're just a nigger.
I'd rather rot in your pig-sty,—
Five thousand is my lowest figure."

At this the Bey blew off his top.
Said he with ire: "Your cell I plan some
For other Knights,—you cannot stop:
Get out!—And I'll *forgo* your ransom."
So there they wrestled, fought and fell,
And as he squashed its swart invader,
Sir Godwin perished in his cell,
An incorruptible Crusader.

WASTED MORNING

My pencil has a pretty point,
    My page is white,
And I can feel in every joint
    The urge to write.
My rhyme is ready, words await
    The errant thought:
Alas! Though they collaborate,
    My mind will not.

There now! I've made a verse, it's true,
    Just to explain.
But how can I make other two
    With empty brain?
Perhaps if on my head I stood,
    And let blood stream
Into my cerebrum it would
    Give me a theme.

No good! I'll put my work away,
    Though sorry I'm,
And hope that I'll have more to say
    Another time.
No longer will I vainly strive:
    Beyond a doubt,—
It's hell to write when nothing I've
    To write about.

THE BUTCHER

They say that ruthless Robespierre,
　　That "sea-green incorruptible,"
To whom the nobs of nobles were
　　By guillotines deductible,—
With necks of dukes at his demand
　　Could peel an orange with one hand.

I've tried to do it only twice,
　　But though the oranges were Sèville,
I made a mush that wasn't nice,
　　And damned old Robbie to the devil:
Well, in the end he went, by heck!
　　For he, too, got it in the neck.

Aye, finally he lost his nob:
　　('Twas his pet "Maiden" did the chopping).
—I'm glad that was the last of Rob,
　　But though the work he did was "topping,"
His triumph was, I understand,
　　To peel an orange with one hand.

THE THREE WISHES

I queried of an ancient Scot:
    "If you had wishes three,
What would you ask?" In sober thought
    He stared a while at me.
Said he: "Since I've a muckle thirst,
    And feelin' gey an' frisky,
I'm thinkin' I'll be wishin' first
    Loch Lomond full o' whisky."

"Ma second wish?" His hoary locks
    He scratched with worried frown,
And then from out a silver box
    He sniffed a powder brown
And sneezed and sneezed, and as his snoot
    He wiped upon his cuff,
He said: "I'll wish, beyond a doot,
    Ben More was made o' snuff."

"And now the third. Think well," said I,
    "Though full o' Mountain Dew
The lads might drink Loch Lomond dry,
    And then what would you do?"
Said he: "That's very, very true,
    So grant the Lord to give it,—
My last wish, sir, depends on you,
    An' I will tak' it here an' noo,
      —A long dram o' Glenlivit."

OSTLER BILL

Oh did it to your mind occur,
   That boy adopted by Aunt Jane
So very much resembles her
   That it is awkward to explain . . .
Nay, do not think I hint of blame,
   But——well, it's funny, just the same.

Of course Aunt has a perfect right
   To leave her money as she will.
'Tis true it puts me in a plight,
   But what about poor Ostler Bill? ——
The lad who taught her how to ride
   To hounds, and cantered by her side.

He was the household handyman,
   An enterprising lad, 'tis true.
Jane's mother swore: "Our William can
   Do anything he tries to do.
Aye, even more than he is bid
   Will William do,"——*and William did.*

Aunt Jane's devout: she frowns on joy,
   So sanctimoniously austere.
Yon Percy, her adopted boy,
   Is her *sole* heritor, I fear . . .
And as my mug of suds I swill,
   I sigh: "Why did you, Ostler Bill!"

RHYMES FOR A RECLUSE

SANCTUARY

I would go up into those holy hills,
And in a humble cottage close my days;
I would forget all human hurts and ills,
And dedicate myself to Nature's praise.
I would arouse with the rejoicing sun,
Hold parley with the peaks in pearly light,
And when the day's resplendent race is run
      Behold star-spangled Night.

Here in serenity my spirit soars
To heights undreamed of in the meads below;
Exultantly my hungry heart adores
The mountains billowing to ancient snow.
Here where the air buoys me like amber wine,
In severance sublime from strife and sin,—
'Mid silence, solitude and joy divine,—
      Here Heaven I may win.

Here where no evil echo shocks the ear,
And all the happy hills are golden gowned,
Only the crickets in the grass I hear,
Of sad humanity no sight, no sound.
Here in this sanctity inviolate,
Of secret trails by human feet untrod,—
An altar to sheer Beauty consecrate,—
      Here I will talk with God.

MAY MORNING

Sitting so quiet in the morning gold
I look down at my aged hands that hold
A pencil pointed with a pretty care,
A patient copy-book that waits it there:
And yet I have but little mind to write,—
My heart is so invested with delight.

What do I see? A mountain silver-grey,
A sea that laps with lace a golden bay,
A sky that seeks a mirror in the sea
Wherein to glass its tranced tranquillity:
A world of placid peace, of pearly sheen,
A world of joy,—as it has always been.

What do I hear? From palm and olive tree,
From pine and cedar, flights of feathered glee;
From softly shimmering, exultant grove
In praise of perfectness a choir of love:
All is as it has been,—I do not need
Discordant sounds and sordid sights to heed.

What do I feel? A rapture of repose,
And yet a quickness that the spirit knows
When gratitude wells up for all the joy
Of Being, no world warfare can destroy,
Saying: What does woe matter unto me?
Have I not birds and trees and sky and sea?

What do I think? Well, see my pencil writes
Amid serene, ineffable delights,
That always have been, always will be mine;
And for all life I know a love divine,
A faith in Nature and in simple ways
Of purity and peace and hope and praise.

So let me thank my God on bended knees:
The rest can go,—I'm overblest with these.

SCOTCH FIR

From June to June it grew in grace,
      Elate, imperially slim;
Precisely and in laddered space
      It put forth slender limb on limb.
Smiling it lofted to the light,
      My love and kinship to invite.

In April rain how it was glad!
      How it rejoiced with summer song!
What glee in wind and snow it had,
      As like a giant it grew strong!
And from my bedroom window I
      Could see it proudly plume the sky.

And then, because so fast it grew
      To prove itself a worthy tree,
One day it shuttered out my view
      Of shining sky and sunny sea:
So urgently it leapt, at last
      A shadow on my bed it cast.

I love a smile, I hate a frown,
      And darkness holds a hint of doom,
So . . . so I told them to cut down
      The source of such untimely gloom:
Because I loved the sunful sea
      Sadly I slew that songful tree.

Still in my heart I hear them chop,
    The sudden crash, the leap of light . . .
Too late I would have bade them stop,
    For now the sun-glare sears my sight,
And weaving in the empty air
    Sad wings I see that nested there . . .

Oh all the hells that wait for me
    Record that once *I killed a tree.*

THE RIVALS

Growing gravely side by side
Are two trees, my garden pride;
And with eagerness each Spring
I await their blossoming.
Oh I'm sure they know I do,
For they sigh the Winter through:
"Sunshine, speed our sap,—to please
This grey worshipper of trees."

Says the first: "My gush of gold
Joyfully he will behold,
And my wealth of sunny boughs
He will drape about the house;
Sprays of yellow, feather-fine,
Making every nook a shrine
As I blazon with delight
All my glory in his sight."

Then the other: "You are first,
But with urgent foam I'll burst
Like a cataract of snow,
Every branch a brilliant glow,
Till but blossom you can see
Gem each twig triumphantly:
Countless fairy lamps alight,
Clustered to bewitch his sight."

Branch of gold and bough of snow
How I joy my heart can know
All the ecstasy of Spring
In your gracious blossoming!
God of Beauty, I implore
Of sweet living give me more,
To behold in Springs to be,
Mimosa and almond tree!

TREE LOVER

From out the wood a thousand trees
      Are calling me to come;
They send their summons on the breeze,
      They know I am not dumb,
That I would with my presence prove
      For them my love.

Oh I am not a talking man,
      A harkener am I;
I look and listen all I can,
      And wistfully I try
To understand with eager ear
      Tree words I hear.

But I must be so all alone,
      From humankind apart,
For leaves to lisp with tender tone
      Unto my hungry heart . . .
Alas, poor me! O'er ledgers bent,
      In city pent.

Oh sunny boughs, beseeching me!
      Your song is in my ear;
For I can see what none can see
      And hear what few may hear . . .
Let sages prattle, give me please,
      The sooth of trees.

DARK PINE

If my life force, by death decree,
Could find green haven in a tree,
And there in peace untroubled years
Could dream, immune from toil and tears,
Though I'm a lover of all trees
I would not favour one of these . . .

I would not choose a brittle palm
Beside a sea of senile calm;
Or willow droopily adream
Above bright babble of a stream.
No cypress would inhibit me
With dark and dour austerity;
Nor olive, shattering the light,
Nor poplar, purple in the night.
The sanctuary of my search
Would not be oak, nor ash, nor birch:
Ah no! Their comfort I decline,—
Let my life-force pervade a Pine.

Aye, when my soul shall sally forth
Let it be to the naked North,
And in a lone pine desolate
Achieve its fit and final fate;
A pine by arctic tempest torn,
Snow-scourged, wind-savaged and forlorn;
A viking trunk, a warrior tree,
A hostage to dark destiny
Of iron earth and icy sky,
That valiantly disdains to die.

There is the home where I would bide,
If trees like men had souls inside,—
Which is, of course, a fantasy
None could conceive but dolts like me . . .
Let others vision Heaven's gate,
Dark Pine, I dream for me you wait.

NATURE'S UNIVERSITY

In touch with Nature I would be
    And hear her holy word,
And know the name of every tree,
    The song of every bird;
Oh I would learn the secret lore
    Of plant and ant and bee,
And flower and leaf and blade before
    God calls the score for me.

For I have laboured overmuch
    In hives of hollow men,
And I have worshipped wisdom such
    As comes from page and pen;
But let me lay my books away,
    And Nature take for tome:
Of sea and sky a student I,
    With all outdoors for home.

Seek knowledge not in crabbèd print
    And arid chunks of type;
Go out into the fields and mint
    Your learning ready ripe.
Let wood and stream and garden teach
    Their lesson to your need:
Just listen to a daisy's speech
    And you'll be wise indeed.

MY MINSTRELS

I may have many a doubt
      Of angel wings;
But how my heart goes out
      To bird that sings.
No matter what its kind,
      Or how its flight,
A boon in it I find,
      Beyond delight.

I say: "Bless you, my dear,
      Is it for me,
So fresh, so pure, so clear
      Your melody?
Is it because you know
      You bring me bliss?
I'd like to think it so,—
      Maybe it is."

Whitethroat in cherry tree,
      Blackbird in bush,
Robin with garden glee,
      Mad missel-thrush;
Linnets with morning mirth,
      Lark lost in blue,—
I'd give my gain on earth
      To sing like you.

So bravely to rejoice
In beauty's praise;
Vast innocence to voice
In golden days . . .
Aye, though my faith be dim
To holy words,
Maybe God's cherubim
Are singing birds.

THE LILY POND

My lily pond is claret clear,
    A cup of luscious light;
I watch the water beetles steer
    Where lily stems are bright.
When flat flies delicately skate
    On surface crystal cool,
Oh how I love to contemplate
    My lily pool.

But when I take a stalk of cane
    And stir its satin bed,
Oh what a foul and fetid stain
    I make to spring and spread!
My lily pond is hideous now,
    A blur its jewelled fire,
And so I say with furrowed brow:
    "Confound the mire!"

In this our life let us be wise,
    And worship loveliness,
Although we know below it lies
    Abysmal muck and mess.
Enjoy the jewelled face of things,
    Where gracious beauty glows:
From rancid mud the lily springs,
    From rot the rose.

NATURE MAN

Oh lucky is the honest man
  Of mellow ways,
Who in a kindly garden can
  Live out his days.
He may have little in his purse,
  And simply fare;
Yet Nature is a gentle nurse
  To fend off care.

But oh how happy he can be,
  If rustic wise
He knows the way of bird and tree,
  And reads the skies!
The world to him can be a book
  Of fairy lore;
Of field and fen, of bush and brook
  In boundless store.

Oh wealthy is the man who sows
  His strip of soil,
And can with gladness greenly close
  His days of toil . . .
So loving heart to Nature give:
  With her for friend
Enthusiastically live
  Unto the end.

BEAUTY IS ALL

Beauty is in the eye and mind,
   And as we stand and stare,
The more we seek the more we find
   Of Beauty everywhere.
Day-long it woos from hill and dale,
   From woods and meadow bars,
Until in holy night we hail
   The beauty of the stars.

Today for long I stood alone
   And watched beside a brook,
A silver rill that leapt a stone
   And spray of jewels shook.
Drowned sunbeams graved the gravel gold,
   And dream-enraptured there,
I thought: Lo! here is wealth untold
   To make me millionaire!

Oh Beauty, stab me wide awake
   To see with quickened eyes;
And through the magic lens of air
   Behold enchanted skies!
Aye, though a vagabond I be,
   My lot of daily dearth,
With wand of wonder make of me
   The richest man on earth!

THE WALL

I have done with strain and strife,
I am in retreat from life;
And remote from humankind
I enjoy a quiet mind;
And behind a lofty wall
Seldom see a face at all.

Prisoner of Peace am I,
With above, a happy sky,
Innocent of smoke and din,
That serenely roofs me in,
With around, a sunny wall,
Shutting out the bray and brawl.

Hermit-happy, drugged with calm,
Heedless of the world I am;
And my wall is greenly climbed,
Gay with vines of every kind;
Gleamy berries, fruits and flowers,
In the bright bee-haunted hours.

Rhymes and roses are my care,
Grateful green is everywhere;
Grateful too my gentle mood
In the sunny solitude;
As with folded hands I wait
In the sunset of my fate.

146

And my roses unto me
Mean more than humanity;
And my rhymes are sweet and gay
As I dream my life away:
All ignored, ignoring all,
Blessing Heaven for my Wall.

SOLITUDE

How I have loved my solitude
    From youth to elding grey,
As in unsociable mood
    Morose I make my way!
Nor care to converse with the Great,
    Nor babble with the small,
But hermit-wise to go my gait,
    Ignoring all.

How I have longed for loneliness
    In city smog and din,
Some forest cedar to caress,
    And sanctuary win!
Most company I find a bore:
    Just let me be, say I,
Acquainted with myself before
    I come to die.

In woodsy quiet, hilly calm,
    From haunts of men afar,
Leave me to wonder why I am,
    And what is yonder star?
Remotely in my evening glow
    I wait for my last call,
Content to know that not to know
    Is best of all.

And so in crowds I isolate
    My spirit from the throng,
For I to peace inviolate
    And loneliness belong.
Aye, though I huddle with the herd,
    I deem God's greatest good,
His blessing and His holy word
      Is Solitude.

THE ROCKY ROAD

Said the Rocky Road to me:
   "Do not take me,—you'll be sorry!
Yon's the broad highway you see,
   Swishing cars your only worry.
Never of its goal in doubt,
   It is wide and smooth and level:
Up and down and in and out
   I am twisty as the devil."

Said I to the Rocky Road:
   "I will take you notwithstanding;
For adventure is my goad,
   And bright danger my demanding.
I despise the jig and jog,
   Of security a scorner:
I'm a lad who's all agog,
   Wondering what's round the corner."

Said the Rocky Road to me:
   "I will bruise your brave boot-leather;
Take you up the scraggy scree,
   Lose you in the homeless heather;
Lead you by the brawly burn,
   Mock you as you blindly blunder;
Zig and zag at every turn
   I will wake your eyes to wonder."

Said I: "That's all right with me;
　　Get as tough as hell and blazes!
I can take it, you will see:
　　I don't look for dales and daisies."
So up to the glacid sky
　　In the hurly-burly weather,
See the Rocky Road and I,
　　Insolent to time and tether,
　　　　　Singing pals together!

LYRICS OF THE LOST

CONTRITION

When I go back to ghost awhile
    The homes and haunts I knew,
I never see my husband smile
    As once he used to do.
He is so silent and so sad
    Where oft he sang with glee:
I pity him, yet I am glad
      He grieves for me.

But why in life did he not show
    How much I meant to him?
For of his kisses he was slow,
    Sometimes his way was grim.
No doubt he had decisions grave,
    My little world above:
Yet oh how often I would crave
    A word of love!

And so I go a weary ghost
    With hapless babe unborn,
And it is now he needs me most,
    For far he is forlorn.
Oh witless husband! Wistful wife!
    So brief is human breath,—
Could there not be more love in life,
    Less rue in death?

154

DEATH OF A DOCTOR

Angina! Lovely word! It chimes
Like music, yet what pain accurst!
As physician how many times
Its cleaving agony I've nursed!
And now I'm down with it myself,
Too young to go upon the shelf.

Too wise with long experience
Of healing and relieving pain.
It would be tragic to go hence
With all my knowledge void and vain.
Unto so many I have been
A tower of strength on which to lean.

So though in clinic bed I lie,
My destiny I do not shirk.
I will not die; I *will* not die;
Again I will take up my work.
I'll be a human Wailing Wall,
And salvage some, and solace all.

Yet oh the midnight telephone!
The climbing up four flights of stairs!
The fear, the fret that, all alone,
My woe may take me unawares!
My patients haunt and harry me;
I'm rowelled by anxiety.

If I should buy a cottage small,
Long years I'd live in garden days;
Go slow, and never work at all,
And read and read, and laze and laze.
I'll be worm-fodder if I don't . . .
Retire! You fool! You know you won't.

WINGS

In San Diego by the sea
    He had a dream of woe.
His lost love cried: "Oh come to me,
        I want you so!"

He took the plane in morning light,
    With presage weirdly grim,
And all the continental flight
        She haunted him.

How good to see Manhattan tower.
    And there a waiting plane
He caught, and cursed through haggard hours
        The callous main.

Then with a London dawn aglow
    Swift to her home he hied . . .
"Alas!" said they, "you are too slow,
Only a little hour ago
        Your ex-wife died."

THE SISTERS

One grieved because her baby died,
      And evermore was sad.
One mourned for motherhood denied—
      The child she never had.

They stood beside a tiny grave,
      And both were bent and grey.
Said one: "Alas! the Lord who gave
      Ruthlessly took away."

The other sighed with bitterness:
      "I envy you your tears;
My heart is void, while you possess
      A mother's souvenirs."

Sweet Reader, if you had to choose
      What fate would you befall:
Would you elect to love and lose,
      Or never love at all?

FEY

I sagged beside the road,
      All in was I.
So weary was my load;
      Cars passed me by.
Yet when I saw that there
      Was space inside,
With gesture of despair
      I thumbed a ride.

But none took heed of me,
      So grimy grey.
No driver seemed to see,
      Or look my way.
Then hope receding far,
      My hand I dropped,
When suddenly a car
      Beside me stopped.

And in it was a youth
      Whose smile was kind.
He bade with boyish ruth
      Me mount behind.
My heart was full of cheer,—
      When winged with woe,
A voice breathed in my ear:
      "Don't go! Don't go!"

"No thank you, son," I said;
    "I guess I'll rest."
He shrugged, as on he sped:
    "Well, you know best."
Then as I hiked a spell,
    What did I see?
His car all smashed to hell
    Against a tree . . .
        Dead, dead was he!

LEONTIASIS

In our Ionian hotel
When I was but a child of four,
She cast on me her lovely spell,
A golden goddess to adore,
     And worship evermore.

I think she must have pitied me,
For Mother used to gamble late.
She gave me cups of china tea
And cherries on a silver plate,
     And Venice chocolate.

One summer day she closed her door,
And though before it I would spend
Sad hours, I knew that nevermore
Would I behold my lovely friend:
     A shut door was the end.

One night it was ajar . . . To peer
I dared,—on silken couch she sat.
But oh I shrieked with sudden fear,
Her face was puffy like a cat:
     She glared at me and spat.

"A weird disease," my Mother said,
"That frightens every one away.
I think she would be better dead."
Poor soul! She saw my mad dismay
     And . . . cut her throat next day.

GLAUCOMA

One eye is dark, the other dim,
And I can never wed with him
        Who loves me so;
But with a heart of sorrowing
I'll give him back his silver ring
        And bid him go.

Ploughing the deep he deems my eyes
As clear as jade or China skies,
        Each orb a gem;
When he is steering at the wheel,
Beneath the moon with even keel,
        He dreams of them.

I love him. 'Twill be hard to tell
There never can be wedding bell
        For him and me;
His bairnies I will never bear:
What mother could give childer care
        Who cannot see?

Another he must take to wife,
And I will grope my way through life
        A lass unwed.
Why did I ever know his kiss?
Why did God give me breath for this?
        I wish me dead!

THE ADMIRAL

Seeing I never had a son
 I prayed Ann's babe might be
A boy and hear as I had done
 The hail of Old Man Sea.
Yet not like me, a feckless fool,
 Who shipped before the mast;
No, he would go to naval school
 For honour classed.

Though skipper of a tramp was I,
 And life-long was my fight,
A bit of brass I'd put me by
 To steer his course aright.
I dreamed of his bright destiny,
 Though he was in the womb.
Said I: "An Admiral he'll be
 When dark's my tomb."

"The lad will have his chance, I swear,"
 To Dick my dog I'd say.
"Cocked hat and gold braid he will wear,
 With medals he'll be gay . . .
Ann lost her man in China seas,
 Three wintry moons ago;
But now the Admiral will ease
 Her widowed woe."

 *   *   *   *   *

God wills! The waxen hand out-thrust
    Was soft and cold as snow;
Despite her poor, pathetic trust
    With babe Ann had to go.
Now by the hearth alone am I,
    Old Dick my only pal,
Who whines as in his ear I sigh:
            "Poor Admiral!"

THE TELEPHONE

As I am sitting all alone
There comes a ringing in my ear;
I think it is the telephone
And haste, but nothing do I hear.
Yet when I seek my chair again,
It seems to sound so sweet, so shrill,
That though I know it's all in vain
           I listen still.

And as I wait in silence there,
The tears that furrow down my cheeks
Are testament to my despair,
For no one speaks,—oh no one speaks!
How aches my heart to hear that voice
That used to greet me every night,
Making the all of me rejoice
           With sheer delight!

How desolate a home can be!
I'd give my life that's left to hear
That tone so treasure-sweet to me,
Saying: "Hello there, Daddy dear!"
. . . Beloved, it is near the dawn
And I'm so terribly alone.
Darling, I wait—please call me on
           God's telephone."

THE BRIDE

Said she: "A carriage I will ride,
        My wedding day.
Oh I will be the happy bride
        With garlands gay.
And I will have a gallant spouse
        To hold my hand,
And lead me to a little house
        So snugly planned."

It happened at the Harvest Ball;
        In robe of white,
Of maids she was the belle of all,
        To lad's delight.
Yet sitting out a dance or two
        A cold she caught,
That lingered all the winter through,
        With menace fraught.

She rides a coach just as she said,
        A year tonight;
But in the place of roses red
        Are lilies white.
She wins a home, as was her dream
        Of happy breath . . .
White, white her wedding garments gleam,
        Her bridegroom—Death.

THE DISASTER

Said Vi: "My dear, you'll miss your train.
   It's nearly eight, you ought to hurry."
I took the short cut by the lane,
   In pea-soup fog the trees were blurry.
And when I reached the wicket gate,
   The station clock was pointing eight.

My train was slowly pulling out.
   "You'll have to run," the porter said.
I could have made it, I've no doubt;
   I sprinted . . . then I shrieked with dread:
I saw my coach upend and smash,
   Then others pile with crash and crash.

Aye, with those eyes I saw it plain,
   The North Express come roaring through,
To telescope our local train,
   And rear in hideous wreckage too:
With devil's din and cloud of steam,
   And crumpled cars, and scream—and scream.

Over a hundred were the dead;
   But what of those who did not die!
I strove to them with hands that bled,
   'Mid twisted steel I saw them lie:
The raving ones who begged in vain
   For morphine to relieve their pain.

" 'Tis Providence you're safe," said Vi.
  Said I: "Oh Providence my hat!
If He knew what would happen, why
  Could He not have prevented that?
Or did He give no sign because
  He could not override His Laws?"

NO GREATER LOVE

A nest of baby ducks I knew,
    Snug in a thick of sedge;
I peered at them from my canoe,
    Close by the water edge;
The mother, sassy as could be,
    Stared back at me.

Of me seemed not a-feared at all,
    But spunky to defend
Each gaping, golden-plushy ball
    Unto the bitter end;
Though heron dared not come a-nigh her.
    She knew not—*fire*.

As flame came leaping from the West
    With osiers a-blaze,
My worry was that happy nest,
    And through the fiery haze,
I paddled with what haste I could
    To save her brood.

Too late, alas! Charred was the sedge,
    The nest was smouldering;
Dead was each babe of silky fledge,
    Beneath a burning wing:
Sad, sad I saw with smoke-stung eyes
    Love's sacrifice.

I saw a heroine unsung
    Amid the sooty stain,
A shielding breast that closely clung,
    Seared eyes that dimmed to pain:
A mother dying for her young,
    In vain . . . in vain.

MARGARET

He lies upon his dying bed,
    Weighed down by years,
And grieves his daughter cannot shed
    For him her tears.

He sees her as a child of three,
    A dancing sprite,
So quick to climb upon his knee
    And hug him tight.

He sees her as a laughing maid
    Whom love enfolds,
All innocent and unafraid
    Of what life holds.

He sees her as a radiant bride
    In altar glow;
His heart is sad as from his side
    She has to go.

He sees her as a mother blest
    With happy brood;
Her life is crowned and in her breast
    Is gratitude.

Vain dreams! She cannot seek his bed
    To shed her tears . . .
For fifty years she has been dead,
    —For fifty years.

Not even at the door of death
    Can he forget . . .
Lost little babe! His dying breath
    Is Margaret.

THE WHITE STICK

My artist eyes knew vast delight
  And gleaned me joy through years;
But now the left is black as night,
  The other vaguely peers;
And so my cane as white as snow
  I paint to weave my woe.

For when I cross a thoroughfare
  I flourish it about;
Although it's little I would care
  If someone knocked me out:
When one is old and poor and blind
  Swift death is often kind.

For I was painter of renown
  Though few remember me;
My pictures all around the town
  In galleries you see:
Although to me they're just a name,
  A canvas and a frame.

There! Now my old black stick is white,
  Though shadowed in my view;
And in the darkling of my sight
  The last brush-work I'll do:
But as I wait the paint to dry,
  O God! I'd like to cry!

ROSE MARIE

The apple-cheeked young female who
    Brings me my morning mail,
At ten o'clock is always due,
    I never knew her fail.
And so I wondered what was wrong,
    (She, punctual as a pin),
When such an old hag came along,
    Ten hairs upon her chin.

"But where is Rose Marie?" said I,
    "Who brings my post to me."
The withered beldame made reply:
    "A widow woman she:
A telegram she got today
    Of husband newly slain,
In cruel fighting far away . . .
    Now Rose Marie has pain."

Then shrugged the crone: "Why should she moan?
    My man gets drunk each night;
Now sweetly she'll be left alone,
    No husband to get tight,
And keep her down in poverty . . .
    A widow beats a wife:
A lucky lass is Rose Marie,—
    Plump pensioner for life!"

RHYMES FOR REVERENCE

THE JUDGE

When those who pray and those who "prey"
Stand side by side on Judgement Day
I deem the Lord of Life will say . . .

"Because I am omnipotent
I am accountable to you;
I traced the every way you went,
I wrote the part and called the cue:
Although you fancied you were free
Your puppet strings were pulled by me.

"How then shall I praise or condemn!
You did not seek the life I gave.
With laws immutable I hem
You from the cradle to the grave:
Strait-jacketed by fate are you,
And all you do you fain must do.

"You mock me with your mercy plea.
I have no heaven and no hell.
I made you, poor humanity!
In me, for good or ill, you dwell.
You are my instrument,— through you
I strive to make my Dream come true.

"My Dream that dark shall bring forth light,
That good forever blot out ill;
That all mankind shall in my sight
Rejoice and glorify my will;
That earth's experiment may prove
My reign of everlasting love."

Then,—then I thought God bowed His head,
And desolate were we, the Dead,
As tears of woe for Him we shed.

GOD'S DESTINY

It is God's destiny, I deem,
    This world of ours to guide;
Sublime fulfilment of His dream,
    And doubtlessly His pride.
By imposition of His Will
    This Fact He brought to be;
And all we do for good or ill
    Is His decree.

With His divine omnipotence
    Could it be otherwise?
And yet God gave us common sense
    His job to criticise.
And so in vain we ask and ask,—
    Though all will end in good,
Why is there to His human task
    Our dark prelude?

Why should we suffer war and woe,
    And plague and pestilence,
And all the evils God doth know
    In His omniscience?
Why should He in His planet-plan,
    To suffering and strife
Condemn not only martyr-man,
    But all of life?

Maybe a greater God there is,
     And ours doth but obey.
'Tis true I vision final bliss,—
     But oh how far away!
And so for gracious God I grieve,
     Who strives in you and me,
Through pain eternal, to achieve
     His Destiny.

EXPERIMENTALIST

Oftentimes I've wondered why
You are you and I am I;
Pondered if the human race,
In its glory or disgrace,
Is not with a blindfold bent
      God's experiment?

No one knows, no one will know;
But suppose that it is so,
Let us all with heart and soul
Strive toward the unseen goal,
Make amid life's storm and stress
      God's plan a success.

Good is good,—that much we know;
Truth is truth, and even though
Unconsidered drop we be
In illimitable sea,
Let us by our worthiness
Try to make a little less
      God's unhappiness.

TOLERANCE

All beliefs are good beliefs
    That make for happiness;
Faiths that solace human griefs
    Are followings to bless:
Let us never mockers be
    Of soul sincerity.

Some folks to a chapel go;
    Others light an altar flame.
What matters it? In each I know
    The God is just the same:
All worship is a worthy thing
    That gives us comforting.

And all is good that makes for good,
    Kirk and cathedral nave;
While mosque and temple offer food
    Some famished soul to save;
But holier than all of them—
    A stall in Bethlehem.

So bless the gift of true belief,
    Whatever form it take,
If it can solace human grief,
    And comfort human ache;
And in a world of woe and strife
    Lift man to higher life.

HIS CROWN

The Coronation rites were o'er,
The Monarch sighed in weary way.
He doffed the jewelled robe he wore,
And by his side his sceptre lay.
Then to his Chamberlain he said,
With just the shadow of a frown:
"Please take this bauble from my head,
        Now I *myself* must crown.

"A crown of Honour I must make,
Of loving thought and kindly deed,
Of sacrifice for freedom's sake,
Of travail for my people's need.
I did not seek a kingly state,
Above my betters thus to sit,
But now my days I dedicate
        That Time may prove me fit.

"So King of Kings, sublimely just,
On your poor servitor look down;
Humble me, Lord, unto the dust
That I may win a worthy Crown.
Uphold me in my holy task,
Sustain me mid a million scorns . . .
A Crown of Sacrifice I ask,—
        Even like His,—*of thorns.*"

THE PRIVATE GOD

God is beneficence and love;
His presence in all life I see.
No need to seek for Him above,
Nor in dim chapels bow the knee:
His Shrine is lit in you and me.

God is to me the sum of good,
The spirit that sustains us all
To give our best in deed and mood,
To answer urgently the call
For sacrifices great and small.

God in our needfulness has birth;
No author He of cosmic plan;
His altar is a humble hearth,
His throne is in the mind of man . . .
Why seek Him in the starry span?

God is no deity divine;
He is within our hearts, a glow
Of living light, aloft to shine,
And from whose source all blessings flow:
That's all we know and need to know.

DAUNTLESS QUEST

Why seek to scale Mount Everest,
    Queen of the air?
Why strive to crown that cruel crest
    And deathward dare?
Said Mallory of dauntless quest:
    "Because it's there."

Why yearn with passion and with pain
    To storm the sky?
Why suffer,—sullen goals to gain,
    And fear defy?
" 'Tis not for glory or for gain
    We darkly die."

Why join the reckless, roving crew
    Of trail and tent?
Why grimly take the roads of rue,
    To doom hell-bent?
"Columbus, Cook and Cabot knew,
    And yet they went."

Why bid the woolly world goodbye
    To follow far,
Adventures under evil sky
    And sullen star?
Let men like Mallory reply:
    "Because they are."

184

WORSHIP

Lord, I have blest Thy Loveliness
        Of sight and sound;
Thy beauty in its sylvan dress
        That robes me round.
I have responded utterly
        To all glad things,
The living evidence of Thee
        That round me rings.

For in this everlasting frame
        Of joy and light,
Insistently I hear Thy name,
        I mark Thy might;
And as with eyes of love I see,
        And heart aglow,
Am I not glorifying Thee
        Who made it so?

And if adoreful of the sun,
        With pensive prayer,
Am I not worshipping the One
        Who set it there?
And if He gave me heart of grace
        His love to see,—
Oh may there not be just a trace
        Of Him in me?

THE GIVER

"God is so kind to me," I cried,
    As weighed with weariness
I laid me down at eventide
    Beneath the sheet's caress.
And yet, for all the gift of good
    That has fulfilled my day,
Though I am glad with gratitude—
    I cannot pray.

For while I speak of Him, 'tis odd,
    (But maybe you're the same),
I don't know what I mean by "God",
    It's like an empty name.
To figure Him I try in vain,
    For vision I appeal . . .
And yet,—when futile is the brain,
    The heart can feel.

So when in quiet even-close
    I deem how life is good,
And gratitude within me glows
    To glorify my mood;
Although no power divine I laud
    For blessings great and small,
My heart of love is praise to God
    Who gives me all.

TOO LATE

For all the days I've squandered
    In prank and play;
For all the ways I've wandered
    From off Thy way;
For all that doth dissever
    My thought from Thee,
O God of High Endeavour
    Forgive Thou me!

For all the faiths I've fathered
    And counted mine;
For all the gain I've gathered,
    Remote from Thine;
For steps my feet have stumbled,
    Despite Thy Word,
And tasks my hands have fumbled:
    Forgive me Lord!

Now that men soon must grave me,
    And swift the moments haste,
Pardon O Lord, who gave me
    Talents I let to waste!
The man you sought to make me,
    Alas! I now discern . . .
But Oh that it should take me
    All Life to learn!

LOVE'S LEAVENING

When God invented man
    For bliss or bale,
To finish off His plan,
    Upon the scale,
—Paternity to prove,—
    He added Love.

He might have left it out,
    And calloused us;
For Love has brought about
    A heap of fuss;
Since human life began
    It's pestered man.

It's brought upon its train
    Such frets and fears;
As sensitized to pain
    We pay in tears,
That we may daily prove
    The curse of Love.

Yet could it be God said?
    "From out my heart,
I give to you, earth-sped,
    Of Me a part,
That it might bring, maybe
    You home to Me!"

So in our final fate,
            Ere ends the tale
Of war and greed and hate
            Love may prevail . . .
Perhaps this is the plan
            Of God for man.

GOODNESS

No thumping pulpiteer I be,
            But think in churchly mood
The most religious man is he
            Who does the greatest good.

I dare to dream, despite the strife,
            That virtue has increased;
I dare to deem the crown of life
            Is happiness and peace.

I dare to think of God—that His
            Love dwells in us alone;
That kindliness His Kingdom is,
            Unselfishness His Throne.

And so I seek no Power above
            To paradise endow:
My God is happiness and love,
            My Heaven—here and now.

THE PARTING

Dear Life, I've known you long;
Sweet Life, I've loved you well.
Now in despite of song
I must depart a spell.
The door of death is wide,
And fain for it am I;
No longer may I bide,—
   Sweet Life, goodbye!

Dear Death, you shepherd me
Into your healing gloom;
And though no light I see,
I have no dread of doom.
For there's another door,
And as to it I grope,
I glimpse, gleaming before,
   A star of hope.

Death guides me through the night
Unto that other door;
Unto that other light
That shines for me once more.
So out of dark and pain,
No more with doubt a-strife,
I greet my friend again,—
   "Good morning, Life!"

ENOUGH

Rest is enough,—my rich reward
        When daylight dies;
No other do I seek, O Lord,
        For aching eyes.
Though day be long, with sweat and strain,
        And road be rough,
Night brings release from woe and pain,
        —Rest is enough.

Death is enough,—why should I seek
        Another life?
Aye, though the way be cold and bleak,
        And stark the strife,
Let me fight on, for I was made
        Of soldier stuff;
But battle won,—with broken blade,
        —Death is enough.

Love is enough,—let it be so;
        My paradise
Let me win in the holy glow
        Of sacrifice.
And though by evil fate opprest,
        Bare to the buff,
Lord, Thee I thank,—With love and rest
        Life is enough.

END PIECE

Friend, though of Faith we be apart,
Of mood remote,
There is in every human heart
A common note.
So wistfully I hope to find
Your soul within,
That brotherhood of simple mind
That makes us kin.

Our sympathy for all who sweat
In toil and strife;
The countless ones who never get
A chance in life;
The sick, the crippled and the blind,
The foiled of fate;
The folks who don't learn to be kind
Until too late.

Of such with all simplicity
I seek to sing;
And though in vain my hope may be,
To it I cling;
Despite I jingle overmuch
I fain would prove
In you and I the saving touch
Of Human Love.

192